RELIGION AND PUBLIC LIFE
IN THE MIDDLE ATLANTIC REGION:
THE FOUNT OF DIVERSITY

D0048021

RELIGION BY REGION

Religion by Region Series
Co-published with the Leonard E. Greenberg Center for the
Study of Religion in Public Life at Trinity College
Mark Silk and Andrew Walsh, Series Editors

The United States is a nation of many distinct regions. But until now, no literature has looked at these regional differences in terms of religion. The Religion by Region Series describes, both quantitatively and qualitatively, the religious character of contemporary America, region by region. Each of the eight regional volumes includes overviews and demographic information to allow comparisons among regions. But at the same time, each volume strives to show what makes its region unique. A concluding volume looks at what these regional variations mean for American religion as a whole.

1. Religion and Public Life in the Pacific Northwest: *The None Zone*
   Edited by Patricia O'Connell Killen (Pacific Lutheran University) and Mark Silk

2. Religion and Public Life in the Mountain West: *Sacred Landscapes in Tension*
   Edited by Jan Shipps (Indiana University–Purdue University, Indianapolis) and Mark Silk

3. Religion and Public Life in New England: *Steady Habits, Changing Slowly*
   Edited by Andrew Walsh and Mark Silk

4. Religion and Public Life in the Midwest: *America's Common Denominator?*
   Edited by Philip Barlow (Hanover College) and Mark Silk

5. Religion and Public Life in the Southern Crossroads Region: *Showdown States*
   Edited by William Lindsey (Philander Smith College) and Mark Silk

6. Religion and Public Life in the South: *In the Evangelical Mode*
   Edited by Charles Reagan Wilson (University of Mississippi) and Mark Silk

7. Religion and Public Life in the Middle Atlantic Region: *The Fount of Diversity*
   Edited by Randall Balmer (Columbia University) and Mark Silk

8. Religion and Public Life in the Pacific Region: *Fluid Identities*
   Edited by Wade Clark Roof (University of California, Santa Barbara) and Mark Silk

9. Religion by Region: *Religion and Public Life in The United States*
   By Mark Silk and Andrew Walsh

RELIGION AND PUBLIC LIFE IN THE MIDDLE ATLANTIC REGION: THE FOUNT OF DIVERSITY

Edited by

Randall Balmer

and

Mark Silk

Published in cooperation with the Leonard E. Greenberg
Center for the Study of Religion in Public Life at
Trinity College, Hartford, Connecticut

A Division of
ROWMAN & LITTLEFIELD PUBLISHERS, INC.
Walnut Creek • Lanham • New York • Toronto • Oxford

Published in cooperation with the Leonard E. Greenberg Center for the Study of Religion in Public Life at Trinity College, Hartford, Connecticut

ALTAMIRA PRESS
A division of Rowman & Littlefield Publishers, Inc.
A wholly owned subsidary of The Rowman & Littlefield Publishing Group, Inc.
4501 Forbes Boulevard, Suite 200
Lanham, MD 20706
www.altamirapress.com

PO Box 317
Oxford
OX2 9RU, UK

British Library Cataloguing in Publication Information Available

Library of Congress Cataloging-in-Publication Data

Religion and public life in the Middle Atlantic region : the fount of diversity / edited by Randall Balmer and Mark Silk.
    p. cm. — (Religion by region)
    Includes bibliographical references and index.
    ISBN-13: 978-0-7591-0636-9 (hardcover : alk. paper)
    ISBN-10: 0-7591-0636-3 (hardcover : alk. paper)
    ISBN-13: 978-0-7591-0637-6 (pbk. : alk. paper)
    ISBN-10: 0-7591-0637-1 (pbk. : alk. paper)
    1. Religion and politics—Middle Atlantic States. 2. Christianity—Middle Atlantic. 3. Christianity and politics—Middle Atlantic States.
    4. Middle Atlantic States—Religion. I. Title. II. Series.

BL2527.M52 R45 2006
200.974 22   2005033247

Printed in the United States of America

♾™ The paper used in this publication meets the minimum requirements of American National Standard for Information Sciences—Permanence of Paper for Printed Library Materials, ANSI/NISO Z39.48–1992.

Contents

PREFACE

Geographical diversity is the hallmark of religion in the United States. There are Catholic zones and evangelical Bible Belts, a Lutheran domain and a Mormon fastness, metropolitan concentrations of Jews and Muslims, and (in a different dimension) parts of the country where religious affiliation of whatever kind is very high and parts where it is far below the norm. This religious heterogeneity is inextricably linked to the character of American places. From Boston to Birmingham, from Salt Lake City to Santa Barbara, even the casual observer perceives public cultures that are intimately connected to the religious identities and habits of the local population.

Yet when the story of religion in American public life gets told, the country's variegated religious landscape tends to be reduced to a series of monochrome portraits of the spiritual state of the union, of piety along the Potomac, of great events or swings of mood that raise or lower the collective religious temperature. Whatever the virtues of compiling such a unified national narrative—and I believe they are considerable—it obscures a great deal. As the famous red-and-blue maps of the 2000 and 2004 presidential votes make clear, region has not ceased to matter in national politics. Indeed, in this era of increasing federalism regions are, state by state, charting ever more distinctive courses.

To understand where each region is headed and why, it is critical to recognize the place of religion in it. Religion by Region, a project of the Leonard E. Greenberg Center for the Study of Religion in Public Life at Trinity College in Hartford, represents the first comprehensive effort to show how religion shapes, and is being shaped by, regional culture in America. The project has been designed to produce edited volumes (of which this is the seventh) on each of eight regions of the country. A ninth volume will sum up the results in order to draw larger conclusions about the way religion and region combine to affect civic culture and public policy in the United States as a whole.

The purpose of the project is not to decompose a national storyline into eight separate narratives. Rather, it is to bring regional realities to bear, in a systematic way, on how American culture is understood at the beginning of the twenty-first century. In line with the Greenberg Center's commitment to enhance public understanding of religion, these volumes are intended for a general audience,

5

with a particular eye towards helping working journalists make better sense of the part religion plays in the public life—local, statewide, regional, and national—that they cover. At the same time, I am persuaded that the accounts and analyses provided in these volumes will make a significant contribution to the academic study of religion in contemporary America.

The project's division of the country into regions will be generally familiar, with the exception of what we are calling the Southern Crossroads—a region roughly equivalent to what American historians know as the Old Southwest, comprising Louisiana, Texas, Arkansas, Oklahoma, and Missouri. Since we are committed to covering every state in the Union (though not the territories—e.g., Puerto Rico), Hawaii has been included in a Pacific region with California and Nevada, and Alaska in the Pacific Northwest.

Cultural geographers may be surprised to discover a few states out of their customary places. Idaho, which is usually considered part of the Pacific Northwest, has been assigned to the Mountain West. In our view, the fact that the bulk of Idaho's population lives in the heavily Mormon southern part of the state links it more closely to Utah than to Oregon and Washington. To be sure, we might have chosen to parcel out certain states between regions, assigning northern Idaho and western Montana to the Pacific Northwest or, to take another example, creating a Catholic band running from southern Louisiana through south Texas and across the lower tiers of New Mexico and Arizona on into southern California. The purpose of the project, however, is not to map the country religiously but to explore the ways that politics, public policies, and civil society relate—or fail to relate—to the religion that is on the ground. States have had to be kept intact because when American laws are not made in Washington, D.C. they are made in statehouses. To understand what is decided in Baton Rouge, Louisiana's Catholic south and evangelical north must be seen as engaged in a single undertaking.

That is not to say that the details of American religious demography are unimportant to our purpose. That demography has undergone notable shifts in recent years, and these have affected public life in any number of ways. To reckon with them, it has been essential to assemble the best data available on the religious identities of Americans and how they correlate with voting patterns and views on public issues. As students of American religion know, however, this is far from an easy task. The U.S. Census is prohibited by law from asking questions about religion, and membership reports provided by religious bodies to non-governmental researchers—when they are provided at all—vary greatly in accuracy. Most public opinion polling does not enable us to draw precise correlations between respondents' views on issues and their religious identity and behavior.

In order to secure the best possible empirical grounding, the project has assembled a range of data from three sources, which are described in detail in the

Appendix. These have supplied us with, among other things, information from religious bodies on their membership; from individuals on their religious identities; and from voters in specific religious categories on their political preferences and opinions. (For purposes of clarity, people are described as "adherents" or "members" only when reported as such by a religious institution. Otherwise, they are "identifiers.") Putting this information together with 2000 census and other survey data, the project has been able to create both the best available picture of religion in America today and the most comprehensive account of its political significance.

Religion by Region does not argue that religion plays the same kind of role in each region of the country; nor does it mean to advance the proposition that religion is the master key that unlocks all the secrets of American public life. As the tables of contents of the individual volumes make clear, each region has its distinctive religious layout, based not only on the numerical strength of particular religious bodies but also on how those bodies, or groups of them, function on the public stage. In some regions, religion serves as a shaping force; in others it is a subtler conditioning agent. Our objective is simply to show what the picture looks like from place to place, and to provide consistent data and a framework of discussion sufficient to enable useful contrasts and comparisons to be drawn.

A project of such scope and ambition does not come cheap. We are deeply indebted to the Lilly Endowment for making it possible.

Mark Silk
Hartford, Connecticut
September 2005

Introduction

The Proving Ground for Pluralism

Randall Balmer

Since the earliest days of European colonization, the Middle Atlantic region has served as the proving ground for pluralism. Giovanni da Verrazano, an Italian navigator in the service of France, discovered the inlet to what is now New York harbor through the narrows that now bears his name. Nearly a century later, Henry Hudson, an Englishman under contract to the Dutch West India Company, nosed the *Half Moon* through the same narrows and up the river later named in his honor. Hudson failed in his search for a northwest passage to Asia, but he opened the way for immigration. The first group of settlers to disembark at Manhattan were Walloons, French-speaking Belgians, followed soon thereafter by a modest influx of Netherlanders, Germans, and French.

The Pluralist Imperative

In the seventeenth century, no less than today, religious affiliation served as a badge of ethnic identity. Early reports filtering back to Amsterdam from New Netherland told of Huguenots, Mennonites, Brownists, Quakers, Presbyterians, Roman Catholics, even, according to a contemporary, "many atheists and various other servants of Baal."[1] English Puritans settled toward the eastern end of Long Island. Jews, seeking asylum, arrived in New Amsterdam from Recifé in 1654, following the Portuguese takeover of the erstwhile Dutch colony there. The English conquest of New Netherland a decade later further added to the diversity of the colony renamed in honor of the Duke of York, and English attempts to tame some of the religious and ethnic diversity of their new colony met with considerable resistance.

Other colonies in the Middle Atlantic were also characterized by pluralism. Quakers and Scots-Irish Presbyterians, among many others, inhabited what is now New Jersey. Further south, the Swedes, flush from their crucial engagement

9

in the Thirty Years War, sought to establish a beachhead in the New World with settlements along the Delaware River, settlements that yielded to Dutch rule in 1665 and then to the English nine years later. Maryland, named for the wife of England's Charles I (not for the Blessed Virgin, as many believe), was founded by Lord Calvert as a refuge for English Catholics, but he recognized even from the beginning that Catholic settlers would have to accommodate believers from other traditions in order to ensure toleration for themselves. William Penn, an English Quaker, founded his "Holy Experiment" in 1680, a place of religious toleration that attracted Lutherans and Quakers, along with smaller groups such as Moravians, Mennonites, Amish, and Schwenckfelders.

The religious and ethnic pluralism in the Middle Atlantic persisted throughout the colonial period, and when it came time for the framers of the Constitution to configure the relationship between church and state for the new nation, they looked both to Roger Williams' notion of a "wall of separation" as well as to the religious diversity in New York and elsewhere. The notion of disestablishment, the absence of a state religion, was utterly unprecedented in the eighteenth century, but New York had been functioning for decades with *de facto* disestablishment, proving that religious pluralism posed no threat to the secular order and that government could function without the backing of a particular religion.

Religious pluralism in the Middle Atlantic has continued unabated to the present. Waves of immigration in the nineteenth century—especially Irish Catholics fleeing the potato famines and, later, Italian Catholics—changed the character of Catholicism in the region, and their growing numbers led to a greater assertiveness in the public arena. Archbishop John Hughes of New York and Archbishop Francis Kenrick of Philadelphia gamely tangled with Protestant-dominated public school societies over the use of the King James Version of the Bible. Slavs, most of them Eastern Orthodox, came to work in the steel mills of western Pennsylvania (and Ohio). Later in the nineteenth century, the arrival of Jews from Eastern Europe led to tensions, and eventually to schisms, within the Jewish community over the allowable levels of assimilation to American culture.

After Lyndon B. Johnson signed the Hart-Cellar Immigration Act of 1965 in the shadow of the Statue of Liberty on July 4, immigrants once again recast religious life in the Middle Atlantic. The abolition of the national-quota system, which had been in place since 1924, opened the harbors of the Middle Atlantic to thousands of immigrants from Asia and Latin America. By the end of the twentieth century Muslim mosques, Buddhist stupas, Hindu temples, Sikh gurdwaras, and Shinto shrines dotted not only the five boroughs of New York City, but the entire region.

Protestant, Catholic, Jew

Paradoxically, for all of its diversity, the Middle Atlantic is also arguably the center of influence for Protestantism, Catholicism, and Judaism, the nation's three most prominent religious traditions. Aside from Québec, Florida, and the Southwest, the cradle of Roman Catholicism in North America was Maryland, and one of the most important meetings of Catholic leaders took place at St. Mary's Seminary in Baltimore—the Third Plenary Council in 1884, which provided for the establishment of Catholic University and, more important, mandated the formation of parochial schools. As parish-based schools spread throughout the region and the nation, Catholic parents no longer needed to worry that their children's faith would be corrupted by attending Protestant-dominated public schools.

In addition to its historic importance as the host for the Third Plenary Council, the Middle Atlantic, with its large population of Catholics, is, together with the Northeast, a major center of influence within the American church. The Roman Catholic archbishop of New York, for instance, often functions as a spokesman for the American bishops and serves as the unofficial head of the Roman Catholic Church in the United States. The Middle Atlantic has also been home to some major Catholic figures, including Dorothy Day of the Catholic Worker movement; John Corridan, the Jesuit "labor priest" depicted in the 1954 motion picture *On the Waterfront*; Thomas Merton, a hedonistic student at Columbia University who converted to the faith and became a Trappist monk and a best-selling author; and Daniel and Philip Berrigan, Catholic priests who vigorously protested the war in Vietnam.

The Jewish presence in the Middle Atlantic is also significant. After the colonial-era migrations to New York and other seaports, many of the early waves of nineteenth-century Jewish immigrants to the United States settled in the so-called German Triangle of the Midwest, an area defined by three points on the triangle: Cincinnati, Milwaukee, and St. Louis. To a remarkable degree, these immigrants established roots in the Midwest (Hebrew Union College was founded in Cincinnati in 1875) and assimilated to the American, overwhelmingly Protestant, society, much to the shock of subsequent Jewish immigrants, mostly from Eastern Europe.

Having dissented from the assimilationist Reform Judaism—the initial course of the dinner celebrating the first graduating class from Hebrew Union College in 1883 was shellfish, a non-kosher (*traif*) food—Eastern European Jews shifted the focus of Jewish life in America to the Eastern seaboard, especially New York. Conservative Jews founded Jewish Theological Seminary in Manhattan in 1886, and Orthodox Jews operate Yeshiva University and Stern College for

Women in New York City. Substantial communities of Hasidic Jews inhabit Brooklyn and Rockland County in New York; Orthodox Jews operate several rabbinical schools: Beth Medrash Govoha, located in Lakewood, New Jersey, and Ner Israel Rabbinical College in Baltimore, another major center of Jewish population. A variety of Jewish institutions and philanthropic organizations, ranging from Mount Sinai Hospital to the American Jewish Committee, are located in New York; the Anti-Defamation League of B'nai B'rith traces its history to Manhattan's Lower East Side. Elsewhere in the region, Reconstructionist Rabbinical College, the school associated with Reconstructionist Judaism, is located near Philadelphia.

Somewhat counter-intuitively, for all of its cultural dominance elsewhere in the United States, Protestantism in recent decades has struggled somewhat in the Middle Atlantic, especially in New York City. The Dutch Reformed Church (now the Reformed Church in America) established such venerable institutions as the Collegiate School in New York City and Queen's College, now Rutgers University, in New Jersey. The revival fires of the Second Great Awakening swept through upstate New York with such regularity in the early part of the nineteenth century that the region came to be known as the "burned-over district." Quakers certainly shaped Pennsylvania society in the colonial period, although a decision to withdraw from politics in 1756 circumscribed their influence. Presbyterians have been important to the culture of New Jersey not only for their many congregations in the region, especially in New Jersey and Delaware, but also for their educational institutions: the College of New Jersey (now Princeton University) and Princeton Theological Seminary. Subsequent to the founding of the Methodist Episcopal Church at the so-called Christmas Conference in Baltimore in 1784, Methodists have been active throughout the region, bestowing such institutional legacies as Wesley College in Delaware, Drew University in New Jersey, and the Ocean Grove Camp Meeting Association on the Jersey shore.

The African Methodist Episcopal Church (AME) traces its history to 1787, when a disillusioned African-American minister, Richard Allen, walked out of the white-dominated St. George Methodist Episcopal Church in Philadelphia to form Bethel Church, the flagship congregation for the new AME denomination. Similarly, in 1796 Peter Williams, Christopher Rush, and James Varick of the John Street Methodist Church in New York City began leading separate meetings for African Americans and eventually chartered the African Methodist Episcopal Zion Church in 1801, the founding congregation of a new denomination by the same name.

But for all of their historical influence, Protestants have not always held their own. When Billy Graham initiated his storied Madison Square Garden "crusade" in 1957, he specifically compared New York City to the biblical cities Sodom and

Gomorrah, and when the (Protestant) National Council of Churches announced plans to construct an office building on Manhattan's Upper West Side, Protestants across the nation criticized the move as misguided and inappropriate, given that Protestants comprised something of a religious minority in New York.

The National Council of Churches proceeded with their plan, however, and on October 12, 1958, President Dwight Eisenhower laid the cornerstone to the Interchuch Center, a massive, hulking, International Style building on Riverside Drive, just across 120th Street from Riverside Church and adjacent to Union Theological Seminary. Many of the Protestant agencies for which the building was intended have since left the structure, relocating to various sites across the nation—Cleveland, Chicago, Louisville—in an effort to reconnect with more salubrious Protestant populations elsewhere. Still, the influence of Protestantism endures in New York and, more generally, in the Middle Atlantic, alongside of Judaism and Catholicism.

The Religious Landscape

In addition to the Interchurch Center, the Middle Atlantic is also home to some important religious structures. The Morningside Heights neighborhood of Manhattan emerged as a kind of "city on a hill" around the turn of the twentieth century and became home to the Cathedral of St. John the Divine, St. Luke's-Presbyterian Hospital, and the Jewish Theological Seminary, in addition to the Interchurch Center, Union Theological Seminary, and Riverside Church, which is sometimes called the cathedral church of liberal Protestantism. Not all of these buildings are architecturally distinguished (by any means), but their sheer bulk and density attest to the importance of religious life in the neighborhood, at least at one time.

Elsewhere in Manhattan, Calvary Baptist Church, a neo-gothic skyscraper on West 57th Street, across from Carnegie Hall, has been home to such firebrand preachers as John Roach Straton, an influential fundamentalist (known as the "pope of fundamentalism") during the 1920s. The headquarters of the American Bible Society, an influential organization, especially during the nation's westward expansion in the nineteenth century, is located on Columbus Circle. The inauspicious-looking Second German Baptist Church, located in Hell's Kitchen (near the Port Authority Bus Terminal), is now an off-Broadway theater, but it was the place where Baptist preacher Walter Rauschenbusch developed his Social Gospel, a Protestant theology of social engagement and reform, around the turn of the twentieth century.

St. Patrick's Cathedral in Midtown forms the symbolic center of Roman Catholicism in New York and, to a remarkable degree, for the nation, as illustrated by the funeral for Robert F. Kennedy after his assassination on June 6, 1968.

Heading north from St. Patrick's on Fifth Avenue (albeit against the vehicular traffic), one encounters St. Thomas Episcopal Church, Fifth Avenue Presbyterian Church, and the Reform Jewish Congregation Emanu-El, all of them architecturally notable buildings in addition to being important and influential congregations within their respective denominations. St. Bartholomew's Episcopal Church on Park Avenue fits that description also, as does Abyssinian Baptist Church, a major center of political and cultural influence for African Americans in Harlem. The huge new Islamic Center on 96th Street announces the presence of Muslims in New York City, and it serves the worship needs of both the neighborhood and the diplomatic community.

Elsewhere in New York City, the world headquarters for the Jehovah's Witnesses is in the Columbia Heights section of Brooklyn, near the Brooklyn Bridge, and Concord Baptist Church in Brooklyn, home of the legendary preacher Gardner C. Taylor, was a major center of influence during the civil rights movement and remains an important congregation for African-American Baptists. Fordham University in the Bronx and St. John's University in Queens are major centers for Roman Catholic life in the city.

Religious landmarks elsewhere in the region include a Sikh gurdwara in Glen Rock, New Jersey; the Swedenborgian Bryn Athyn Cathedral in Bryn Athyn, Pennsylvania, near Philadelphia; a Thai Buddhist temple, Wat Mongkoltempunee, in the suburbs of Philadelphia; and the Sri Venkateswara Temple in Penn Hills, Pennsylvania, in the eastern suburbs of Pittsburgh. The Mormon Temple in Kensington, Maryland, outside of Washington, D.C., can be seen from the Beltway, and its architectural style reminds many travelers of Oz. The neo-gothic National Cathedral in northwest Washington, D.C., serves as the seat for the presiding bishop of the Episcopal Church, but it also provides the venue for national religious observances; the memorial service for victims of the September 11, 2001 terrorist attacks, for example, was held at the National Cathedral.

"Judeo-Christian"

The Middle Atlantic has also had a hand in shaping even the nomenclature of American religious life. The term "Judeo-Christian tradition" was virtually unheard of at the turn of the twentieth century, but a growing and diversifying religious population coupled with the gathering storm in Europe in the 1930s prompted reconsideration of America as an exclusively Christian nation. The new "Judeo-Christian" formulation was intended to bracket others—Pentecostals, Mormons, Jehovah's Witnesses, Baha'is, Eastern Orthodox, and others—out of the ambit of respectability, and the new formula took shape symbolically in the Temple of Religion at the New York World's Fair in 1939-40, which limited its scope to Christians and Jews, thereby enshrining "the Judeo-Christian tradition."

By the mid-1950s, following World War II, the atrocities of the Holocaust, and the assimilation of Roman Catholics into middle-class society, it was time to expand the boundaries of religious acceptability once again in order specifically to include Catholics. Will Herberg, a professor at Drew University in Madison, New Jersey, provided the manifesto for this new inclusiveness with the publication in 1955 of *Protestant - Catholic - Jew*.

Herberg enlarged the boundaries of "the American way of life," but in doing so he effectively excluded all others, just as the term "Judeo-Christian" had done a few years earlier. "The outstanding feature of the religious situation in America today," Herberg wrote, "is the pervasiveness of religious self-identification along the tripartite scheme of Protestant, Catholic, Jew. From the 'land of immigrants,' America has," he concluded, "become the 'triple melting pot,' restructured in the three great communities with religious labels, defining three great 'communions' or faiths.'"[2] Herberg called the three—Protestantism, Catholicism, and Judaism—the "religions of democracy." Significantly (and not surprisingly), Herberg quoted Eisenhower's comments at the launch of the American Legion's "back to God" campaign in 1955. Recognition of a supreme being, the president declared, "is the first, most basic expression of Americanism. Without God, there could be no American form of government, nor an American way of life."[3]

A decade later, another New York World's Fair, in 1964-65, embodied further changes. The most popular pavilion by far was that sponsored by the Vatican, which had loaned Michelangelo's *Pieta* to the fair. Jews had grown so confident about their standing in American society that they looked toward broader horizons across the Atlantic; their exhibition was called the American-Israel Pavilion. Another major attraction was the Billy Graham Pavilion, sponsored by the twentieth century's foremost preacher, an evangelical Protestant.

Even then, however, the region's religious configuration was again in transition, heralding changes that would eventually be felt across the nation. The Mormon Pavilion at the 1964-65 World's Fair attracted as many as 34,000 visitors a day, and a recent book credits that exhibition with providing Latter-day Saints a foothold in New York City, part of a broader and more aggressive proselytization initiative across the nation and throughout the world.[4] At the same moment that queues snaked around the *Pieta*, however, President Johnson's signature on the Immigration Act just a couple of nautical miles away from the World's Fair site in Flushing, Queens, ensured that future reckonings of religious life in the United States would never again be so tidy and circumscribed.

Religious Minorities

Religious minorities have always been part of the patchwork of the Middle Atlantic. A small group called the Labadists, followers of Jean de Labadie, established a colony in Maryland in the seventeenth century. Johann Conrad Beissel set up a Protestant monastic community in Ephrata, Pennsylvania, in 1732, and Moravians arrived in Bethlehem, Pennsylvania, from Georgia on Christmas Eve, 1741. Mother Ann Lee first convened her followers, the Shakers, in Niskeyuna, New York, in 1774, and the Community of True Inspiration settled in Ebenezer, New York (near Buffalo), in 1842 before relocating to the undulating hills of eastern Iowa 13 years later, where they established the Amana Colonies. John Humphrey Noyes's ideas about "complex marriage" created a scandal among his Victorian neighbors in Oneida, New York, eventually forcing the colony to relocate to Canada.

The Jehovah's Witnesses, begun by Charles Taze Russsell in Allegheny, Pennsylvania, now make their home in Brooklyn. The Salvation Army, which is both a social-service organization as well as a holiness denomination, began its North American operations in New York City, and it has its national headquarters in Verona, New Jersey. After a starring role at the World's Parliament of Religions in Chicago in 1893, Swami Vivekanada established North America's first Vedanta Society the following year in New York City.

A number of African-American religious movements trace their history to the Middle Atlantic, especially after the "Great Migration" of blacks from the South to northern cities beginning around the turn of the twentieth century. Examples include the Universal Negro Improvement Association, a quasi-religious movement founded by Marcus Garvey, an immigrant from Jamaica; the United House of Prayer for all People, begun by Daddy Grace in Harlem and Long Island; and Father Divine's Peace Mission Movement, now headquartered in the Woodmont estate in suburban Philadelphia. The Moorish Science Temple, founded in 1913 in Newark, New Jersey, spread to New York and other northern cities. The Nation of Islam first appeared in the ghettos of Detroit, and Elijah Muhammad moved its base of operations to the south side of Chicago. But Harlem became a center of influence for the separatist movement because of the charismatic presence of Muhammad's most famous convert, Malcolm Little, better known as Minister Malcolm X. In 1989, George Augustus Stallings, an African-American priest in the Roman Catholic Church, left the church because of what he regarded as its persistent racism and formed the African-American Catholic Congregation, now known as the Imani Temple, in Washington, D.C., near the U.S. Capitol.

Since 1965, religious minorities and new religious groups have multiplied in the Middle Atlantic region. Muslims have flourished, along with Buddhists, Hindus, Jains, and other religions generally associated with Asia and South Asia. Vodou has taken hold among Haitian immigrants in Brooklyn and elsewhere. The Hare Krishna movement has its major base of operations for North America in New Vrindiban, West Virginia, not far from Pittsburgh. On Long Island, the Ave

Maria Chapel in Westbury serves as a beachhead for traditionalist, pre-Vatican II Catholicism, another sort of religious minority.

Pluralism in the Middle Atlantic

This volume examines the religious pluralism of the Middle Atlantic region, but it does so against the background of Herberg's Protestant-Catholic-Jew paradigm. If Herberg's formula works anywhere in America, the Middle Atlantic would be the most likely venue. Despite the presence and the persistence of Protestantism, Catholicism, and Judaism, however, the Middle Atlantic has always provided a haven for other religious groups, whose numbers today are greater than they have ever been in history. A recent survey, for instance, revealed that 36 percent of those in New York City were born in another nation.[5]

Vivian Klaff's chapter on demographics shows that the percentage of whites in the Middle Atlantic is 72.6 percent, just slightly below the national average, although whites constitute a minority in each of the region's three largest metropolitan areas: New York, Philadelphia, and Baltimore-Washington. Immigration from Latin America, Asia, and Africa (in descending order) means that a lower percentage of residents in the Middle Atlantic claim English as their home language (79 percent) than in any other region of the country. All of this makes for a pluralistic religious environment, although Klaff also points out that numbers are all relative. Muslims represent a higher percentage of the population in the Middle Atlantic than in any other region, for instance, but still only 1.7 percent. Corroborating the Protestant-Catholic-Jew synthesis, Klaff points out that, relative to the national population, Jews and Catholics are overrepresented in New Jersey and New York, while the percentage of mainline Protestants in Delaware, Pennsylvania, and Maryland exceeds the national average.

James Hudnut-Beumler notes that 34 percent of the Middle Atlantic population is Protestant, but the internal diversity within that number exceeds that of any other religious grouping. Roman Catholics, because of the nature of their church, are much more religiously homogeneous, though by no means ethnically homogeneous. Jews, of course, are ethnically homogeneous—or nearly so—and they divide themselves into only a few "denominations." The splintering of Protestantism into diverse and numberless denominations is amply demonstrated in the Middle Atlantic: Lutherans, Presbyterians, Congregationalists, Methodists, Episcopalians, Reformed, Quakers, Brethren, Moravians, Amish, Mennonites, and an infinite variety of Baptists and Pentecostals, to name only a few. Hudnut-Beumler suggests that Protestants in the Middle Atlantic can be divided by a line drawn through the Catskill, Pocono, and Appalachian mountains; Protestants to the west of that divide tend to be more conservative or evangelical, while Protestants in the region east of the line tend to affiliate more with mainline or liberal denominations. Although the percentage of evangelical Protestants in the Middle Atlantic is lower than in the remainder of the country, the mainline congregations in the western part of the region skew toward the conservative end of their denominations.

James Fisher finds the annual Alfred E. Smith dinner, sponsored by the Roman Catholic Archdiocese of New York, a fitting symbol of Catholic presence in the Middle Atlantic. Catholic immigrants in the nineteenth century survived various attempts to torch their buildings, proselytize their children, and deny them their rights as citizens. Due to the efforts of such bishops as John Hughes and Francis Kenrick, Roman Catholics tenaciously defended their rights and prerogatives, eventually securing for themselves a place in American society that, at various times and places, has approached political dominance. Smith's election as governor of New York and his nomination in 1928 as the first Roman Catholic to run for president on a major party ticket attest to the influence of the Catholic vote—even as his drubbing at the hands of Herbert Hoover, the Republican nominee, illustrates the extent to which Americans in the rest of the country lagged behind the Middle Atlantic in their acceptance of Roman Catholics in positions of authority. (Smith received only 41 percent of the popular vote nationwide, and he lost the Electoral College vote 444 to 87.)

The Smith dinner provided the second Roman Catholic nominee, John F. Kennedy, an important forum during the 1960 campaign; in subsequent years the Smith dinner became a required stop on the itinerary of presidential candidates, although more recently the archbishop of New York has tried to demonstrate his displeasure with politicians who support "choice" on abortion by refusing to extend them invitations to the dinner. Smith himself was an assimilated Catholic who at one point in the 1928 campaign demanded to know what a papal encyclical was; but, as Fisher points out, ethnic dynamics are once again being played out in Catholic parishes. Whereas the Irish hierarchy generally prevailed in transforming "ethnic parishes" into assimilated, American parishes around the turn of the twentieth century, increased immigration and changing neighborhoods have led to demands for the saying of mass in a host of languages other than English.

After noting the difficulties of quantifying the Jewish presence in the region and the nation, Lawrence Grossman states that 45 percent of America's Jews live in the Middle Atlantic, and an overwhelming majority of the country's Jewish organizations have their offices in the region, as do the major Jewish denominations. From the earliest days of settlement, Jews found in America a level of religious tolerance they found nowhere else (with the possible exception of the seventeenth-century Netherlands); Grossman notes that "there has never been anything approaching an anti-Semitic political party in the United States, Jewish civic equality has never been threatened, and today anti-Semitism is at an all-time low in the country," though that tolerance, coupled with the small number of Jews relative to the larger population, made it easier for Jews to assimilate, often at the cost of religious observance and even (for some) ethnic consciousness. For others, however, the trappings of Jewish life and identity persist, from dietary observances to the Kabbalah, the Jewish mystical tradition.

Jews, as Grossman points out, exert a political influence far disproportionate to their numbers. Generally their politics lean toward the left, especially on matters of racial equality and church-state separation, but the Republican Party in recent years has harvested substantial contributions from the Jewish community, and some of the region's most prominent Republicans—Michael Bloomberg, mayor of New York City, and Senator Arlen Specter of Pennsylvania, for instance—are Jewish. Most of all, Jews in the Middle Atlantic (and elsewhere) are concerned about two issues, support for Israel and quashing anti-Semitism, such as that many detected in Mel Gibson's movie, *The Passion of the Christ*, in 2004.

Finally, Wendy Cadge (like others before her) has identified Queens, New York—and Bowne Street in particular—as the emblem of the new religious pluralism in America. The arrival of immigrants from Latin America and Asia has undoubtedly altered the complexion of the Middle Atlantic, but it has done little overall to change the Christian dominance of the religious landscape, due to the fact that the overwhelming majority of immigrants are Christian. Just as settlement houses around the turn of the twentieth century provided essential services and helped immigrants acclimate to American society, so too religious organizations now offer assistance while also reinforcing ethnic and religious identity. While there is little evidence that large numbers of new immigrants are running for political office, these new religious groups have tried to make their voices heard in the public arena as advocates for such issues as housing and fair employment. Following the terrorist attacks of September 11, 2001, Muslim organizations in particular have been eager to educate the larger public about Islam, seeking in so doing to dissociate the vast majority of American Muslims from the extremists. Above all, new immigrants to the United States have discovered the power of the franchise, with many religious organizations encouraging their constituencies to register and vote.

Collectively, these essays paint a picture of a region of extraordinary diversity, a diversity that can be traced all the way back to seventeenth-century New Amsterdam. Will Herberg's Protestant-Catholic-Jew paradigm persists in the Middle Atlantic, however, not so much because of the internal vitality of these traditions as because of their entrenched institutions, which, due to their longevity, their cultural (and physical) location, and their endowments, continue to shape the politics and culture both of the region and the nation. At the same time, however, the region's long tradition of religious toleration impels these older traditions to make room for newcomers and religious minorities. From the seventeenth century to the present, that has been the pluralist imperative in the Middle Atlantic region.

Endnotes

1 Jameson, J. Franklin, ed., *Narratives of New Netherland, 1609-1664* (New York, 1909), 123-125.

2 Herberg, Will, *Protestant – Catholic – Jew* (Garden City, N.Y.: Doubleday, 1956), 272-273.

3 Quoted in ibid., 274-275.

4 Larsen, Kent S., 2nd, "A Stake in Babylon," in *City Saints: Mormons in the New York Metropolis*, ed. Scott Tiffany (New York: Nauvoo Books, 2004), 44.

5 See chapter by Vivian Klaff in this volume; cited also in Carnes, Tony, "New York's New Hope," *Christianity Today*, December 2004, 36.

RELIGIOUS AFFILIATION IN THE
MIDDLE ATLANTIC AND THE NATION

The charts on the following pages compare two measures of religious identification: self-identification by individuals responding to a survey and adherents claimed by religious institutions. The charts compare regional data for the Middle Atlantic and national data for both measures. The sources of the data are described below.

On page 22
Adherents Claimed by Religious Groups
The Polis Center at Indiana University-Purdue University Indianapolis provided the Religion by Region Project with estimates of adherents claimed by religious groups in the Middle Atlantic and the nation at large. These results are identified as the North American Religion Atlas (NARA). NARA combines 2000 census data with the Glenmary Research Center's 2000 Religious Congregations and Membership Survey (RCMS). Polis Center demographers supplemented the RCMS reports with data from other sources to produce estimates for groups that did not report to Glenmary.

On page 23
Religious Self-Identification
Drawn from the American Religious Identification Survey (ARIS 2001), these charts contrast how Americans in the Middle Atlantic and the nation at large describe their own religious identities. The ARIS study, conducted by Barry A. Kosmin, Egon Mayer, and Ariela Keysar at the Graduate Center of the City University of New York, includes the responses of 50,283 U.S. households gathered in a series of national, random-digit dialing, telephone surveys.

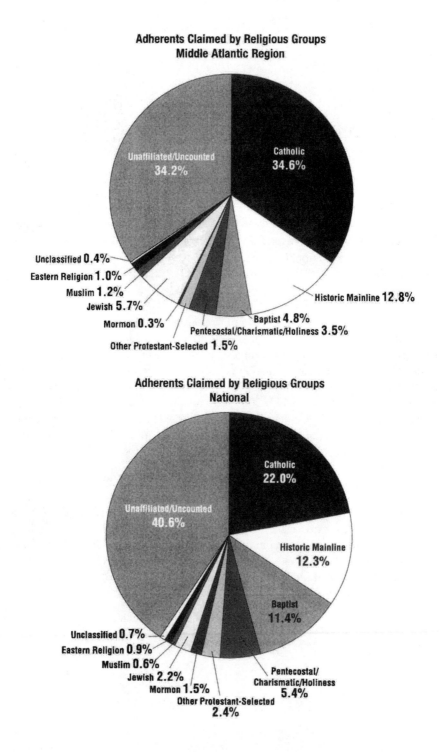

Adherents Claimed by Religious Groups
Middle Atlantic Region

Catholic
34.6%

Unaffiliated/Uncounted
34.2%

Historic Mainline 12.8%

Baptist 4.8%

Pentecostal/Charismatic/Holiness 3.5%

Other Protestant-Selected 1.5%

Mormon 0.3%

Jewish 5.7%

Muslim 1.2%

Eastern Religion 1.0%

Unclassified 0.4%

Adherents Claimed by Religious Groups
National

Catholic
22.0%

Unaffiliated/Uncounted
40.6%

Historic Mainline
12.3%

Baptist
11.4%

Pentecostal/
Charismatic/Holiness
5.4%

Other Protestant-Selected
2.4%

Mormon 1.5%

Jewish 2.2%

Muslim 0.6%

Eastern Religion 0.9%

Unclassified 0.7%

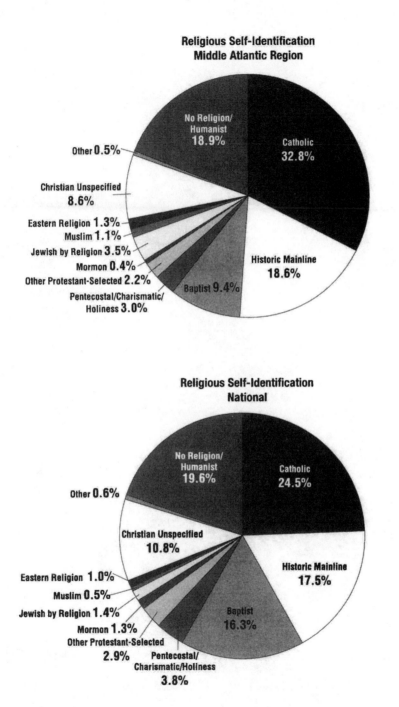

**Religious Self-Identification
Middle Atlantic Region**

No Religion/Humanist 18.9%

Catholic 32.8%

Other 0.5%

Christian Unspecified 8.6%

Eastern Religion 1.3%
Muslim 1.1%
Jewish by Religion 3.5%
Mormon 0.4%
Other Protestant-Selected 2.2%
Pentecostal/Charismatic/Holiness 3.0%

Baptist 9.4%

Historic Mainline 18.6%

**Religious Self-Identification
National**

No Religion/Humanist 19.6%

Catholic 24.5%

Other 0.6%

Christian Unspecified 10.8%

Eastern Religion 1.0%
Muslim 0.5%
Jewish by Religion 1.4%
Mormon 1.3%
Other Protestant-Selected 2.9%
Pentecostal/Charismatic/Holiness 3.8%

Baptist 16.3%

Historic Mainline 17.5%

CHAPTER ONE

THE RELIGIOUS DIVERSITY
OF AN IMMIGRANT REGION

Vivian Z. Klaff

A typical journey across the American landscape reveals to even the most casual of travelers the extent of the racial, ethnic, and religious diversity found in the society. In almost every corner of the land one finds Catholics, Lutherans, Buddhists, and people who profess no religion among the hundreds of religious configurations. Churches of one or other denomination, synagogues, mosques, and other religious buildings and holy sites are evident in every corner of the country. It is in the Middle Atlantic states that the dynamics of this American religious diversity were established.

The Middle Atlantic region covers 3.2 percent of the United States' land mass, and at the time of the first national census in 1790 contained 1.3 million people, 33.6 percent of the nearly 4 million American people. Between the nation's first census in 1790 and its twelfth in 1900, the population of the Middle Atlantic increased to about 17 million; by 1920 it had reached 34 million, and by 2000 the number was 46 million.

Over the years, as the country has filled up to the south and west, the region's portion of the U.S. population has steadily declined. From 1900 to 2000, it grew by 171 percent while the population of the nation as a whole increased by 270 percent. In the last decade of the twentieth century the region grew by 6.1 percent—less than half the nation's rate of 13.2 percent. Thus, as of the 2000 census, the Middle Atlantic's 46.3 million people constituted 16.5 percent of the U.S. population, making it third in population among the eight *Religion by Region* regions, behind the South and the Midwest. Eighty-six percent of the Middle Atlantic's population was urban in 2000—up from 80.7 percent in 1990 and now second only to the Pacific region. The most populous state in the region is

New York, with 41 percent of the region's population; followed by Pennsylvania, 26.5 percent; New Jersey, 18.2 percent; Maryland, 11.4 percent; and finally the District of Columbia and Delaware, each with less than 2 percent.

In the past, the Middle Atlantic was the point of entry into America for the vast majority of immigrants. It continues to attract a large number and to be the principal area from which newcomers disperse to other parts of the country. The region's population remains heterogeneous in the aggregate, with recent immigrants adding to the racial, ethnic, and religious mix. But as in the colonial period, when different ethno-religious groups staked out their own geographic territories, there are great demographic differences from one part of the region to another.

Race and Ethnicity

In racial and ethnic terms the Middle Atlantic region as a whole very closely resembles the national population. Close to three quarters (72.6 percent) of its people are classified as white, as compared to 75.1 percent nationwide. (New England ranked highest, with 86.5 percent, and the Pacific lowest, with 59.2 percent.) The Middle Atlantic's 15.7 percent black population is somewhat higher than the 12.2 percent for the nation as a whole, falling between the extremes of 20 percent in the South and 2 percent in the Mountain West. For their part, Asians comprise 4.3 percent in the Middle Atlantic, just modestly higher than the 3.6 percent for the country and falling between a high of 11.5 percent in the Pacific and a low of 1.6 percent in the South. In addition, 10.1 percent of the Middle Atlantic population was classified as Hispanic of all races, far closer to the national figure of 12.5 percent than the Pacific's 30.8 percent or the Midwest's 5.1 percent.

Within the region, however, significant racial and ethnic differences exist from state to state, as indicated in Figure 1.1. The proportion of whites varies from a high of 85 percent in Pennsylvania to a low of 31 percent in the District of Columbia. The inverse holds for the black population, which is highest in the nation's capital (60 percent) and lowest in Pennsylvania (9.9 percent). The proportion of Asians is roughly three times larger in New Jersey (5.7 percent) and New York (5.5 percent) than in Delaware (2.0 percent) and Pennsylvania (1.8 percent). Hispanics range from a high of 15.1 percent in New York to a modest 3.2 percent in Pennsylvania. Looking at the region's three major metropolitan/urbanized areas—New York, Philadelphia, and Baltimore-Washington, D.C.—the white population constitutes a minority within each city but a majority in all of the combinations of metropolitan or urbanized areas outside of the cities themselves. Hispanics and people defining themselves as other than white tend to be considerably overrepresented in New York City and the surrounding areas; Asians are also fairly well represented in the three metropolitan groupings.

	U.S.	Middle Atlantic	DE	D.C.	MD	NJ	NY	PA
Variable								
Percent White	75.1	72.6	74.6	30.6	64.0	72.5	67.9	85.4
Percent Black	12.2	15.7	19.0	60.0	27.7	13.4	15.7	9.9
Percent Asian	3.6	4.3	2.0	2.6	4.0	5.7	5.5	1.8
Percent Hispanic of all races	12.5	10.1	4.8	7.9	4.3	13.3	15.1	3.2
Percent foreign-born	11.1	14.0	5.7	12.9	9.8	17.5	20.4	4.1
Percent entered 1990-2000	42.4	41.2	47.2	51.0	44.1	41.6	40.4	41.1
Percent entered 1970-1989	42.3	41.4	32.4	37.8	2.3	41.2	42.3	35.2
Percent entered before 1970	15.4	17.5	20.4	11.2	13.6	17.2	17.3	23.6
Born in Europe as percent of foreign-born	15.8	23.4	22.1	17.5	16.7	3.9	2.7	35.9
Born in Asia as percent of foreign-born	26.4	26.4	30.0	16.9	35.0	27.7	23.6	35.9
Born in Africa as percent of foreign-born	2.8	4.2	45.0	2.5	12.0	4.0	3.0	5.0
Born in Latin America as percent of foreign-born	51.7	44.0	38.9	50.4	33.9	42.9	48.9	19.5
Born in state of residence		74.4	51.3	5.0	54.6	64.7	82.0	81.1
Language spoken at home (18+)								
English		78.7	89.8	81.4	86.3	72.6	70.7	91.4
Spanish		10.1	5.1	9.9	5.0	13.4	14.5	3.3
Other		11.2	5.1	8.7	8.7	14.0	14.8	5.3

Figure 1.1 Socio-Demographic Characteristics of the Middle Atlantic Region and States (U.S. Census 2000)

Foreign Born, Country of Origin, and Language Spoken

According to the 2000 census, 11.1 percent of the U.S. population is foreign born. As seen in Figure 1.1 15.4 percent of immigrants entered the country before 1970, 42.3 percent entered from 1970 to 1989, and 42.4 percent entered after 1990. These numbers provide dramatic evidence of the continuing importance of immigration in the nation's demography. Indeed, given the declining U.S. fertility rate, which is currently running at or below the replacement rate of slightly more than two children per woman (down from 3.6 at the height of the post-war baby boom), immigration will be responsible for whatever population growth takes place in the United States for the foreseeable future. Of the approximately 750,000 people who now immigrate legally to the United States every year, 81 percent come from non-European locations—Latin America (52 percent), Asia (26 percent), and Africa (3 percent)—areas of the world whose cultures, languages, and, in many cases, religious traditions differ profoundly from the Anglo-Saxon Protestant civilization that dominated the United States at the time of the Declaration of Independence and shaped the social and political core of American society for many generations.

The proportion of foreign born in the Middle Atlantic is 14 percent, second only to—but much lower than—the 25.3 percent in the Pacific. It is considerably higher, however, than the remaining six regions, which all come in below 10 percent. While there is little regional variation in dates of arrival, countries of origin vary considerably. Immigrants from Latin America, Asia, and Africa account for 90.9 percent of immigrants in the Southern Crossroads (including 70 percent from Latin America and 18.3 percent from Asia) and 87.4 percent in the Pacific (54.5 percent from Latin America and 33.7 percent from Asia) to a low of 58.1 percent in New England. Again, the Middle Atlantic falls in the middle of the range, with 74.6 percent of all immigrants coming from these three areas of origin (Latin America, 44 percent; Asia, 26.4 percent; and Africa, 4.2 percent). It is important to note that the proportion of foreign born in the Middle Atlantic increased considerably, from 9.9 percent to 14 percent, between 1990 and 2000. Thus, while the Middle Atlantic's share of the national population is declining, its share of new immigrants is increasing.

Within the region itself there is great variation in immigration patterns. Consistent with its history, New York leads the region, with 20.4 of its residents foreign born, in stark contrast to Pennsylvania, where the number is only 4.1 percent. Date of arrival varies little; a high of 51 percent in the District of Columbia and a low of 41 percent in New York arrived during the 1990s. This was a decade that saw an increase in the percentage of foreign born throughout the region. Immigrants from Latin America, Africa, and Asia range from a high of about 80 percent of all immigrants in both Maryland and the District of Columbia to a low of 60 percent in Pennsylvania. With the exception of the Keystone State (20 percent), Latin American immigrants constitute more than a third of all immigrants everywhere, ranging from 34 percent in Maryland to 50 percent in the District of Columbia. Asians constitute a quarter or more of all immigrants in every state, but not the District of Columbia; D.C. and Maryland stand out in the number of African immigrants, each with about 12 percent.

This variation in the immigrant population is reflected linguistically.

Seventy-nine percent of residents 18 and older in the Middle Atlantic speak English at home—just three percentage points lower than the national figure. But the range within the region extends from a high of just over 90 percent in Pennsylvania and Delaware to lows of 73 percent in New Jersey and 71 percent in New York.

Among the region's important urban areas, New York City and Washington, D.C. have by far the highest percentage of foreign born, with 36 percent in New York City proper, 27 percent in the New York metropolitan area, and 20 percent in metropolitan Washington. By contrast, less than 10 percent of the populations of Philadelphia, Baltimore, and Pittsburgh are foreign born, a figure that also applies to the surrounding metropolitan areas. Looking at the three largest sources of origin (Latin America, Europe, and Asia), the Washington and Baltimore areas have high concentrations of Latin American immigrants (ranging from 36 percent to 50 percent), followed by Asians (26 percent to 39 percent) and Europeans (11 percent to 24 percent). In the New York metropolitan area, Latin Americans constitute about half of all immigrants, with Asians at nearly a quarter and Europeans somewhat more than one fifth. Among the considerably smaller immigrant populations of the two Pennsylvania metropolitan areas, Asians lead in Philadelphia, with 36 percent, followed by Europeans, at 30 percent; in Pittsburgh the Europeans lead the Asians by 46 percent to 42 percent. In both metropolises, Latin American immigrants fall into the 21-22 percent range. Based on this profile of immigrant diversity, it comes as no surprise that the religious character of the Middle Atlantic would be in flux, leading to a complex mosaic of religious identification and affiliation.

With respect to migration within the United States, 74 percent of the Middle Atlantic's American-born population were born in the Middle Atlantic, but as shown in Figure 1.1, the regional variation is substantial. At the high end, about 80 percent of the native-born populations of both New York and Pennsylvania come from the region, while to the south the number ranges from 45 percent in the District of Columbia to the low 50s in Maryland and Delaware. Unsurprisingly, the Washington, D.C. area displays a high rate of mobility, whereas the states of New York and Pennsylvania have unexpectedly low mobility rates. If you're born in either state, it seems, you're very likely to stay there—wherever your forebears came from. One possible explanation is that these are large states and that outside the major metropolitan areas that attract immigrants seeking economic and social opportunities, the rest of the state population is less mobile.

Income and Education

In 2000, about 35 percent of American households had annual incomes of less than $30,000, while about 12 percent had incomes of $100,000 and above. The Middle Atlantic region falls toward the upper end of this income distribution, not as high as the New England and Pacific regions but considerably higher than the South and Southern Crossroads. As shown in Figure 1.2, Pennsylvania and the District of Columbia had the highest percentage of households in the Middle Atlantic with incomes of $30,000 or less, while Maryland and New Jersey had the highest percentage of households with incomes of $100,000 or more, both considerably above the national average.

In terms of education, 20 percent of men over 25 nationwide have less than a high school diploma, ranging from about 14 percent in the Pacific Northwest to about 23 percent in the South, the Southern Crossroads, and the Pacific. The Middle Atlantic falls slightly toward the less-educated end of the distribution, with 19 percent. While the numbers are slightly different, the picture is the same for women. At the upper end of the educational spectrum, 52.5 percent of men over 25 nation-wide have some college education, with Middle Atlantic men again falling slightly below the norm (and, again, with comparable numbers for women). Across the region, as shown in Figure 1.2, New York and the District of Columbia have the largest percentages of the least educated, even as the District of Columbia (along with Maryland) has the highest proportion of people with some college education. Pennsylvania has smaller proportions of both the less educated and the college educated. Across the region, Pennsylvania has the weakest socio-economic profile in the aggregate, while Maryland has the strongest.

Like the rest of the nation, the Middle Atlantic has an aging population, with 21.7 percent of the population under the age of 15 and 11.2 percent aged 65 and over. The marital status of the Middle Atlantic population also parallels the nation, reflecting a downturn in the percentage of married households and an increase in the percentage of people remaining single. About 55 percent of adults aged 18 and over were married in 2000, with 30 percent never married and the remainder separated, divorced, or widowed. Overall, if current fertility and mortality conditions continue, the population will reach zero growth within the next few decades unless immigration continues. But because the Middle Atlantic is a region of high immigration, and is likely to remain so, it presents a dynamic environment—as it always has—for changes in culture, language, social structure, and, of course, religion. At the same time, because of the pronounced demographic variations across the region, such changes will vary greatly from state to state, and within the states themselves.

Figure 1.2 Socio-Demographic Characteristics of
the Middle Atlantic Region and States
(U.S. Census 2000)

Variable	U.S.	Middle Atlantic	DE	D.C.	MD	NJ	NY	PA
Income								
Up to $29,999	35.1	33.1	29.5	38.2	25.8	26.0	35.3	37.2
$100,000 and over	12.3	15.3	14.0	16.4	18.1	21.3	15.3	10.3
Education								
Male: 0-12 years	19.9	19.1	18.3	22.1	16.5	17.7	21.1	18.0
Some college and above	52.7	51.5	51.4	58.6	57.6	54.8	52.3	45.3
Female: 0-12 years	19.3	19.0	16.6	22.3	15.9	18.1	20.8	18.2
Some college and above	52.9	49.2	51.0	56.1	56.7	50.8	50.5	42.5

Religious Roots: Early History of the Region

It could be suggested that the history of European Christian influence in the Middle Atlantic began when Columbus and other European explorers landed in the new world. However, it was not until the arrival of larger numbers of European settlers in the seventeenth century that the region's religious-political structure began to take shape.

In the early years of European settlement, white society in the Middle Atlantic was religiously diverse. Early on, there were Dutch Calvinists, who founded the colony of New Amsterdam in what is now New York City in 1626; Swedish Lutherans, who established the colony of New Sweden in present-day Delaware in 1638; and Sephardic Jews, who in 1654 arrived in New Amsterdam from Brazil. William Penn arrived in 1682 in what came to be Pennsylvania and established an area of comfort for the Quakers. Maryland was set up as a haven for Catholics in the mid-seventeenth century, although Catholics quickly became a minority when Anglicans and other Protestants streamed in.

Describing the religious composition of the Middle Atlantic region at the birth of the nation necessitates turning to historical data on congregations that existed in 1776.[1] While these figures offer only a shadowy indication of the number of adherents, they do provide some sense of the relative strength of the region's denominational bodies. Thus, the proportion of Presbyterian congregations was high in all five states, ranging from 37 percent in Delaware to 14 percent in Maryland. Anglican (Episcopal) congregations were somewhat less prevalent, with a high of 27 in Maryland to a low of 6 percent in Pennsylvania. Quaker congregations were situated evenly and in significant numbers in all states, ranging from 19 percent of congregations in Delaware to 15 percent in New Jersey. In addition—and counting only those denominations with 10 percent or more of the congregational total—we find a Catholic concentration in Maryland (16 percent), Baptist strength in New Jersey (18 percent), a powerful Dutch Reformed presence in New York (26 percent), and numerous German Reformed in Pennsylvania (18 percent), the latter being the forerunners of the contemporary Amish and Mennonite communities centered in Lancaster County.

In 1776, Congregationalists, Presbyterians, and Anglicans dominated the region, but, dependent as they were on permanent institutional structures, these three colonial denominations were ill equipped to prosper in an emerging frontier society. By the Second Great Awakening, Baptists and Methodists had begun to attract increasing numbers of adherents, emerging as the largest Protestant groups by the mid-1800s. In the later nineteenth century, Catholic immigration from Europe transformed the region's religious composition. Through the 1890s the vast majority of immigrants came from western and northern Europe. The end of the century saw the arrival of large numbers of Southern-, Central-, and Eastern-European immigrants, including especially Italian Catholics and Eastern-European Jews. Data from the *New Historical Atlas of Religion in America* contained in Figure 1.3 demonstrate this transformation.[2] By 1890 Catholics represented the majority of members of religious bodies in all Middle Atlantic states with the exception of Delaware, where most adherents were Methodists. Methodists were generally the second largest group, followed by Baptists, Episcopalians, and Lutherans. Other Christian groups had very small numbers, while significant numbers of Jews existed only in New York.

A hundred years later, Catholics represented the highest percentage of adherents in all states; in the District of Columbia Baptists constituted the majority. Jews were now found in substantial numbers throughout the region.

Religion in the Middle Atlantic in 2000

By the end of the twentieth century the original Protestant immigrant groups from western Europe that populated the Northeast and the Middle Atlantic had made way for a diverse array of long-standing Christian denominations as well as quantitatively small but nevertheless culturally significant new-immigrant religions. In all of the states in this region there is a considerable variety of religious groups. The discussion in this section

Figure 1.3 Proportionate Judeo-Christian Denominational Strength by State in Middle Atlantic Region, 1890 & 1990
(Gaustad, Edwin S. New Historical Atlas of Religion in America, Oxford University Press, 2001)

	DE	D.C.	MD	NJ	NY	PA
1890						
Catholics	24.2	40.0	37.3	43.9	53.1	32.4
Methodists	53.0	17.4	32.6	19.0	12.2	15.1
Presbyterians	9.5	5.4	3.3	11.7	7.8	12.5
Baptists	4.1	20.6	4.3	7.8	6.6	5.0
Episcopalians	5.9	7.9	6.4	6.0	5.9	3.3
Lutherans		3.2	6.5	2.5	1.3	12.7
Reformed			2.8	5.2		7.2
Evangelical Associations						2.5
United Brethren						2.0
Congregationalists		1.5			2.1	
German Evangelical Synod			1.2			
Jews					2.1	
Other	3.3	4.0	5.6	3.9	8.9	7.3
Total	**100.0**	**100.0**	**100.0**	**100.0**	**100.0**	**100.0**
1990						
Catholics	38.0	20.7	36.0	67.4	61.6	50.4
Methodists	20.1	15.5	14.2	4.4	5.5	10.9
Presbyterians	5.9	2.6	2.6	3.0	1.7	5.6
Baptists	16.7	41.2	18.6	6.8	6.4	4.9
Episcopalians	4.3	4.3	3.6	2.2	2.0	1.9
Lutherans	3.0	1.5	6.0	2.4	2.4	9.7
Jews	3.1	6.8	9.1	9.1	15.6	4.5
Other	8.9	7.4	4.7	4.7	4.8	12.1
Total	**100.0**	**100.0**	**100.0**	**100.0**	**100.0**	**100.0**

focuses on the numerically dominant groups in each state and the principal areas of concentration of these groups. The logic followed is that the size of a group has a significant cultural influence on an area. However, this analysis should not be allowed to obscure the distinctive influence of smaller denominational groups in specific areas, such as the Amish in central Pennsylvania and Pentecostal Christians on the eastern shore of the Chesapeake Bay.

The population of the Middle Atlantic is more "churched" than the nation as a whole, as seen in Figure 1.4. With only 34.1 percent unaffiliated, the region approaches the church membership rate of the Southern Crossroads, the most church-going region in the country. About half the region's adherents are Catholic—not as high as the 68 percent in New England, but well above the 13 percent in the South. The Hispanic Catholic population in the Middle Atlantic region is considerably lower, of course, than among Catholics in the Pacific, the Mountain West, and the Southern Crossroads regions, pointing toward an important regional distinction within this religious tradition. New York is the only state in the region with a substantial number of Hispanic Catholics. The only other groups overrepresented in the Middle Atlantic compared to the nation are Jews and Muslims. The former have a long history of settlement in the Middle Atlantic, but have declined slightly as they inter-marry with non-Jews and integrate into the society at large, and as younger Jews migrate out of the region. Muslims have grown from a very small base as a result of immigration and conversion.

These broad regional data, however, disguise important subregional differences among and within individual states.

New York

The Empire State is generally viewed as a crucible of ethnic and religious diversity. In fact, much of this image of diversity has to do with the tendency to focus on groups in New York City that have very low numerical representation in the state—as is the case, for example, in a recent book entitled *New York Glory: Religions in the City*.[3] In fact, however, in the city itself Catholics, Baptists, and Jews comprise roughly two-thirds of the population. Statewide, four out of every five adherents fall into these groups, and three of these are Catholic. Catholic prominence is particularly high to the north and east, less so along the Pennsylvania border. (In two counties, Clinton and Putnam, Catholics comprise about 85 percent of all adherents.) In no county is the Catholic rate lower than 30 percent.

Jews constitute the second largest group of religious adherents in the state, with 12.8 percent. This population is highly concentrated around New York City, where it has had a powerful influence on the city's social, cultural, and economic institutions. In the five counties surrounding the city, Jewish adherents represent 20 percent or more of the total; in Rockland County they represent just over a third. Despite the fact that the Jewish population now exists in substantial numbers in met-ropolitan areas across the country, New York City can still legitimately claim to be the heart of American Jewish cultural and institutional life. But in the remainder of the state, as in much of the nation, the Jewish population tends to be quite small.

Figure 1.4   Denominational Adherents for States in Middle Atlantic: Percent of Persons who are Adherents of a Specific Denomination (NARA)

	U.S.	Middle Atlantic	D.C.	DE	MD	NJ	NY	PA
Total population	281,421,906	46,389,480		783,600	5,296,486	8,414,350	18,976,457	12,281,054
Total adherents	167,452,161	30,462,957	unavailable	440,077	2,908,285	5,620,503	12,944,632	7,977,401
(*Percentages*)								
Catholic adherents	37.0	52.5	--	34.5	32.7	60.5	58.3	47.7
Baptist adherents	14.3	3.0	--	3.3	7.0	2.2	2.1	2.6
Historically African-American Protestant adherents	12.4	10.5	--	25.7	17.7	10.7	8.8	8.2
United Methodist adherents	6.2	5.2	--	13.5	10.2	2.5	3.1	8.3
Other Conservative Christian adherents	4.7	2.1	--	2.5	3.6	1.5	1.7	2.8
Holiness/Wesleyan Pentecostal adherents	4.6	2.7	--	3.6	4.0	1.8	2.2	3.7
Jewish adherents	3.7	8.7	--	3.1	7.4	8.3	12.8	3.5
Lutheran (ELCA) adherents	3.1	3.2	--	1.5	3.6	1.4	1.3	7.7
Confessional/Reformed/Non-UCC Congregational adherents	2.6	1.2	--	1.6	1.7	1.3	1.3	1.0
Mormon adherents	2.5	0.4	--	0.6	0.9	0.4	0.3	0.4
Muslim adherents	0.9	1.7	--	0.8	1.8	2.1	1.7	0.9
Eastern religion adherents	1.5	1.6	--	1.0	2.4	1.7	1.8	0.7
Other (small group) adherents	6.5	7.2	--	8.3	7.0	5.5	4.6	12.6
Total adherents	100.0	100.0	--	100.0	100.0	100.0	100.0	100.0
Percent of population who are adherents, by region	59.5	65.9	--	56.2	54.9	66.8	68.2	65.0
Percent of population who have no religion, by region	40.5	34.1		43.8	45.1	33.2	31.8	35.0
Total population	100.0	100.0	--	100.0	100.0	100.0	100.0	100.0

African-American Protestants, most of whom are Baptists, make up the third largest group in the state, with 8.8 percent of all adherents. While concentrated in the New York City area, a fair number of counties in the northwest sector near the Canadian border have relatively high concentrations of African-American

Protestants. The only other group with 3 percent or more of all adherents is the United Methodists (3.1 percent), who tend to be spread out across the state, particularly in counties with lower population densities. Counties along the Pennsylvania border have relatively high concentrations of United Methodists, comparable to counties in northern Pennsylvania. A band of Lutheran strength begins in the south-central sector of New York, running down through the mid-section of Pennsylvania and into the northern counties of Maryland.

New Jersey

Catholics comprise over 60 percent of adherents in New Jersey, while only two other groups—African-American Protestants (10.7 percent) and Jews (8.3 percent)—exceed 3 percent. In 16 of the state's 21 counties, Catholics hold the majority, and in only one of the remaining five counties are they less than 45 percent; they are fairly evenly distributed across the state with the exception of the southern portion, where they compete with the Historically African-American Protestants in Atlantic County (Catholic, 45 percent; Historically African-American Protestant, 25.1 percent), and Salem County (Catholic, 25.4 percent; Historically African-American Protestant, 32.8 percent). In the rest of the state, Historically African-American Protestants are concentrated in urban areas adjacent to New York City (Newark) and Philadelphia (Camden and Trenton).

Jews, who comprise about 8 percent of the state's adherents, are represented most strongly in three central counties (Monmouth, 13.6 percent; Essex, 12.6 percent; and Bergen, 11.8 percent) but otherwise have fairly low concentrations. They tend to live in residential communities with fewer cultural institutions of national prominence than the higher density Jewish areas of New York City.

Non-Judeo-Christian communities are making inroads into the Garden State's cultural mix. The city of Patterson is home to a large number of Muslims, who constitute 8.1 percent of adherents in Passaic County. In four other New Jersey counties—Essex, Hudson, Mercer, and Burlington—more than 3 percent of adherents are Muslims. In Warren County in the northwest and in Somerset County in the central part of the state, 7.7 percent and 3.8 percent of adherents, respectively, belong to an Eastern religion.

Pennsylvania

In Pennsylvania there is a fairly large drop in Catholic adherents (to 47.7 percent). This is partially related to the lower proportion of Latinos—Pennsylvania has the lowest proportion of foreign born and new immigrants of all the region's states—and partially to the traditional strength of the mainline Protestant denominations, especially Methodists and Lutherans, who predominate in the central part of the state. In just 19 of the state's 67 counties do Catholics constitute a majority of adherents. The largest concentration is in the east, in and around the Philadelphia metropolitan area, and in the counties closest to the New York and New Jersey borders. Catholics are also concentrated in the western portion of the state, in and around metropolitan Pittsburgh.

In addition, Pennsylvania boasts five other religious groups with 3 percent or more of all religious adherents, the largest being the United Methodists (8.3 percent) and Historically African-American Protestants (8.2 percent). So, while less diverse along racial and ethnic lines, Pennsylvania is perhaps the most religiously diverse of the Middle Atlantic states, as seen in Figure 1.4. For example, about 12 percent of the state's adherents are classified as "other," a far larger percentage than in the other states. These consist mainly of smaller Christian denominations.

The Historically African-American Protestant denominations represent 8.2 percent of the adherent population. They are highly concentrated, 70 percent living in the four metropolitan counties in and around Philadelphia (Philadelphia, Delaware, Chester, and Montgomery) and in the Pittsburgh metropolitan county (Allegheny). The Historically African-American Protestants are clearly a highly urbanized population, with a strong influence on the metropolitan political and social environments. Pennsylvania's Jewish adherents, constituting 3.5 percent of the population, are likewise highly urbanized and concentrated in the southeast corner of the state. About 73 percent live in the five counties in and around the Philadelphia metropolitan area (Philadelphia, Montgomery, Bucks, Delaware, and Chester).

Maryland/Delaware

Moving south to Maryland and Delaware, the Catholic numbers decline further, to roughly one-third of all adherents. Yet Catholics are still clearly the dominant religious group. They predominate in 15 of Maryland's 24 counties, mainly on the western side of the Chesapeake Bay, which divides Maryland into two parts. In both states, Catholics are followed by Historically African-American Protestants, who constitute nearly a fifth of Maryland's adherents and a quarter of Delaware's. They are concentrated in Delaware's two southernmost counties and on the eastern shore of Maryland. Pentecostals, who make up 4 percent of Maryland's adherents, are also disproportionately located on the eastern shore. This provides a considerable population of religiously conservative, but politically complex, denominations in this area.

United Methodists come in third in both Delaware and Maryland, comprising 13.5 percent and 10.2 percent of adherents respectively. Like the African Americans, they are concentrated in southern Delaware and on the eastern shore. Across the bay, the Methodists cluster in the north along the Pennsylvania line.

As in Pennsylvania and New York, they are generally located away from the major population centers.

Jews, who constitute 7.4 percent of adherents in Maryland and 3.1 percent in Delaware, are highly concentrated and urbanized. In Delaware, they live mostly in the northern part of the state, in and around Wilmington. In Maryland, about 83 percent live in the city of Baltimore, in Baltimore County, and in Montgomery County (on the border of the District of Columbia). Adding two more counties, Prince Georges and Howard, creates a contiguous area that contains about 96 percent of the Jewish adherents in Maryland. Such demographic concentration has enabled Maryland's Jewish community to establish communal institutions with great efficiency.

The population of white Baptist adherents in Maryland, at 7 percent, is higher than in any other state in the Middle Atlantic region, with Delaware coming in second, at 3.3 percent. The majority of Maryland's white Baptists are found west of the Chesapeake, and just over half are located in a five-county central-western section from Montgomery County down to St. Mary's County. There is also a relatively heavy concentration of white Baptists in the northeast corner of the state—part of a band of significant Baptist adherence that extends across northern Delaware and into southwestern New Jersey.

Middle Atlantic Self-identifiers in National Context

With 81.1 percent of the population associating themselves with a religion, according to the American Religious Identification Survey (ARIS), the Middle Atlantic falls between a high of 83 percent religious self-identification in the South and a low of 67.7 percent in the Pacific Northwest. The percentage of individuals identifying with one or other religion is considerably higher than the North American Religion Atlas (NARA) adherence rate of 66 percent for the Middle Atlantic region. This tends to corroborate much of the literature, which suggests that a higher proportion of Americans identify with religion than attend religious services or belong to religious institutions. Although the General Social Survey—a national random opinion survey conducted every year—does not ask whether respondents are members of a religious organization, it does ask to what extent they believe in God and how often they attend religious services. While about 85 percent of respondents now claim some level of belief in a deity, 50 percent say they never or hardly ever attend a religious service. While this is not conclusive evidence, it does lead to an expectation of a significant differ-ence between religious adherence and religious identity across the country. The Middle Atlantic's gap in this regard is relatively small; while the proportion of those claiming a religious identity is less than one percentage point greater than in the nation as a whole, the membership rate is 6.4 percentage points higher. By way of comparison, the proportion of Southerners claiming a religious identity is 3.5 percentage points higher than in the nation, but membership is virtually identical.

According to ARIS, Catholics are over-represented in the Middle Atlantic as compared to the nation as a whole, 41.1 percent of the population to 31.2 percent. Jews are likewise over-represented in the region (4.3 percent versus 1.7 percent in the nation as a whole), as are Eastern Orthodox (.7 percent versus .4 percent). So, too, the region features twice as large a proportion of Muslims as the nation (1.4 percent versus .7 percent), and more than a third as large a proportion of Hindus (.8 per cent versus .5 percent). By contrast, Baptists are significantly underrepresented (5.6 percent versus 14.9 percent), as are Mormons (.5 percent versus 1.6 percent) and Pentecostals (1.6 percent versus 2.7 percent).

Bearing in mind that the Middle Atlantic contains 16.7 percent of the national population, Figure 1.5 (page 41) shows the percentages of religious groups residing in the region; 26.3 percent of white non-Latino Catholics and 30.2 percent of all black Catholics in the nation, for instance, live in the Middle Atlantic. Likewise, Reformed (28.7 percent), Quaker (25 percent), and Mennonite (28.4 percent). A remarkable 42.5 percent of all American Jews reside in the Middle Atlantic region, and almost a third of all the nation's Eastern Orthodox (32.5 percent) and Hindus (30.7 percent).

Growth and Decline in the Middle Atlantic

Comparing the ARIS data to the National Survey of Religious Identification (NSRI)—a comparable study conducted in 1990— it is possible to assess recent patterns of religious growth and decline in the region. In both 1990 and 2000 six denominational groupings accounted for 78 percent of the region's total population—Catholic, Baptist, Mainline, Evangelical, Jewish, and None. Nationally, all three of the largest denominational groups (Catholic, Baptist, and "mainline") saw proportional losses. In the Middle Atlantic, the mainline Protestants held steady, and the Baptists saw only modest losses. The greatest changes in proportional representation were experienced by Catholics (6 percent loss) and those claiming no religion (8.7 percent gain).

The Eastern religions such as Hinduism and Buddhism, as well as Islam, increased. But due to small base numbers it was not possible to determine the extent of the increase. Nevertheless, these non-Christian groups remain proportionally modest (Muslims, 1.7 percent; Eastern Religions, 1.5 percent). Thus, while these minority religions, along with a variety of Native-American and New-Age religions, are becoming important actors on the local and national social and political scene, it is difficult to identify and analyze them with the demographic data currently available.

A Liberal Tilt

This series of books uses a set of public opinion items that, while limited, offer a way to assess how the religious demographics of a region affect its public life. These indicators, described here as "Akron/Pew" data cover three broad areas. First are two indicators of political ideology: self-described political party preference and ideological self-description (as liberal, moderate, or conservative). Second is a set of indicators related to the so-called "hot-button" issues of abortion, gay rights, and school vouchers. Finally, four indicators cover attitudes related to the modern regulatory state: Welfare spending, national health insurance, programs to encourage minority achievement, and environmental protection.

On all these indicators, the population of the Middle Atlantic is modestly more liberal than the nation as a whole, but the differences are quite modest. Whereas 42 percent of the national population identify as Democratic, for instance, 46.5 percent identify themselves as Democratic in the Middle Atlantic. Likewise, on hot-button issues, Middle Atlantic residents are more likely to favor school vouchers (46.8 percent vs. 42.6 percent nationally), support gay rights (64.6 percent vs. 56.7 percent nationally), and support legal abortion (46.9 percent vs. 41.1 percent nationally).[4] On issues related to the welfare state, the differences between the region and the nation as a whole are negligible, with the exception of attitudes about welfare spending, an item on which Middle Atlantic residents are modestly more liberal (55 percent supporting greater spending compared to 51.4 percent nation-wide).

This tendency to follow the national patterns repeats itself among the five major religious groups in the region, with only a few notable exceptions. Catholics, the largest religious group in the region, mirror their co-religionists nationally on all but two of the indicators. Like their co-religionists nationally, Catholics in the region are more likely to identify as Democrats (45.4 percent) than Republicans (36.6 percent), and more likely to describe themselves as ideologically conservative (40.7 percent) than liberal (31.4 percent). On abortion, they are more pro-life (44.7 percent) than pro-choice (40.6 percent). They support greater welfare spending (54.7 percent), national health insurance (47.2 percent compared to 33.6 percent opposed), and environmental protection (54.7 percent). They are evenly divided on programs to encourage minority achievement (36.6 percent in favor, 39.6 percent opposed). On only two indicators do Catholics in the region differ from Catholics in the nation as a whole. They are more likely to support school vouchers (54 percent compared to 46 percent nationally) and more supportive of gay rights (66.2 percent compared to 62.6 percent nationally).

Mainline Protestants in the region are more likely to say they are Democrats (37.1 percent) than are their co-religionists nationally (33.3 percent), and

Figure 1.5   Denominational Self-Identification (ARIS) for the Nation,
Middle Atlantic, and Comparisons With Regions
Percent of Denominational Self-Identifiers Who Reside in the Middle Atlantic
(ARIS 2001)

Denominations	Mid-Atlantic	Region	High	Region	Low	Percent of religion in U.S.
White Catholic, non-Hispanic	26.3	MW	26.5	NW	2.4	20.1
Minority Catholic						
Hispanic Catholic	13.3	P	33.6	NW	1.7	8.6
Black Catholic, non-Hispanic	30.2	S	29.7	M	0.0	0.9
Other minority Catholic	15.6	P	35.9	M	5.3	1.3
White Protestant, non-Hispanic						
Methodist	17.4	S/MW	27.5	NW	2.2	7.3
Lutheran	14.9	MW	48.9	NE	2.0	5.6
Presbyterian	19.7	S	27.7	NE	1.8	3.1
Episcopalian	18.2	S	25.3	NW	3.4	1.8
Congregational / UCC	17.3	MW	30.2	M	3.4	0.8
Disciples of Christ	3.9	MW	34.9	NE	1.9	0.3
Reformed Tradition	28.7	MW	42.9	M	0.9	0.2
Quaker	25.0	MW	24.0	NW	2.5	0.1
Baptist / Baptist Tradtion	6.3	S	45.4	NW	1.9	14.9
Pentecostal/ Charismatic Tradition	10.4	S	31.8	NE	2.6	2.7
Evangelical / Fundamentalist / Non-denominational	11.1	S	20.5	NE	3.4	1.7
Holiness Tradition	9.3	S	26.6	NE	2.1	0.4
Mennonite / Brethren	28.4	MW	42.8	NE	0.8	0.4
Protestant / Christian unspecified	11.9	MW	25.7	NW	6.1	8.1
Minority Protestant						
Hispanic Protestant	12.5	P	30.8	NW	2.5	3.5
Black Protestant, non-Hispanic	18.1	S	41.1	NW	0.5	9.9
Other minority Protestant	17.3	P	23.9	NE	1.2	2.2
Eastern Orthodox	32.5	MW	20.8	SC	1.4	0.4
Mormon	4.9	M	47.2	NE	3.1	1.6
Jehovah Witness	17.6	S	20.4	NE	3.4	0.8
Jewish by religion	42.5	S	19.0	NW	2.3	1.7
Muslim	35.5	MW	24.5	NW	0.5	1.7
Buddhist	17.3	P	39.9	NE	3.0	0.7
Hindu	30.7	P	30.8	M/NW	1.8	0.5
Yes Religion	16.9	S	23.8	NW	2.9	**100.0**
All other religious group	14.0	S	19.3	NW	5.0	
Percent no religion	15.7	MW	21.2	NE	5.5	
Percent refused answer / Don't know	17.0	S	22.1	NW	3.8	
No religion	15.9	MW	20.6	NW	5.2	
Total	16.7	S	22.7	NW	2.2	

somewhat less likely to describe themselves as ideologically conservative (40.4 percent vs. 47.1 percent nationally). On all other indicators, they mirror the national statistics for this denominational family almost precisely, opposing school vouchers (50.3 percent) but favoring legal abortion (49.6 percent) and gay rights (60.3 percent); favoring increased welfare spending (50 percent), national health insurance (42.1 percent), and environmental protection (61.4 percent); and divided on assistance to minorities (35.9 percent in favor, 39.7 percent opposed).

As is the case nationally, African-American Protestants vote Democratic by large margins (78.1 percent), but are only somewhat more likely to describe themselves as ideologically liberal (43.1 percent) than conservative (32.7 percent). They are substantially more likely than their co-religionists nationally to support school vouchers (61.8 percent as opposed to 50.6 percent nationally) and somewhat more likely to support increased welfare spending (71 percent vs. 65.6 percent nationally), programs to encourage minority achievement (67.3 percent vs. 63.9 percent), and environmental protection (48.6 percent vs. 43 percent). On the remaining attitudinal items, they mirror African-American Protestants nationally—divided on abortion (41.5 percent pro-choice; 41.9 percent pro-life) and favoring gay rights (58.8 percent compared to 22.3 percent opposed) and national health insurance (56 percent).

Taken together, these three groups account for almost two-thirds of the Middle Atlantic population. Although, as a rule, they tend to resemble their co-religionists nationally, their combined influence largely accounts for the modest leftward tilt in the region as a whole. That tendency is further explained by the two groups that do differ notably from their co-religionists nationally: Evangelical Protestants and seculars, both being more liberal than the national data would lead one to predict.

Although evangelical Protestants resemble their co-religionists nationally in terms of party identification (54.2 percent Republican; 32.8 percent Democrat) and ideology (27.1 percent liberal; 54.5 percent conservative), they differ substantially from their co-religionists on the hot-button issues. Indeed, attitudes about abortion and gay rights would suggest that evangelicals in the region have been influenced by the surrounding environment. Evangelicals in the Middle Atlantic region are considerably more likely to favor both legal abortion (36.6 percent) and gay rights (53.4 percent) than are their co-religionists elsewhere in the nation (27.8 percent and 41.3 percent, respectively). Middle-Atlantic evangelicals support school vouchers at a rate of 54.6 percent (compared to 46.8 percent nationally). This may reflect their awareness of the prevalence of Catholic parochial school education or, conceivably, signal resistance to the prevailing culture. On issues related to the regulatory state, by contrast, Middle Atlantic evangelicals look like evangelicals nationwide.

Ironically, evangelical Protestants in the region are much like those who profess no religion, the "nones" or "seculars," who resemble secular Americans nationally in terms of political identity and ideology, and attitudes about the regulatory state, but who are substantially more liberal on the hot-button "values" issues. Secular Middle Atlantic residents are more likely than their co-secularists nationally to favor school vouchers (42.3 percent vs. 34.1 percent), legal abortion (62.3 percent vs. 56.4 percent), and gay rights (73.7 percent vs. 65.5 percent nationally).

Conclusion

The mandate for this chapter is first to describe the demographic and religious profile of the Middle Atlantic region in the context of the nation as a whole and the other seven regions and second to provide a picture of the religious landscape. This is done in order to provide the reader with a background to the more descriptive and qualitative presentations that form the remainder of this volume. It is a difficult task to generalize about 46 million people across five states and the District of Columbia, using data based on a variety of methodologies and that use a variety of definitions of religious connections. In exploring similarities and differences in socio-demographic characteristics, and in religious composition, distribution, and attitude, the object has been to identify a distinctive profile for the region.

In the aggregate, these data contribute to an explanation of the small but significant shift of the Middle Atlantic states in recent years towards the Democratic Party. On secular measures, increased urbanization combined with greater number of immigrants has strengthened Democratic ranks. Religiously, the Democrats have been aided by the growing numbers of non-Christians in the region, including those who identify themselves as having no religion. The proportion of white Catholics, who have shifted to the right, is in decline, while mainline Protestants, who appear to be shifting to the left, are holding steady. Combined with the region's liberal tilt on social issues, these trends combined to help make the Middle Atlantic the only region in the country other than New England in which every state voted for John Kerry in the 2004 election.

Endnotes

1. Finke, Roger and Stark, Rodney, *The Churching of America: Winners and Losers in our Religious Economy* (New Brunswick, NJ: Rutgers University Press, 1992).

2. Gaustad, Edwin Scott and Barlow, Philip L., *New Historical Atlas of Religion in America* (New York: Oxford University Press, 2001).

3. Carnes, Tony and Karpathakis, Anna (ed.), *New York Glory: Religions in the City* (New York: New York University Press, 2001).

4. While support for school vouchers is often seen associated with conservative views, it is related to the other indicators in this set in that support for vouchers can be taken as support for greater individual liberty in making private life choices; thus, a liberal, rather than conservative position.

CHAPTER TWO

PROTESTANTS IN THE MIDDLE ATLANTIC REGION

James Hudnut-Beumler

Containing the three key American cities of New York, Philadelphia, and Washington, D.C., the Middle Atlantic region is often thought of as the center of commercial culture for the United States. Massive financial, transportation, manufacturing, shipping, and governmental activities are indeed transacted in and through the region. This association with commerce might lead some to assume that the region is less religiously identified than other regions such as the South or the Midwest. This region, composed of five states and the District of Columbia, has a greater proportion of its population affiliated with religious bodies than any other region defined for the purposes of this series except the "Southern Crossroads" region of Texas, Oklahoma, Arkansas, Louisiana, and Missouri.

As noted elsewhere in this volume, part of the high adherence rate is due to the strength of the Roman Catholic Church and Catholic culture in the region. Still, Catholics account for only 52.5 percent of the more than 30 million religious adherents in the region. Another 13.5 percent of adherents are accounted for by Orthodox (1.1 percent), Mormon (.4 percent), Jewish (8.7 percent), Muslim (1.7 percent), and all Eastern religions combined (1 percent). This leaves 34 percent of the region's religious population to be counted as Protestant of one type or another.[1]

Who are these Protestants? What generalizations can be made about them and what important exceptions to those generalizations might be observed? Which groups are key to the culture of the region? Finally, how does a many-hued Protestantism function in the cultural and political life of these states and the District of Columbia? These questions structure the balance of this essay.

Protestant Homeland

The place of Protestantism in this region is only partially revealed by the numerical prevalence of Protestant adherents. Two other measures must be utilized to plumb the significance of Protestantism in the Middle Atlantic region. The first can be briefly noted. That is the importance the region plays in certain denominational and faith traditions more generally.

For instance, while only 3.2 percent of adherents in the region are associated with the Evangelical Lutheran Church of America (ELCA), this constitutes the largest concentration of Lutherans outside the Midwest and the largest concentration of the Church's Lutherans who are descended out of German, as opposed to Scandinavian, ethnic stock. The Episcopal Church has more members in only one other region, and the Middle Atlantic states constitute one of the three regional power bases of the Presbyterian Church (USA). Pietists and Anabaptists—members of Moravian, Brethren, and Mennonite churches, for example—are likewise, though small in number next to Roman Catholics or even Presbyterians, only more prevalent in the Midwestern region than they are in the Middle Atlantic. Finally, the United Church of Christ has nearly as many adherents in the Middle Atlantic region as in the New England states, where it once was an established church in the form of Congregationalism. For several Protestant denominations, then, the Middle Atlantic region is home turf, a place where they are numerically strong (for them) and where congregations, denominational leaders, and key support institutions such as denominational headquarters, colleges, and seminaries are located.

But the numbers of various Protestant denominations indicates only part of their significance to the region. Equally important is the history of particular Protestant groups in the region. Outside of Maryland, it was Protestants of one sort of another who founded the seventeenth-century colonies that became the region's states. Formal religious establishment had a short and somewhat checkered career in the region relative to the Standing Congregational Order in New England or to Anglicanism in Virginia and the Carolinas. Each of the colonies had multiple strong denominational presences throughout the era leading up to the revolution.

Therefore, the story of the middle colonies can be placed in a narrative of the origins of American pluralism and church-state separation. It is also the case that, collectively, the free denominations and traditions formed a *de facto* Protestant hegemony for most of the region's history. This *de facto* hegemony pertained even in Maryland and continued until Roman Catholic immigration from Ireland began to turn the demographic tide in the mid nineteenth century. Even so, the churches, institutions, and cultural patterns set in place over the 375 years since the Dutch set up for business in New Netherland continue to influence the character of the region out of proportion to Protestants in the total population.

Understanding Protestantism in the Region

Protestantism is not just a catchall classification, but a classification that encompasses more diversity in theological, political, and ecclesiastical expression than it excludes. Therefore, this chapter will discuss families of Protestants and even provide some extended discussion of particularly large and influential American Christian denominations that are significant to the Middle Atlantic region.

The region as a whole is characterized by a combination of cities, suburbs, and rural areas. This inter- and intra-state geographic and demographic diversity has a tendency to be obscured or flattened in discussions that take the state as their unit of analysis. Thus, to take one example, Roman Catholics and Protestants of various types are both prevalent in Pennsylvania taken as a whole. Yet examining the state on a county-by-county basis quickly reveals that Catholics are much stronger the closer one gets to Philadelphia and Pittsburgh, while conservative, Evangelical Protestants are dominant in the state's western or more rural counties. Moreover, mainline Protestants, while present everywhere throughout the state, have as their natural homes the suburbs ringing the major cities together with the state's larger towns. People associated with Historically African-American churches are more likely to be found in the two principal cities than are any other Protestant faith group.

All of this indicates that the gross category "Protestant" does not have much examining value when explaining voting patterns, statewide social controversies, or even local school board disputes that have a religious dimension. The interpreter will want to know more about what kind of Protestants he or she is dealing with and the role they play in the local ecological system, however large that system might be. As it turns out, intra-regional factors are also highly significant.

Regional Generalization: The Mountains Divide Protestants

The region as a whole falls into two dominant Protestant types. The western half, consisting of the area west of the Catskills, Poconos, and Appalachian mountains, is more conservative and the eastern portion is more mainstream and liberal. The western portion is also more decisively Protestant, while in the eastern portion Protestants, though numerous, are outnumbered by Catholics and share religious influence with both Catholics and Jews in urban and metropolitan areas.

If one draws a straight line from Baltimore to New York City and then northward up the Hudson River Valley and beyond to Montreal and then visualizes a zone extending approximately 50 miles west of that line eastward to the Atlantic Ocean, one has roughly defined the more mainline and liberal Protestant zone. The remainder of each state west of the thus-defined zone constitutes the conservative Protestant zone. Here then, in upstate New York, in western Pennsylvania, and in western Maryland, are large concentrations of "Bible believing" Protestants who tend to vote more conservatively in state and national elections than their down-state and eastern counterparts. Here, too, are the towns and cities where Bible reading in the public schools persisted well into the 1960s and student prayer fellowships continue to flourish in public high schools only somewhat tempered by the attempts of various civil liberties groups to do away with them.

Of all regions in the United States, it is the Middle Atlantic that has the smallest conservative and evangelical adherence rates among Protestants. Adherents classed as mainline and liberal outnumbered those classified as evangelical and conservative in all the metropolitan areas in the region in the *North American Religion Atlas* (NARA). Only when moving southward toward the Baltimore/Washington metropolitan area does the pattern even begin to tip away from mainline dominance as more Southern Baptists are added into the denominational mix.

But this generalization, that mainline Protestants dominate in the region, is misleading. It relies upon the classification of certain adherents as liberal and/or mainline based upon associations with national denominations that clearly break down when subjected to regional analysis. The Presbyterians, Episcopalians, and United Methodists of western Pennsylvania, for example, have been among the most conservative in their voting patterns within their respective denominational families when it comes to proposals for women's ordination, gay ordination, church recognition of gay marriage, evangelization of Jews, and the morality of abortion. Mainline-church membership, therefore, does not mean liberal strength in all places, and the East/West split of Middle Atlantic Protestantism proves to be the key to understanding the paradox that evangelicals appear to be weak in the region only because in the western side of the region one does not have to leave a mainline church in order to be part of a conservative and evangelical Christian fellowship.

This is demonstrated by high levels of mainline adherence precisely in the areas where the mainline denominations are at their most conservative and evangelical. With thousands of congregations throughout the Middle Atlantic region, not every local church will map precisely onto the East/West split that has been here introduced for heuristic purposes. Nevertheless, observers long used to patterns of socially liberal voting in urban and metropolitan areas and more conservative candidates and issues being favored by rural and "upstate" counties will note a certain symmetry between religious and political preferences for Protestants by sub-region.

Protestants and Politics—A Cautionary Note

Ever since the signal failures of J. Milton Yinger and Gerhard Lenski in the 1960s to find highly predictive value between Protestant or Catholic identification in voting patterns, social scientists, pollsters, and social historians have worked at refining markers associated with religion so as to turn out stronger predictions. Richard Jensen, examining Protestant voting in the nineteenth century, concluded that if Protestants in the Midwest were divided into liturgicals (e.g., Lutherans and Anglicans) and evangelicals (e.g., Methodists, Baptists, and Presbyterians) some fairly strong Democrat/Republican patterns of party association could be established.

Most recently, pollsters believe they found a strong association between those who attended church and a vote for George W. Bush in the 2000 presidential election on the one hand, and an equally strong association between ever watching a pornographic movie and voting for Al Gore in the same election. Closer analysis subsequently demonstrated that the so-called religious edge for Bush evaporated when church-going frequency was shifted from "attended church in the last week" to "attended church in the last month." Part of that "every week" vs. "at least once in the last month" difference in voting may involve differences between kinds of Christian believers and especially distinctions between types of Protestants. For the 2004 election, Bush picked up more support among evangelicals attending monthly (from 64 percent support in 2000 to 79 percent in 2004). On the other hand, among mainline Protestant monthly attendees, he lost support (from 62 percent to 54 percent).[2]

Given decades of later discounted observation about the "religious factor" in politics, the reader is cautioned against drawing overly broad generalizations of religion's role in public affairs. This caution is doubly important for interpreting religion and culture issues in the Middle Atlantic region, which incorporates some of nearly every group in America within each state in states that themselves are demographically and geographically diverse. Assessing the role of religion here is not as simple as explaining the role of the Mormon Church in Utah or secularity in the Pacific Northwest.

Beyond all of these cautions, however, there are several helpful things that may be said about the kind of Protestants one encounters in the region, what issues are most significant in their own group histories, and how particular blends of religion that are found in each state help constitute that state's composite character. This chapter, therefore, now turns to a discussion of particular groups of Protestants and their characteristic issues and beliefs, followed by a discussion of the states and their blends of Protestant emphasis.

Three Waves of American Protestantism

One way Protestant churches can be classified is according to when and how they were founded. For the purpose of this chapter, Protestant churches fall into three classes. In the first wave are churches of the so-called Magisterial Reformation. These were state churches at least somewhere in Europe that were transplanted to American soil. These churches include the Episcopal, Reformed, Presbyterian, Congregational, German Reformed, and Lutheran churches. These churches often have a fairly developed political ethic because they have at some time in their past thought about the obligations of the church in a land where the church was to be the nation's soul and conscience.

Second-wave churches are the product of European pietism and American revivalism. They include the Baptist and Methodist churches, including the African-American denominations of those two traditions, together with the Disciples of Christ, Church of Christ, and Christian churches. An important subclass of these churches are the Mennonite, Brethren, and Amish churches, which are pacifist in their approach to the use of coercion in public and international affairs. Each of these second-wave traditions arose out of an application of the Protestant principle—taking scripture as the only rule of the faith and life in the church—in a context where there was already a Protestant church, or several, in place. They can be seen, therefore, as the historical products of purification movements within Protestantism. The Historically African-American churches within this second wave are the products of early-nineteenth-century separation of the races within revivalistic Methodist and Baptist churches. Due to their early histories, the political ethic in many of these churches tends to insist on separation of church and state and to rely on the power of witness and moral suasion in politics.

A third wave of Protestant churches is constituted by the churches founded in roughly the last 100 years, including many Pentecostal and holiness churches, together with independent congregations of almost infinite variety. Many of these recent churches are evangelical in belief and practice. They are distinguished from second-wave churches insofar as they have not developed as movements away from establishment churches. Rather they are often the result of charismatic leadership taking the Protestant principle of Biblical fidelity to the extent of founding churches that are faithful to the founding leaders' understanding of the Christian life. Twentieth-century America proved to be fruitful soil for fresh varieties of Protestantism. Churches of this type range from tiny urban storefront missions to the so-called megachurches that dot the suburbs with their 5,000-plus memberships and colossal campuses. Because of the fragmented and idiosyncratic histories of churches in the third wave, it is difficult to classify their political ethic. Some congregations are quiet enclaves of escape from secular culture. These churches emphasize that the Christian life is an alternative lifestyle with minimal engagement with the world outside the enclave. Others, taking their cues from television preachers like Pat Robertson and Jerry Falwell, urge their members to "take back America" from the forces of Godless secularism.

A few churches in the first wave are present throughout the nation, but do not dominate the range of ecclesiastical options the way they did on the eve of the American Revolution. The dominant type since the nineteenth century has been the second-wave churches. Baptists and Methodists of all types are the most common affiliations nationally. It is the share of all Protestant adherents possessed by the third-wave churches that has grown the most in the last 50 years, however. In some regions, believers of this sort are becoming dominant. In contrast with this aggregate national picture, the Middle Atlantic region features a strong first-wave church presence and a relatively weak second- and third-wave church presence. What follows is a discussion of eight of the most significant bodies of Protestants in the region.

The Episcopal Church

The Episcopal Church was one of the first of the colonial powerhouse traditions to feature a presence in the Middle Atlantic states. The Episcopal Church is the American body of the Anglican Communion, formally established in 1789 as a distinct American denomination separate from its parent Church of England. The Episcopal Church was an ecclesial power throughout the region until the close of the eighteenth century. The Church was established to varying degrees and at various times in New York and Maryland.

Maryland had a considerable number of Anglican parishes dating back to the seventeenth century, owing to the energetic work of the Bishop of London's representative, Thomas Bray. Alongside churches, Bray founded numerous libraries and schools in that colony. The Church established significant institutions in the era, including Trinity Church in New York, Christ Church in Philadelphia, and King's College (now Columbia University) in New York.

The Anglican Church on the eve of the revolution had made considerable progress in New York, Pennsylvania, New Jersey, and Delaware. The American Revolution posed an acute challenge to the Anglican clergy, many of whom were educated and ordained in England, and returned there during the conflict. This led to a period of stagnation in the years of the early Republic. The number of Episcopal churches in the nation as a whole did not return to its 1780 highpoint of approximately 400 parishes until nearly 60 years later.[3]

The Episcopal Church went through a period of exponential growth in the later nineteenth century, and again in the 1940s and 1950s. The Church grew in tandem with the population of the Northeast, and particularly with the Empire State. Throughout the region today, one is likely to find multiple Episcopal Churches in each county, except those in central Pennsylvania.[4] A large number of Episcopalians, nationally speaking, live in the Middle Atlantic region. In each state they contribute at least 3 percent of the total membership of the denomination, and the Episcopal Church continues to maintain its denominational headquarters in New York City.

Episcopalians tend to be well educated, possess much higher than average household incomes—paralleling those of members of the Reformed Church in America and the Presbyterian Church (USA)—and are over-represented relative to population in the ranks of political leaders in the region, in both major parties. The Episcopal Church has been divided nationally over issues pertaining to women's ordination, gay clergy, and the recognition of holy unions between people of the same sex. Though there are conservative pockets in the Episcopal Church in the region, notably in western Pennsylvania, the region as a whole has tended to favor the liberal and inclusive side of contemporary debates.

Presbyterians

The largest of American Reformed denominations owing their theological roots to John Calvin, the Presbyterians were strong in Scotland and in England under Oliver Cromwell. They observe a church government that balances lay and clerical authority, both locally and at regional assemblies of church elders called "presbyteries." Presbyterianism was effectively introduced by the Scottish missionary Francis Mackemie, whose work began in Maryland in 1683. By 1706 enough churches had been established there and in the Delaware Valley to form the Philadelphia Presbytery.

Philadelphia became associated in the eighteenth century with "Old Side" rationalists. Meanwhile, "New Side" evangelicals embraced revivalism and eventually founded both the Synod of New York and the College of New Jersey (later known as Princeton) to educate ministers. By the eve of the revolution, Presbyterians claimed more adherents in the 13 colonies than any other body save the Congregationalists. Subsequent development found some Presbyterians at the forefront of revivals and abolitionist groups in the Western Reserve of New York and in twentieth-century fundamentalist struggles centered in Pittsburgh, Philadelphia, Princeton, and New York.

Claiming two-thirds of a million adherents in the region, they are present throughout the region and constitute over 10 percent of all religious adherents in many western Pennsylvania counties, with other strong areas of presence in northern New Jersey and southeastern Pennsylvania. Perhaps because of their association with higher education and lay participation in church governance, a disproportionate number of Presbyterians can be found in the legislatures and congressional delegations of the region.

Lutherans

Followers of Martin Luther came to the American setting as early as 1638 with the founding of New Sweden in the Delaware Valley, which brought both Swedish and Finnish Lutherans to America for the first time. Congregations were formed by these immigrants, including "Old Swedes" and Gloria Dei in Philadelphia, and Trinity Church in Wilmington, though these churches were later received into the Anglican Community.[5] Danish Lutherans followed, but it was the Germans, and particularly those connected to the Pietist stronghold Halle University, who would make the largest mark on behalf of Lutherans in the Middle Atlantic.

By the 1720s, aided by a wave of German immigration filtering through the port of Philadelphia, German Lutherans began to form multiple congregations in Pennsylvania. In 1742 Henry Melchior Muhlenberg was sent from Halle as a missionary to German Lutherans in Pennsylvania. Muhlenberg organized the Pennsylvania Ministerium as the first Lutheran Synod in 1747 to gather the multiple congregations operating within Pennsylvania at the time.[6]

Though the kinds of Lutherans proliferated through the nineteenth century to the point that there were, by Sydney Ahlstrom's calculations, more than 400 different denominations of Lutherans at the opening of the twentieth century, most Lutherans in the Mid-Atlantic region belonged to the Evangelical Lutheran Church in America (ELCA). Today, Muhlenberg, Gettysburg, Thiel, and Wagner colleges, Susquehanna University, and the Lutheran Theological Seminary at Philadelphia and Gettysburg Theological Seminary, all serve the ELCA and the nearly 1 million ELCA adherents in the region.

All Lutherans believe in salvation by God's grace through faith alone (*sola fides*), that scripture is the only and final authority in all matters of faith and practice (*sola scriptura*), and declare that their faith is expressed in the Apostles, Nicene, and Athenasian creeds. Most also accept the Book of Concord, including the Augsburg Confession, as a reliable exposition on the faith, the church, and its ministry.

The United Church of Christ

The United Church of Christ was formed in 1957 by the merger of two Reformed bodies of differing governmental structures, the Congregational Churches and the Evangelical and Reformed Church. The former was greatest in strength in New England, while the Evangelical and Reformed Church was strong both in Pennsylvania and the Midwest. Prior to the 1957 merger there were numerous Congregational Christian churches in the western reserve of New York, where Connecticut residents settled in the early nineteenth century and brought their religion with them in the migration from New England. A large number of Evangelical and Reformed Christians in Pennsylvania, especially concentrated in eastern and south central Pennsylvania, were associated with the large populations descended from ethnically German stock.

The name Evangelical and Reformed denoted a merger both in the United States and in Germany between Lutheran (Evangelical) and Calvinist (Reformed) Christian churches, but the much greater influence in the American context was the German Reformed Church, whose members constituted some of Pennsylvania's earliest and most numerous settlers, coming as they did out of the Palatinate and Rhine regions where their faith was merely tolerated among other more powerful Christian churches.

The German Reformed Church featured a polity in which lay and clerical representatives directed regional affairs in Synods. The current denomination operates with both strong congregational governance and area associations that take on more or less significance, depending on the prior denomination associated with the area. For eastern and central Pennsylvania, then, this means a highly connectional church where church leaders are known from town to town, and where congregations are often the first Protestant churches in their communities, dating from the earliest days of German migration to the region in the early eighteenth century and possessing relatively large membership and influence in local affairs down to the present.

Quakers, Anabaptists, and the Reformed Church

Three traditions that significantly figured in the founding years of the region have been largely eclipsed by other, more dominant, groups. Quakers, or "Friends" as they preferred, gravitated toward Pennsylvania, the commonwealth established by William Penn. Penn was himself a Quaker and his colony was tolerant by design to people of various faiths. The Quakers, having themselves been oppressed for nonconformist religious beliefs in England and in other American colonies, sought first and foremost the freedom to follow their own consciences guided by God's spirit expressed in an "inner light."[7]

In Pennsylvania and parts of western New Jersey, Quakers also became very successful as farmers, but observed several practices that virtually assured slow growth in the American setting. The first was the austere nature of the Friends' Meeting, which required time and patience on the part of participants. The second was the fact that early Quakers disinherited those men and women who "married out" to non-Quakers. "Marrying out" signaled a decisive break from one's family and the church. Third, from the very beginning Penn began recruiting German settlers to his colony, thus assuring cultural competition for the English Quakers. Finally, as pacifists, Quakers became reliant at an early stage of development upon others, and particularly Scots-Irish Presbyterians, for the enforcement of colonial law and order among the burgeoning number of non-Quaker immigrants.

Not wholly unlike the Quakers, German followers of Menno Simons, known as Mennonites, and related representatives of the radical reformation in Europe, made Pennsylvania their initial home in the colonial era. These groups, centered in Lancaster and York counties, are present throughout Pennsylvania and western Maryland. The Amish and Old Order Mennonites are notable for their observation of pre-modern modes of life and their cautious approach to modern implements. The buggies, dress, folkways, and furniture of the Amish attract tourists to south-central Pennsylvania, but all Mennonites and members of the Church of the Brethren continue the characteristic Anabaptist renunciation of violence as unchristian. It is for this reason that these believers, roughly 400,000 strong across the region, are known together with Friends as members of "peace churches," whose members are routinely exempted on religious grounds from military service.

The Reformed Church in America continues today what was the Dutch Reformed Church, a Calvinist Protestant church in the Colonial era. The Reformed Church was the first church to be established in the Middle Colonies, in both what are now New York and New Jersey. The English takeover in 1689 began the steady dismantling of Dutch hegemony in these areas. Today the church is largely restricted in the Middle Atlantic to areas of early Dutch settlement and continues to have congregations in the Hudson River valley of New York and New Jersey. As with so many other groups that established an early presence in the region, regional importance for today's Reformed Church is more significant than the tradition's contemporary significance in the total political and social culture of the region. Places with names like "Quakerbridge Road" or "Dutch Neck" that survive in common usage to this day also testify to the early impact of religious groups now small in number.

Historically African-American Churches

The Middle Atlantic region is home to many of the most significant sites in the development of the Historically African-American churches, particularly those of Methodist origin. The African Methodist Episcopal Church (AME) came into being in 1787 in Philadelphia, begun by a 27-year-old Methodist minister, Richard Allen. The church he founded, Bethel AME (also known as Mother Bethel), began as a withdrawal in protest from the St. George Methodist Episcopal Church, owing to the second-class treatment people of African descent received at the hands of white church members. [Begun in an old blacksmith's shop and later moved to the corner of Sixth and Lombard Streets in Philadelphia, Mother Bethel stands today as one of the historic shrines of Philadelphia.]

The AME Zion Church, founded in New York City, similarly grew out of a 1796 withdrawal from the white-dominated Methodist Episcopal Society of that city. Though the Methodist Episcopal Church in New York had licensed a number of African-American men to preach, they nevertheless prevented them from preaching even to those of their own race except on rare occasions, and prohibited them from joining the conference as itinerant preachers.[8]

Early African-American church leaders were noted for their determination. Both Richard Allen and Absalom Jones, founding pastor of Philadelphia's St. Thomas Episcopal Church, were born into slavery and purchased their freedom. Richard Allen's preaching also deeply affected Jarena Lee to the point where she, likewise, felt called to preach. After initially telling her that women could not preach in the Methodist Church, Allen changed his mind after hearing her give a spontaneous exhortation during a sermon at Bethel AME. Henceforth, he opened his pulpit to her and Lee traveled throughout the eastern United States preaching her gospel of freedom, including preaching forays into the South to preach among slaves.

Somewhat later she was joined as an outstanding preacher by Rebecca Cox Jackson, who won over Morris Brown, Allen's successor as Bishop of the AME, in a similar way as had Lee won over Allen earlier. Sarah Allen, Richard Allen's wife, was active in church leadership in a way more typical for women in the nineteenth century, organizing a women's group called the Daughters of Conference that provided support to church ministers. All of these early leaders, women and men, set an independent course for the future of the black church, such that demonstrated gifts in preaching and leadership have continued to overcome socially conscribed gender and race barriers.[9]

In the very early years, when slave gatherings and even slave evangelization were being outlawed in the Deep South, the Middle Atlantic region was home to a growing and vibrant autonomous African-American Christianity. Today, the strength that characterized the early years of the nineteenth century can be seen through the region, but especially in the old seaboard and harbor towns of New York, Philadelphia, and southward to Washington, D.C.

In Philadelphia, Wilmington, or Baltimore, the AME and AME Zion clergy, joined with National Baptist ministers, have the clout to stop, or bless, on moral grounds, a needle exchange program aimed at harm reduction for addicts in AIDS prevention efforts. Political careers and the careers of school superintendents and police chiefs are made and lost with the help or opposition of the black church and its leaders. Yet while these churches are often noticed for their external effects upon their communities, for their members, the churches of the AME, AME Zion, the Christian Methodist Episcopal Church (CME), National Baptist, Progressive Baptist, and Church of God in Christ denominations, are mostly remarkable for the preaching and worship that goes on week after week and the reinforcement of community norms to a mostly middle-class following.

Black church people are, as C. Eric Lincoln and Lawrence Mamiya have demonstrated, a "respectable" people (read: more middle-class and more afflu-ent) relative to non-churchgoers within the black community.[10] While many dominant-culture churches are experimenting with informal dress in the current decades, Historically African-American churches across the theological spectrum maintain the tradition of dressing in one's "Sunday best." More formal dress does not, however, connote in this instance stiffness in worship. The Methodist, Baptist, and Pentecostal streams of the black church are all known for joyful praise and ecstatic worship. Mainstream culture gets a glimpse into the character of black church praise when a gospel singer like Philadelphia's Whitney Houston enters popular music. For most black churches, however, gifted singers and dynamic preaching constitute a weekly expectation.

Protestantism Viewed from the States and the District of Columbia

New York

It is easy to read religion as a mere dimension of ethnicity in New York, for it so often functions that way in cultural and political affairs. It is widely assumed, for instance, that the people marching on Columbus Day, St. Patrick's Day, and Puerto Rican Pride Day, are Catholic. Likewise, African Americans in Harlem and Washington Heights are assumed to be Protestants and members of African-American denominations. Conversely, Episcopalians are assumed to be white and non-immigrant. Like most generalizations, there is much truth to these particular characterizations, even though there are a sizeable number of Catholics in Washington Heights and New York Episcopalians include not a few members from the Caribbean islands such as Barbados. The generalization points to one of the most important functions religion plays in New York and in the region more generally; that is, religion provides a separate social space for like-minded people from similar backgrounds to gather even in the midst of stunning metropolitan diversity. Indeed, what makes the diversity tenable is, in part, the ability to resist homogenization to some centralizing norm.

New York provides one of the models for the American way of religious life. Whereas Pennsylvania embraced a certain amount of religious liberty by design. New York simply became a thriving marketplace of religious competi-tion. Without waiting for official sanction on a theory of religious co-existence, early New Yorkers simply made co-existence and competition work. In this sense New York was a model for all that would follow in the way Americans "do" religion.

New York, as a city and as a state, began as a Protestant endeavor, or rather several. Dutch Reformed clergy in Manhattan, Brooklyn, Albany, and the Hudson River valley soon found themselves vying for authority with English Anglicans around New York, Presbyterians on Long Island, and Swedish Lutherans dotting the Hudson River. New York was diverse, but only slowly did it become significantly Catholic, and the nineteenth-century transformation from a generalized Protestant culture to the state in the East with the greatest religious diversity was one that featured immense cultural battles that still mark the psyche of New York City and account for its unusual blend of philanthropic institutions.

The foundations for later disputes were laid in early New York State history. In 1792, George Clinton, the state's first governor, argued the importance of public education for a new republic when he said, "Diffusion of knowledge is essential to the promotion of virtue and the preservation of liberty."[11] Clinton's views were widely shared, and the state began funding public education in 1795, with upstate elementary education becoming nearly universally available and New York City education being available through private "charity schools" to most non-immigrant, non-poor children by the early nineteenth century.

The Free School Society, a voluntary association, worked to gather poor and working-class children into its schools, which it explicitly defined as non-denominational, but with a clear aim at suppressing vice through elevation of the spirit, including Bible reading and lessons in general Christianity. What was meant by non-denominational can be seen through the exclusion of Baptist and Catholic schools for receipt of funds provided by the Free School Society. The growing numbers of Catholics in New York City and Brooklyn began to object to *de facto* Protestant hegemony, with a result that the schools in both of these major downstate cities were turned over to local political control in the 1840s.

During these same years, Protestants from the respectable denominations funded numerous freestanding benevolent groups. As in the schools case, some had very local mission orientations. These groups included the New York City Mission Society (founded in 1812), the New York Female Moral Reform Society (aimed at keeping women out of prostitution and reclaiming prostitutes from that life), and the New York Society for the Relief of Widows and Orphans of Medical Men. Other groups, such as the American Bible Society and the American Tract Society, sought to extend the reach of the Protestant faith throughout the nation. The latter two organizations used New York as a printing and management base for enterprises that, at their peaks, employed hundreds of "colporters" to sell religious books across the land.

The nature of the local organizations was reflective of the Protestant ethic of benevolence dominant at the time, wherein a congregation's members were expected to take a moral interest in the lives and difficulties of those less fortunate than themselves. There was, as one detects from the titles, a determination not simply to provide alternatives but to actually reform the behavior of prostitutes, drinkers, immigrants, and orphans. Protestants in New York throughout the nineteenth century acted as though the disposition of the welfare of the entire population was theirs alone to dispose. Today, the clearest remaining sign of this benevolent empire is that nearly all the city's private hospitals are identified with a faith group that started them, at least in name. St. Luke's was Episcopalian, Columbia-Presbyterian was obviously Presbyterian, Mt. Sinai was Jewish, and so forth. To a remarkable degree, when compared to, say, the South or West, the not-for-profit sector of New York (and Philadelphia and Pittsburgh, for that matter) is a religiously tinged sector. Only the strength of organized Protestantism—and other faith groups' response to that strength—can explain this city wherein the most secular person looks forward to being taken to St. Vincent's rather than Bellevue Hospital.

Organizations of moral reform were joined by revivalist preaching in both congregations and in special halls set up as venues for mass revivals in nineteenth century New York. The philanthropists Arthur and Lewis Tappan supported both kinds of activities and one of their chosen instruments, Charles Grandison Finney, led successful revivals in both Rochester and New York City in the 1830s. Revivalism was so much a part of upstate New York life that the region west of the Catskills became known as "the burned-over district."

The modern legacy of this revivalism is the countless small Protestant churches left dotting the upstate countryside that owe their founding to the heat of revival. The legacy of the "benevolent empire" of reform and revivalism downstate was more complicated, for driven by outraged resistance to the corrupt politics of William Marcy Tweed's Tammany Hall political organization, the Protestant clergy tended to turn politics into moral crusades. Liquor, prostitution, and even theater were frequent objects of clergy-led protests. In the second half of the century, preachers like Henry Ward Beecher and William Rainsford were effective in building "institutional churches," churches that served as urban villages unto themselves, offering wholesome recreation and educational opportunities for their members throughout the week. In the same vein, Protestants established YMCAs—Young Men's Christian Associations—in many neighborhoods.

Neighborhoods changed in social class and ethnicity in the nineteenth century more rapidly than they have in the last 100 years. Congregations initially coped with this change by selling their buildings to other religious groups and for other uses and moving to follow their membership to new residential areas. In the last years of the nineteenth and first years of the twentieth centuries, some churches whose memberships had moved remained behind and attempted to do their religious business with new groups of people. This could lead, in the case of a German Baptist leader like Walter Rauschenbusch, to a more radical engagement with the poor than the prior tendency to moralize about them. Rauschenbusch became the intellectual leader of a movement called the Social Gospel, with his determination that the social order of advanced industrial urban capitalism must be Christianized.

The Social Gospel's heyday can be limited, perhaps, to the years between 1890 and 1918, but the basic social orientation of Protestantism in New York City to this day is a reflection of the Social Gospel's take on modern life. Protestantism in New York City is liberal, engaged, and political to the point of being confrontational at times. Nowhere is this perhaps more obviously the case than in the black church in New York City. For example, a succession of pastors of the Abyssinian Baptist Church in Harlem, from Adam Clayton Powell, Sr. and Jr., to Samuel Proctor, to Calvin Butts have inspired a large following of middle-class blacks to see social and political causes as an essential part of Christian life in twentieth-century America. At the height of his power in the 1960s, Adam Clayton Powell, Jr. was one of the most visible members of the United States House of Representatives. More recently Rev. Floyd Flake represented the Sixth District of New York in the U.S. House from 1986 to 1997, all the while serving as senior pastor of the Allen African Methodist Episcopal Church in Jamaica, Queens. Still more recently, the long-time minister activist Rev. Al Sharpton, a Pentecostal minister and former road manager for the singer James Brown, ran for President of the United States. Meanwhile, the current Abyssinian Baptist Church pastor, Calvin Butts, has exhibited political leadership not through seeking political office but by establishing a successful community development corporation and by crusading against alcohol and tobacco marketers that target black neighborhoods and consumers with stereotyped appeals.

If religious political leadership is the hallmark of much of African-American Protestantism, it is not a black church phenomenon alone. William Sloane Coffin, during his years at the Riverside Church on the upper west side of Manhattan, used his pulpit and energized his congregation to push for a reduction of nuclear armaments and to resist the policies of the Reagan Administration in Central America. Riverside and other New York City churches became active in the sanctuary movement, sheltering human rights abuse victims from Latin America and visibly addressing the AIDS crisis, periodic crises in the administration of the Health and Hospitals Corporation, and violence perpetuated on people of color by the New York City Police Department. Indeed, to a remarkable degree, the political role of Protestant ministers in New York City to push for moral reform and resist various forms of evil has recapitulated itself repeatedly down to the present day. To be part of the clergy in New York is to have a public leadership role, whether one accepts that role or not, for the city's congregations are some of the most enduring and effective outlets for democratic participation, as they have been for over two centuries.

Finally, New York has historically served as an important center of organized Protestantism for the rest of the United States and even the world. New York City is the headquarter city for the National Council of Churches, which represents most mainline Protestant bodies in an ecumenical council. For decades the Interchurch Center at 475 Riverside Drive was the headquarters building not only of the National Council of Churches but also of the Presbyterian Church (USA), the Reformed Church in America, the United Church of Christ, Church World Service, several international mission agencies, and the Board of Global Missions of the United Methodist Church. Several of these denominations moved to locations that were geographically more central to the rest of the United States in the 1980s and 1990s, but all continue to maintain a presence in New York.

Ecumenism and interfaith cooperation are so ingrained in the New York metropolitan area that what seems natural to representatives of even conservative Protestant groups can appear unintelligible and unforgivable to their co-religionists in other regions. The Rev. David Benke, the regional leader of the theologically conservative Lutheran Church-Missouri Synod (LCMS), found himself being ordered to apologize for mixing Christian and non-Christian beliefs at the nationally televised prayer service held at Yankee Stadium following the September 11 terrorist attacks. On September 23, 2001, he took part in the service, standing alongside representatives of other Christian, Muslim, Jewish, Hindu, and Sikh groups. Benke asked those in the stadium to join hands and pray with him "on this field of dreams turned into God's house of prayer." Though he ended his prayer "in the precious name of Jesus," Benke soon found himself charged with offenses that ultimately led to his suspension.

In a denominational decision reached the next summer, the Rev. Wallace Schulz wrote: "To participate with pagans in an interfaith service and, additionally, to give the impression that there might be more than one God, is an extremely serious offense against the God of the Bible." The New York press treated the story with outrage and LCMS adherents in the region expressed disappointment, but clearly ecumenism in New York extends farther than it does in many other regions of the United States.[12]

New Jersey

The Garden State is characterized by such substantial diversity of equally diverse forms that it is often seen as a state lacking in identity. This is partly because New Jersey is part of two tri-state media markets (New York/Connecticut/New Jersey on the one hand, and Pennsylvania/Delaware/New Jersey on the other) that each constitute one of the nation's principal metropolitan areas. New Jersey, since colonial times, has been both its own entity and part of greater New York and Philadelphia.

But rather than continuing to see New Jersey as a mere artifact of these two metropolitan centers, one might prefer to see New Jersey as the quintessential Middle Atlantic state. It is highly dense, with numerous urban municipalities the size of principal cities in the Midwest and Mountain West states. Not far from these often poor cities are vast middle- and upper-middle-class suburban areas. These suburbs, taken collectively, are the home of some of the wealthiest Americans, so many indeed that the state, together with Connecticut, perennially boasts the nation's highest median household incomes. Finally, New Jersey is a state of seashore, small towns, and rural hamlets.

Religiously, the groups of New Jersey tend to distribute themselves along these demographic and geospatial lines. While Catholics predominate in many areas, first-wave Protestants are strong in the New York and Philadelphia suburbs and in the towns of central New Jersey. Methodists are found there and in the smaller towns of the more rural areas. Finally, Protestants in the city are likely to be members of Historically African-American churches, or first- or second-generation American members of third-wave, often independent, churches. Even when city churches in places like Newark, Passaic, and Patterson are of colonial derivation such as Episcopalian, Reformed, or Presbyterian, it is likely that they are neither native-born white, nor exclusively English-speaking. The cities and more urban suburbs of New Jersey provide these older denominations with substantial measures of Korean, Chinese, African, and Caribbean members and congregations.

In contrast to the radical Protestant ethnic diversity of New Jersey's cities are the Protestant churches whose members are white and native born. Perhaps more than any other state, to be white and Protestant in New Jersey is to likely be Republican, for it is in the suburbs and small towns among Protestants where New Jersey's Republicans are strongest. The Protestant-Republican connection, however, is one with extraordinary features, for in New Jersey Republicans are more apt to be pro-choice than is the norm. They are also Republican for very local reasons insofar as they—as suburban and town dwellers—are determined to resist the urban-inflected taxation, public works, and education-equalization policies of the Democrats in Trenton's state house. Conversely, leaders of African-American churches in New

Jersey cities have played such a key role in Democratic Party politics that their ability to "get out the vote" is widely viewed as a determinant of statewide and local election results. Thus, once again, the *kind* of Protestant one is proves to be much more important than the mere fact of *being* Protestant.

Delaware

While small, Delaware is host to a full spectrum of Protestants in Wilmington, New Castle, and its rural areas. The state perhaps deserves to be best known for its role in the effective founding of Methodism in the United States. Begun as an evangelical movement within the Anglican Church by John Wesley in England, Methodism took root in the new world as members of Methodist societies came to the American colonies. In the years leading up to the American Revolution Wesley sent eight Methodist lay preachers from England to minister to these growing societies. When the Revolutionary War began, only two of the lay preachers chose to remain and only one, Francis Asbury, remained in active ministry, itinerating to the various societies.

Upon the conclusion of hostilities in 1784, Wesley sent Thomas Coke to America with the mission of finding Asbury and discussing the future of American Methodism. The two finally met on November 14, 1784, at Barratt's Chapel, a building erected in 1780 for Methodist worship in Kent County, Delaware. The meeting was dramatic as Asbury arrived while Coke, a Church of England priest, was preaching. Coke descended from the pulpit and embraced Asbury and the sacraments of baptism and communion were administered for the first time by ordained Methodist clergy. Coke and Asbury then organized a meeting to call together all Methodist preachers on Christmas Day 1784 in Baltimore.

At this so-called Christmas Conference, the Methodist Episcopal Church was organized as a distinct American denomination. Within five years, the Methodists had opened Cokesbury College in Abingdon, Maryland, and established the Methodist Book Concern in Philadelphia. By 1800 German pietists adhering to Wesleyan views, led by Jacob Albright and Phillip William Otterbein, had founded the Evangelical Association and the Church of the United Brethren in Christ, respectively.[13]

By the middle of the nineteenth century Methodists and Baptists had leapfrogged the colonial powerhouse denominations to become the most numerous types of Protestants throughout the United States. Though Baptists and Methodists could be found throughout the United States, Methodists were stronger in the North, Baptists in the South. To this day Delaware, where the Methodist movement took permanent root, illustrates how this tremendous growth and expansion took place.

Nearly every community, however small, has a Methodist church, however small its congregation might be. United Methodists constitute over 9 percent of

Delaware's population, a very large proportion of the population for any non-Catholic group in the North. Throughout the Middle Atlantic region, United Methodism is, likewise, ubiquitous. Methodists owe their geographical presence to two factors. First, their evangelical message, a plainspoken gospel Christianity that offered conversion and the assurance of salvation without the theological qualifiers offered by most Calvinists in the early nation. Second, Methodists did not simply found churches with settled pastors, but rather itinerated preachers between areas where Sunday Schools and churches might be established such that Methodist presence was begun among groups too small to gain the attention of Congregationalist, Anglican, or Presbyterian groups, let alone to sustain one of their ministers.

Methodism's unique polity is also backed by an economic system that makes it possible to be in places where there is not enough money to support a minister on a freestanding congregational basis. Clergy in all Methodist denominations are subject to being moved to a new charge by their conferences each year. This practice, still termed "itinerancy," was initiated to keep clergy pressing on for new converts, but continues mostly in smaller and rural churches, whereas large and wealthy congregations often keep ministers of whom they approve for many years.

Maryland

As is appropriate for this state on the Chesapeake, where freshwater and saltwater meet, Protestantism in Maryland forms a kind of a transitional zone. While Baptists constitute 14.26 percent of all adherents nationally, only 3 percent of all religious adherents in the Middle Atlantic region are Baptists. In Maryland, this changes to 7 percent. Moving into Maryland from Pennsylvania or Delaware, religiously speaking, therefore, means transitioning into a Protestant religious culture that is more like Virginia, a state where Baptists are the most numerous group in virtually every county and where a Methodist affiliation is second in popularity.

In Maryland, however, the United Methodist record 10.2 percent of all religious adherents as their own, and adherents to Historically African-American denominations make up 17.7 percent of all adherents. Again, this is a pattern that makes the state look more like a southern state than does, say, New York or Pennsylvania, where fewer than 9 percent of all adherents belong to Historically African-American denominations. The final characteristic that makes Maryland look like a southern state is its relatively high number of Episcopal adherents, at 2.8 percent roughly twice the national average and a clear legacy of its colonial strength indicated above. Yet Maryland resists being classified as entirely southern in its Protestantism, for in other respects it more closely resembles Pennsylvania, with relatively large numbers of Lutherans (the ELCA has 3.6

percent of all religious adherents) and Anabaptist adherents (.6 percent), both of which exceed national averages for these groups. Looking from the north, then, Maryland appears to be the beginning of the South. Viewed from Virginia and the Carolinas, however, even leaving aside the huge Catholic population of Maryland, the state looks to be the beginning of the North.[14]

Washington, D.C.

The most significant religious building in the nation's capital may be the capitol building itself. For despite the official separation of church and state, 435 representatives and 100 senators are quick to preach, cajole, and seek to manipulate the religious sentiments of the American people from the floors and conference rooms of the two bodies' chambers. Outside these public rooms, in the hallways and offices, lobbyists and interest groups push issues with religious overtones— abortion rights and abortion bans, prayer in public schools, faith-based charitable social service, human rights certification, food aid, and AIDS assistance to Africa. Doing good and preventing evil are on the agenda of both America's mainline and evangelical Protestants (as well as other groups). Members of Congress, nearly all of whom are affiliated with a Protestant, Catholic, or Jewish congregation, reflect the concerns of their own groups, to be sure, but reflect even more so the religious concerns of their constituencies. Political piety on the Potomac is alive and well in the first decade of the new millennium.

Not all Protestantism is political in this city that exists for politics. The Washington National Cathedral of the Episcopal Church is the *de facto* chapel of the United States in mourning. When thousands were killed in the attacks of September 11, 2001, it was in the National Cathedral that the nation's leaders, the President and cabinet, senators, representatives, Supreme Court justices, and foreign ambassadors, gathered to pray, to grieve, and to pledge fidelity to the memory of those killed. Though the Roman Catholics and the Presbyterians also have self-described "National" churches capable of hosting large services of this type, it is the Gothic structure set in a cathedral close that mimics the religious precincts of its English archetypes that presents itself as a place for the faithful of all faiths to gather.

Moreover, it is the quiet confidence of the denomination formerly established in this very city carved out of Maryland and Virginia that is open to prayer by members of other faiths in a way Roman Catholics and the more evangelical Presbyterians would find uncomfortable that makes it possible for the politicians to gather across faith lines to pray with nary a thought that their actions might have First Amendment implications.

Power of an entirely different sort is reflected in the city's black churches. Washington, D.C. is a majority African-American city whose brief years of supposed home-rule have brought leaders up from the ranks of the churches but where the finances of the city, its purse strings, and ultimately its destiny are still determined by the 535 members of Congress who determine the length of the municipal leash. The power of the African-American congregations in the city's neighborhoods is not the power to make laws, but rather the power to maintain and sustain life in the midst of urban life poised between government service jobs on the one hand and street crime and drug violence that threaten to swallow the loved ones of church members each week on the other.

A Tale of Two Western Cities

Early in this chapter the insight was offered that the mountains divide the Middle Atlantic region when it comes to religion. The cities of Pittsburgh and Buffalo, lying far to the west of Washington, D.C., help illustrate how politics, policy, and Protestantism are affected by this intra-regional diversity and how these differences are more than simply reflections of city-country differences. The area west of the Catskill and Allegheny mountains is not entirely rural, and though Protestantism in various fairly conservative forms is characteristic of smaller towns in this sub region it is not the central religious attribute of the urban centers such as Pittsburgh and Buffalo. Nevertheless, the Protestantism practiced in these two population centers on the western edge of the region helps to show how Protestantism can continue to shape areas where it is no longer numerically dominant.

Both of these cities owe their success in becoming large and important cities to being located at opportune places for trade between the East and West. Pittsburgh was a trading city dominated early on by an elite of Scots-Irish Presbyterian merchants. By 1803 they were already numerous enough to found a Second Presbyterian Church. A historian, John Newton Boucher, writing later in the nineteenth century about the Scots-Irish, called them "very independent, if not arrogant in the world," noting that, "They always looked down on the Puritans and Quakers, who in turn despised them. They abhorred the Pennsylvania Dutch ... and yet from the beginning to the end, they ruled the Quaker, Puritan and Dutchman as though with a rod of iron."[15]

Meanwhile in Buffalo, the local elites almost universally possessed English surnames at the time when they founded the First Church of Christ of Buffalo in 1812. These two early elite groups founded not only churches but libraries, schools, and other cultural institutions throughout the rest of the century. Yet during these same years the success of their business enterprises brought in massive numbers of workers who were neither of English or Scots-Irish stock. German-born and descended people composed more than half of Buffalo's population by 1875. Despite the Catholics among its immigrant population, Buffalo was and remains heavily Republican, owing in part to the fact that German Americans, as well as Anglo Americans, found political success in that party.

Today, Protestantism in Pittsburgh and Buffalo is strongest in the outlying suburbs, but huge church edifices and congregations remain from the heyday of their industrial elites. African Americans who came north in the great migration of the 1920s and later have also left a religious mark on these cities, as have more recent immigrant communities. Still, the Catholic and Orthodox populations are stronger by far than all the Protestants put together in these cities, but a conservative tinge remains in the collective values of all these traditions expressed in political life.

Whereas in Brooklyn or Philadelphia Al Gore recorded roughly four votes for every one vote marked for George W. Bush in the 2000 presidential election, in Allegheny (Pittsburgh) and Erie (Buffalo) counties votes between the two were far closer to even (with neither exceeding 59 percent for the Democrat). When it came to voting patterns for the 2000 election then, Buffalo and Pittsburgh more closely resembled Columbus, Ohio, or Davenport, Iowa, than they did any of their eastern urban counterparts. Religious support for the right-to-life movement is also strong in these cities.

The picture that emerges for religion in the western portion of the Middle Atlantic region is a relatively conservative one, whether the setting be rural or urban. The results of the 2004 presidential election simply confirmed the overall pattern, since western Pennsylvania and New York counties went relatively more "red" (Republican) in 2004 than in 2000, while the eastern portions of those states became more "blue" and tipped their states' electoral votes toward John Kerry.

The Pennsylvania Experience and the American Way of Religion

As the reader will have noticed by now, Pennsylvania is the state in the region where nearly every Protestant faith group found an early home and many went on to thrive in a place where no church or sect predominated, but nearly all found the respect of their neighbors. Pennsylvania also is the living embodiment of a trend observed about the region more generally, namely that the mountains divide Protestants into zones of like-minded piety and observance. The experience of many of these groups in Pennsylvania has been detailed elsewhere in this chapter. But the way in which Pennsylvania, along with the area surrounding New York City, prefigure the contemporary American scene and even continue to exemplify that scene, deserves a further note.

While other colonies and later states—save New York—were still wondering which form of Protestantism to establish, or to gently disestablish, Pennsylvania was reveling in its diversity. Lutherans, Quakers, Anglicans, Swiss Brethren,

Presbyterians, Moravians, Mennonites, and German Reformed Christians all found homes, village by village, in the Pennsylvanian Commonwealth. This of course became the pattern in the nineteenth and twentieth centuries throughout the nation. Real liberty of worship in the American republic probably owes more to the fact that William Penn's "Holy Experiment" worked than to any theory of the separation of church and state articulated and advanced by Thomas Jefferson. Yet it can be argued that Pennsylvania is not merely a model for development in the past. Rather, Pennsylvania is also a model of the present, for perhaps nowhere else is it clear in a single state that in today's America differently minded Protestants, while somewhat dispersed, do not live in randomly dispersed residences and houses of worship across the American landscape.

The western Pennsylvania conservative Anglo Protestants and the more moderate German-descended Protestants of eastern Pennsylvania have more in common with the other Protestants in their sub-regions than their apparent denominational diversity within sub-regions might indicate. And within denominational groupings, it is exceedingly important to know where someone is from before one can reasonably calculate the probabilities of holding this or that position on a given theological or social issue of the day.

In sum, the different varieties of Protestantism help shape a region, or subregion, and then in turn the region shapes its characteristic forms of Protestantism. In late modern America Pennsylvania again leads the way as neither state nor religious affiliation by itself can capture or explain religious outlook and behavior, but location and tradition, combined with other political and economic indicators, can tell much about what people believe, what they value, and how they might choose to live.

Endnotes

1. Unless otherwise indicated statistics concerning adherence rates and denominational affiliation are derived from the 2000 Glenmary Religious Congregations and Membership Survey, available at http://www.religionatlas.org.

2. Green, John C., "Religion Gap Swings New Ways," in *Religion in the News*, Spring 2005, Vol. 7, No. 3.

3. Gaustad, Edwin Scott, Barlow, Philip L. and Dishno, Richard W., *New Historical Atlas of Religion in America*, New York: Oxford University Press, 2001, 18.

4. Gasutad and Barlow, 105.

5. ELCA Family History: 1600s, website www.elca.org/co/timeline/16.html.

6. The Lutheran Theological Seminary at Philadelphia, The Philadelphia Tradition, www.ltsp.edu/about/about3.html.

7. Levy, Barry, "Tender Plants': Quaker Farmers and Children in the Delaware Valley, 1681-1735," *Journal of Family History* 3 (Summer 1978): 116-129.

8. Moore, John Jamison, *History of the AME Zion Church in America*, York, Penn.: Teachers' Journal Office, 1884, pp. 15-18.

9. See Allen, Richard, *The Life, Experience, and Gospel Labours of the Rt. Rev. Richard Allen. To Which is Annexed the Rise and Progress of the African Methodist Episcopal Church in the United States of America. Containing a Narrative of the Yellow Fever in the Year of Our Lord 1793: With an Address to the People of Colour in the United States.* Philadelphia: Martin & Boden, Printers, 1833.

10. Lincoln, C. Eric and Mamiya, Lawrence H., *The Black Church in the African-American Experience*, Durham: Duke University Press, 1990.

11. Quoted in Ment, David, "Public Schools," in Jackson, Kenneth T., ed., *The Encyclopedia of New York City*, New Haven: Yale University Press, 1993, 956.

12. Stem, Gary, "The Lutheran minister suspended for 9/11 service" in *The Journal News* July 10, 2002, (http://www.thejournalnews.com/newsroom/071002/10lutheran.html); and Hertz, Todd, "Benke Suspended for 'Syncretism' after 9/11 Event" in *Christianity Today*, Week of July 29 (http://www.christianitytoday.com/ct/2002/129/31.0.html)

13. "A brief timeline of the United Methodist Church and its American heritage." (http://www.gcah.org/umc_timeline.html)

14. Source: North American Religious Atlas, 2000 Glenmary Religious

a major party. He was also the quintessential Catholic urban Democrat, a multiethnic product of the streets of New York (his was a mix of Irish, Italian, and
German ancestry), schooled not in the Ivy League but, as he put it, the Fulton
Fish Market. He was a loyal Catholic whose most trusted advisers were Jewish.
He was a progressive governor of New York who enjoyed the ardent backing of
secular urban reformers as well as Tammany Hall chieftains. From the vantage
point of New York City in 1928 Smith's national appeal was irresistible, especially after the Catholic issue was seemingly defused by Smith's deeply genuine
reaffirmation of the primacy of the constitution in church-state relations. (It was
asked during the campaign whether, if elected, he would implement teachings
of the papal encyclicals. He reportedly later implored his aides: "Would someone please tell me what the hell a papal encyclical is?") The vehemently hostile
reaction to Smith's candidacy in many parts of the nation shocked the "Happy
Warrior" and his handlers. While no Democrat could likely have defeated Herbert
Hoover in 1928, the repudiation of Smith on religious grounds indicated that the
ethno-political style he represented was not yet capable of surmounting nativist
distrust. [1]

New York City is surely not wholly representative of the entire Middle
Atlantic region or its Catholic population. Yet until recent decades Catholicism
throughout the region was an overwhelmingly urban phenomenon and the
extraordinary density of Catholic populations meant that these cities were
largely Catholic-made and operated. A substantial majority of Catholics in
the Middle Atlantic could trace their origins in the region to the areas in and
around New York City, Albany, Baltimore, and Philadelphia. In Jersey City,
New Jersey, in the first half of the twentieth century, for example (just across
the river from Manhattan, Jersey City occupies a distinct cultural location),
the Irish-Catholic machine of Frank Hague orchestrated the electoral politics
of Hudson County—one of the most Catholic places on earth—while exerting
statewide power as well. Most of New Jersey's 21 counties were largely rural
and Protestant, but Hudson County alone could make or break statewide candidacies of Republicans and Democrats alike (Hague occasionally muted his
opposition to Republican candidates for strategic purposes). Hudson County
also enjoyed national clout. Hague supported Al Smith in his quixotic effort to
recapture the Democratic presidential nomination in 1932, but after Franklin D.
Roosevelt won the nod Hague promptly organized a massive rally at the Jersey
Shore for FDR, who repaid the debt regularly as president.

Hague was pilloried by the organs of liberal reform as un-American and was
condemned as a fascist in the pages of the *Nation* and the *New Republic*. While
the proximate cause of this outrage was Hague's militant resistance to Congress
of Industrial Organizations (CIO) organizing campaigns in Jersey City, the rheto-

ric of his critics evoked an older nativist tradition that haunted Catholics across the nation but enjoyed a particular resonance in the Middle Atlantic region.

Unlike in New England, Catholics had been present in the Middle Atlantic for nearly as long as Anglo Protestants (albeit in much smaller numbers in the early days). At the same time, there was no hereditary Catholic elite in the Middle Atlantic akin to those of St. Louis, New Orleans, or St. Paul, Minnesota. Catholics in the Middle Atlantic inhabited an intermediate place marked by contentious yet engaged relations with outsiders, internecine conflicts and genuine if hard-won social and economic mobility. As the historian R. Laurence Moore wrote in *Religious Outsiders and the Making of Americans*, "Catholics encountered hatred, but Catholic leaders had the relative luxury of being able to imagine more than one way to press their collective fortunes in America."[2]

American Catholicism Stakes its Claim

The immigrant church and its ethnic diversity is such a dominant motif in the Catholic history of the Middle Atlantic that it is easy to forget it was not always so. Maryland was settled in 1634 by relatives and associates of a British convert to Catholicism, George Calvert, Lord Baltimore, who died in England the same year as the colony's founding. Calvert's "vision," according to the historian Thomas W. Spalding, entailed "interfaith harmony, public service, and attachment to such American principles as religious liberty and separation of Church and state." This "Maryland tradition" stands over against "attitudes and institutions that developed with the immigrant church." Catholic Marylanders enjoyed an enormous advantage not always acknowledged by their admirers: Though never comprising a majority of citizens in the colony, they were heavily concentrated within the social and economic elite. Within a decade of Maryland's founding, however, the Calverts were overthrown by Puritans, who sailed into the colony aboard the aptly named vessel the *Reformation*.[3]

The Calverts regained control in 1649 and three years later the proprietors encouraged the passage of the Act of Religious Toleration, which introduced limited religious freedom to the British colonies. The Calverts were less invested in Catholic hegemony in the colony than in the peace and prosperity of their enterprise. A policy of official toleration protected Catholics, the only non-Protestant Christian denomination found in Maryland. The 1649 Act made denial of the Trinity punishable by death, but it also mandated:

> 'noe person or persons whatsoever within this Province ... professing to believe in Jesus Christ, shall from henceforth bee in any ways troubled, Molested or discountenanced for or in respect of his or her religion nor in the free exercise thereof ... nor anyway compelled

to the belief or exercise of any other Religion against his or her consent.[4]

The early years of the Maryland experiment indicated that Catholics fared best in British colonies when Christian fervor was at low tide. This was certainly the case in New York. While on a tour in the mid 1680s Captain William Byrd of Virginia remarked that the New York colony's inhabitants "seem not concerned with what religion their neighbor is, or whether he hath any or none." New York's Irish-Catholic governor at the time, Thomas Dongan, made his own denominational inventory and found "not many of the Church of England; few Roman Catholics; abundance of Quakers ... Singing Quakers; Ranting Quakers; Sabbatarians; Anti-Sabbitarians, some Anabaptists, some Independents, some Jews; in short, of all sorts of opinions there are some, and the most part of none at all."

Dongan was appointed governor in 1682 by James, the Catholic Duke of York, and the following year promoted passage by the colony's representative assembly of a Charter of Liberties and Privileges granting religious freedom to all Christians in the colony. Dongan was a pragmatist like most of the successful New York Catholic politicians that followed him, but he became a victim of religious zealotry spilling across the Atlantic. After King James II was overthrown at the end of 1688 a new, robustly anti-Catholic colonial regime issued arrest warrants for all suspected "papists" in New York. Dongan fled to England but many of the small community of disfranchised New York Catholics eventually found a nearer refuge in Quaker Pennsylvania, site of William Penn's "holy experiment" in religious liberty.[5]

Catholics were prohibited from holding public office in Pennsylvania until 1775; nevertheless, the historian John Tracy Ellis still described the Catholic experience there as "the most pleasant and positive of any of the original thirteen colonies." St. Joseph's Church, established on Walnut Street in Philadelphia in 1733, was the first permanent urban Catholic foundation in the British colonies. The small Catholic community in Philadelphia was bolstered by a steady migration from neighboring Maryland, as well as by immigrants from Germany.

By the beginning of American nationhood in 1789 there were an estimated 2,000 Catholics in Philadelphia and another 5,000 scattered throughout the state. In that same year John Carroll was elected bishop of the nation's first "See," the diocese of Baltimore, which initially included the entire United States. Carroll, scion of Maryland's leading Catholic family, was chosen by the roughly 30 Catholic priests in active ministry in the United States at the time. His election—as distinct from the customary papal appointment—was partly the result of diplomacy by Benjamin Franklin, U.S. Minister to France, and others with an interest in promoting the compatibility of the Church with American democracy. Carroll himself had "contracted the language of a republican" as early as 1782. He advocated the election of bishops by those he termed "the older and more worthy clergy." Under his leadership the Middle Atlantic Church grew more responsive at the local level: In 1808 Philadelphia was made the seat of a new diocese that included all of Pennsylvania and Delaware, along with western and southern New Jersey. The Diocese of New York was established at the same time, encompassing New York state and northern New Jersey.

In the early national period these new dioceses became the sites of sometimes bitter conflict over Church governance. A system of lay trustees overseeing parishes was established, in keeping with American law and custom, but it was frequently resisted by bishops and pastors alike. The most contentious dispute occurred in the early 1820s at Philadelphia's affluent St. Mary's Church, where a fiery, recently arrived Irish priest, William Hogan, sided with lay trustees against a new bishop, Henry Conwell. The dispute was not settled by an election campaign marked by brawling outside the church. Hogan's faction, which called for the trustees to choose pastors and bishops, won the election but he subsequently submitted to a papal order limiting the power of trustees. Hogan then changed his mind, left the country and later left the priesthood and the Church. Conwell's successor, Bishop Francis Kenrick, reasserted episcopal authority in Philadelphia and set the tone for a national trend toward centralized authority in American dioceses.

That emerging structure of authority was quickly and sorely tested by the tidal wave of mass immigration of European Catholics to the United States. Between 1815 and 1845 nearly 1 million Irish emigrants made their way to the United States; this cohort was roughly equally divided between Catholics and Protestants and many were ambitious and skilled. After 1845, however, the overwhelming majority of Irish immigrants were Catholic peasants in flight from the devastating impact of the Great Famine that broke out that year. "The air was laded with a sickly odor of decay," recalled an immigrant, "as if the hand of death had stricken the potato field, and...everything growing in it was rotten." Most of these refugees landed in New York, and most remained in the city and region, especially when compared with the vast numbers of German Protestant and Catholic immigrants who succeeded the waves of Irish: these latter groups were much more likely to settle in the nation's interior regions.[6]

The Catholic Church played the central role in transforming famine migrants from peasants into urban Americans. In the absence of public agencies dedicated to serving newly arrived immigrants, the Church tended to newcomer's material as well as spiritual needs. The support was particularly welcome since the Irish did not receive the warmest of welcomes in Philadelphia, New York, or the smaller cities of the Middle Atlantic region. In Philadelphia's Kensington neighborhood two Catholic churches were burned by nativists in May 1844. In July of that year more than 20 people were killed when a mob of thousands attacked members of the state militia guarding St. Philip Neri Church in nearby Southwark. In New York the Irish-born bishop John Hughes announced that if any Catholic churches in the city were burned, "New York would be another Moscow." His churches went unharmed.

Hughes signaled the growth of urban Catholic political power in 1841 when, disappointed by Democrats who failed to back his proposals for religious instruction in public schools, he ran his own independent slate of candidates in local elections. Hughes was incensed by anti-Catholic rhetoric in textbooks supplied by New York's Public School Society, an organization of leading Protestants who devised curricula for the city's public schools. Hughes' candidates swept to victory and New York's Democrats would not again fail to court the Catholic vote. The links between Church and Party grew closer as the Irish moved toward full control of Tammany in the 1870s.

John Hughes was the most powerful American prelate of the mid-nineteenth century. When he laid the cornerstone of Manhattan's massive St. Patrick's Cathedral in 1858 he triumphantly proclaimed before a crowd of more than 100,000 that New York's Irish Catholics could "laugh to scorn" those who ridiculed their customs and religion. Hughes' confrontational remarks aroused the ire of *The New York Times*, which chided the bishop for his "bad taste, which, of late years, has more or less characterized everything His Grace has said or written outside the immediate sphere of his archiepiscopal duties." In July 1863, however, in the final months of his life, Hughes was lauded for his efforts to quell the terrible Draft Riots, in which mobs of Irish-Americans, resentful of the Union Army's conscription policy, rampaged through the streets of Manhattan. One hundred five people were killed, including 11 African Americans, targeted both for their race and their role as competitors for scarce jobs. The Draft Riots marked the nadir of the Irish-American experience in urban America, but the rioters were far outnumbered by volunteers of the "Corcoran Legion" and other Irish- and German-American battalions from Middle Atlantic cities serving in the Union Army. The Church's prestige and self-confidence grew quickly in the post-Civil War era.[7]

Nowhere was this confidence more apparent than in the rapidly expanding system of Catholic schools. Despite his triumph over New York's Public School Society in 1841, Hughes decided to build a separate, costly, and extensive network of private Catholic schools. Hughes led and the leaders of other dioceses followed. By 1884, when the American bishops declared that "every Catholic child in the land" should enjoy access to a parish (parochial) school, enrollments in Catholic schools in New York, Philadelphia, and other Middle Atlantic cities equaled roughly one-third that of public school enrollments. The impact of such a costly system of parochial schools was nowhere more evident than in such Middle Atlantic locales as Jersey City, Philadelphia, and New York. As Daniel Patrick Moynihan wrote in a landmark 1963 essay on the New York Irish: "there is nothing in the history of organized religion comparable with the effort of the American Catholic Church to maintain a complete, comprehensive educational system."[8]

Though Catholic schools have often been viewed by critics as separatist, they performed a highly public function in acculturating immigrant children to urban American life. This role was especially critical in the Middle Atlantic region because schools there were almost invariably housed in ethnic, or "national," parishes, as they were known until the mid-twentieth century.

Ethnic parishes were the principal vehicle of Catholic Americanization, a paradox rooted in the nature of ethnic and neighborhood politics in the urban Northeast. Immigrants did not simply replicate the traditions of the old country but created new hybrid forms of identity: Italian Americans, for example, initially identified themselves almost entirely with a village or at most a region of Italy, but found themselves part of a much larger collectivity in American cities. Members of these newly constituted ethnic groups sought to worship with their compatriots in a parish led by a pastor who shared their language and culture. The first Italian-American parish in the United States, St. Mary Magdalen da Pazzi, was founded in Philadelphia in 1857. By the early twentieth century Italian Americans outnumbered the Irish in many of the largest cities in the region, including Jersey City, Newark, and New York City.

Inter-ethnic discord was a major element of the "Americanism" controversy of the late nineteenth century, a conflict that pitted largely Irish-American bishops against Germans and others that believed the Church was adapting too readily to the American environment at the expense of cultural traditions imported by non-Irish immigrants. The ethnic tensions unleashed by the controversy were stronger in the less-populated western regions of the Middle Atlantic than on the East Coast, where the dominance of the Irish was reflected in *intraethnic* ideological conflicts. In New York City, for example, Archbishop Michael Corrigan in 1886 suspended a local priest, Edward McGlynn, not once but twice over his support for the mayoral candidacy of Henry George, the controversial advocate of a "single tax" on land. McGlynn was also an outspoken critic of Tammany Hall, a position the Archbishop found unacceptable. McGlynn was a hero of "Americanist" Catholics for his critique of papal infallibility and his preference for public over parochial schooling. When Corrigan appointed another priest to take McGlynn's place at St. Stephen's parish on the East Side of Manhattan, a crowd of 7,000 McGlynn supporters prevented the new man from entering the church. The struggle between the strong-willed Irish priest and the authoritarian Irish bishop grabbed the attention of New Yorkers of all faiths.

Irish-American bishops were the first shepherds of the dioceses of Albany and Buffalo (both established in 1847), Pittsburgh (1843), and Scranton (1868). These latter three "inland" dioceses quickly attracted a larger percentage of Eastern-European immigrants than their counterpart dioceses on the Eastern Seaboard. The nation's first Slovak (St. Joseph's in Hazelton) and Croatian (St. Nicholas in Pittsburgh) parishes were established in Pennsylvania in the 1870s. Ethnic conflicts with Irish bishops in the interior Middle Atlantic grew common by the late nineteenth century.

In 1897 Polish Catholics at Sacred Heart parish in Scranton built their own church after clashing with Bishop William O'Hara over control of the parish. In 1904 they joined with other disaffected Polish Americans and established the Polish National Catholic Church. A recently excommunicated priest from Scranton, Francis Hodur, served as the church's first bishop. The Polish National Church was the most significant "schismatic" movement in American Catholic history. As of 2000 the church was divided into four dioceses, with 20 parishes found in the Buffalo-Pittsburgh diocese and an additional 49 parishes located in the Central diocese, covering Eastern and Central Pennsylvania, and New York, New Jersey, and Maryland.

Cardinal James Gibbons of Baltimore emerged during the late nineteenth century as both the leader of the national hierarchy and the most influential spokesmen for the "Americanist" camp. The son of Irish immigrants, Gibbons was named archbishop of the "Premier See" in 1877 and presided over the Third Plenary Council of Baltimore in 1884. Despite his initial lack of enthusiasm for an event called by the Vatican, the Council "produced the most comprehensive body of legislation for the Catholic Church in America." In addition to mandating a parochial education for every Catholic child, a committee led by Gibbons also produced a new catechism that became the standard catechetical text nationwide. Although the *Baltimore Catechism* was largely a compilation of earlier works, it provided a uniform method of religious instruction that prevailed until the 1960s. Gibbons was elevated to the cardinalate in 1886, the second American prelate so honored (Archbishop John McCloskey of New York was the first, in 1875).[9]

The Irish stranglehold on the hierarchy in the Middle Atlantic was near total from the mid-nineteenth century to the mid-twentieth. The "hibernarchy" tended to view Irish-American parishes as simply "American" with all others classified as "national." German-American Catholics, located mostly in the Midwest, were the most vocal to resist the "Americanizing" impulse of Irish-American bishops. Leaders of this community called on Rome to condemn "Americanism" and they found substantial support for their cause. Cardinal Gibbons of Baltimore objected to intervention in U.S. Catholic affairs by "officious gentlemen" in Europe and promised: "We will prove to our countrymen that the ties formed by grace and faith are stronger than flesh and blood. God and our country—this [is] our watchword. Loyalty to God's church and to our country—this [is] our religious and political faith." "Americanism" as misunderstood by Pope Leo XIII was condemned in an 1899 papal letter addressed to Gibbons, *Testem Benevolentiae.*[10]

Gibbons' territory included Washington, D.C., which did not become a separate archdiocese until 1939. Washington was a sleepy southern city with few Catholics and none of the immigrant parish communities that dominated the Middle Atlantic. But as the national capital it became a major site of Catholic activity. Cardinal Gibbons was instrumental in winning Vatican approval for the Catholic University of America, which was opened in Washington in 1889. Catholic University represented a triumph for Gibbons and his "Americanist" allies in the church, many of whom came from other regions of the country but took advantage of Gibbons' political clout in establishing their imprint in the nation's capital. John A. Ryan, a young priest from St. Paul sent to Catholic University for graduate studies in 1898, returned in 1915 as a member of the faculty and became a highly influential social thinker. In 1917, with Gibbons still in charge, the National Catholic War Council was established in Washington: Two years later the organization was renamed the National Catholic Welfare Conference (NCWC) and quickly emerged as the voice of the American bishops on public issues. Msgr. John A. Ryan was commissioned in 1919 to draft a *Bishop's Program on Social Reconstruction.* This landmark document signaled the American church's commitment to the pursuit of social justice for all Americans, and it may be rooted at least to some extent in the activist, optimistic Maryland tradition that ran from John Carroll through James Gibbons. In 1920, a year before he died, Gibbons laid the cornerstone for the National Shrine of the Immaculate Conception on the grounds of Catholic University. It is the largest Catholic church in the Western Hemisphere.

The Making of an Urban Mass Culture

While historians of American Catholicism have been preoccupied with "Americanism" as an ecclesiastical controversy, a more enduring, non-theological variant of Americanism emerged among the urban laity in the Middle Atlantic region in the late nineteenth and early twentieth centuries. The invention of urban popular culture in New York and other cities in the region can be largely attributed to Catholics. In part this was due to the sheer numbers of Catholics found in the urban Middle Atlantic: By the early twentieth century the larger cities in the region were home to Catholic majorities ranging from 50 to 75 per cent of the populace. As the historian R. Laurence Moore explained, the birth of urban mass culture was "specifically a non-Protestant and working-class accomplishment."

Immigrant Catholics, whether Irish, German, Italian, Polish, or Latino, carried to the United States a great variety of street entertainments and a zest for holiday and carnival rooted in folk traditions. Not only could these things be commercialized but they also reflected an untroubled acceptance of gaiety that made possible an enormous range of other commercial pastimes. Mass-circulation newspapers, nickelodeons, movie palaces, and commercial radio broadcasting outlets all targeted Catholic audiences. These new institutions in turn reflected Catholic sensibilities, which were never shaped in isolation but were the product of interactions with other urban groups, particularly Jews and—especially in the years following World War I—African Americans.[11]

This model of popular Catholicism as highly interactive was particularly evident in New York City. The connections between Jews and Catholics on the streets of Lower Manhattan, for example, prefigured the almost reflexive tendency of Jewish producers in Hollywood to "synthesize the Christian religion," as Daniel Patrick Moynihan put it, "in the person of an Irish priest." Similarly, "when it came to playing a tough American, up from the streets…James Cagney was the quintessential figure."

In New York, Albany, Jersey City, and other Middle Atlantic locales, second-generation Irish political machines provided for both the circuses of popular culture and the bread that sustained them. In the late nineteenth century the Irish machines took care of their own; in the twentieth they continued to do that while also brokering the multiethnic metropolis. In most of these cities Democratic machines collaborated with Church officials while observing a division of spiritual and material labors.

In places such as Jersey City, where municipal employees routinely cleared snow from the steps of parochial schools, the lines separating church and state were blurred beyond recognition. In Albany, where the machine established by Dan O'Connell in 1922 ruled New York's capital city for the balance of the century, the local Catholic diocese received "gifts of money, land, moral stricture" (in the form of district attorneys prosecuting morally objectionable literary and artistic works), along with "gifts of special services, such as paving, snowplowing, and sewer work, whose like did not necessarily accrue to other denominations. As in Jersey City and other urban locales run by Democratic machines, the diocese returned the favors.[12]

In other places, however, where Protestant and/or Republican bosses ruled, bishops enjoyed even greater power because they faced no Catholic competition. This was especially true in Philadelphia, where Cardinal Dennis Dougherty reigned supreme between the world wars. From the late nineteenth through the mid-twentieth centuries Philadelphia was governed by an Anglo-Protestant Republican machine that fully acknowledged the dimensions of Catholic power. Dougherty fancied himself "God's Bricklayer" for his massive efforts to build up the Catholic infrastructure of Philadelphia, but he was also a power broker who in 1934 issued an edict forbidding Catholics from attending movies because he viewed theaters as "occasions of sin." Despite the canonical (he did not consult with other bishops before issuing the edict) and theological (a theater cannot be an occasion of sin as distinct from the particular film playing there) inadequacies of his position, Philadelphia's Catholics generally obeyed his orders, at least for a while. Dougherty was an absolutist who symbolized the era of prelate-as-CEO, general, and monarch rolled into one. Like many such figures, as the author Charles R. Morris showed in *American Catholic* (1997), he was a bundle of contradictions. According to Morris, Dougherty

> treated his priests harshly, sometimes even cruelly, but forged one of the most effective diocesan clergies. His views on sexuality were among the most conventional of his time, but alone among the hierarchy, he took the feminist position on issues affecting both laywomen and nuns. The most secure and strongly entrenched of churchmen, he was the most servile toward Rome. The Philadelphia Catholic subculture that he created was among the most carapaced and separatist in the country, but he drew his own friends from outside the Church, indeed, the men who may have been closest to him were Jews. He was shy and private and hated speaking or preaching in public, but loved the pomp and princely luxury that came with his office.[13]

These contradictory traits were not unique to Dougherty but seem characteristic of urban Middle Atlantic prelates of the twentieth century. These bishops needed to sustain the Church's aristocratic prerogatives while forging an increasingly public role for the Church. Their dioceses were not only the most ethnically and religious diverse in the nation, they also featured the highest level of interaction between members of ethnic and religious traditions, some of it harmonious, some contentious. Given these challenges it is hardly surprising that Dougherty, like his better-known counterpart in New York, Cardinal Spellman (who ruled from 1939-1967), was not a model of consistency. As Morris noted: "Dennis Dougherty was a difficult man, although undeniably a great cardinal, and while he was called many names during his long career, no one ever accused him of being reasonable."[14]

Like Dougherty, Cardinal Spellman grew wary of "national" parishes and preferred to see immigrant groups "Americanized" as quickly as possibly through the tender ministrations of Irish-American priests and parochial school teachers. Spellman was a militant anti-communist and ostentatious patriot as vicar of the nation's armed services. He was fully prepared to guard the church from enemies foreign and domestic but was no better prepared than his brethren for challenges emanating from *within* the Church.

The most enduring challenge to the "triumphalist" model of church leadership provided by Dougherty, Spellman, and others came from the Catholic Worker movement, a radically apostolic community founded in Lower Manhattan in 1933. The Catholic Worker resulted from an encounter between Peter Maurin, a 54-year-old French itinerant philosopher, and Dorothy Day, a 35-year-old journalist who had converted to Catholicism just five years earlier.

Dorothy Day is often described as a former communist, but she was a much more intuitive radical than a Party functionary, moving from one bohemian enthusiasm to another during her years as a vivid denizen of New York's Greenwich Village. Her conversion was linked to experiences surrounding the birth of her only child in 1926 and was not informed by the Church's social teachings, since she believed the Church offered none. Peter Maurin indoctrinated her in the tradition of the "social encyclicals," the two most significant of which were issued in 1891 and 1931 by popes Leo XIII and Pius XI, respectively. The social encyclicals affirmed the Church's solidarity with working people. Maurin urged Day to take the further step of *applying* these teachings directly, opening her modest apartment to the homeless and unemployed in the spirit of Christ. Soon the fledgling apostolate established "houses of hospitality" to serve the poor, and Day also launched an extraordinarily influential monthly newspaper, *The Catholic Worker*.

The Catholic Worker movement was a quintessentially New York phenomenon, though this characteristic has strangely evaded scholars and critics. Catholic Workers took their place amid the contentious din of Union Square and other public venues where radicals and reformers vied for influence in the 1930s. The newspaper was distributed with cries of "read the *Catholic Worker* daily," a play on the title of the Communist Party newspaper, *The Daily Worker*. Peter Maurin wanted the paper to be called "The Catholic Agitator," which was in fact a more accurate title since he disdained the organized labor movement for its gradualism and its concessions to the logic of industrial capitalism. The paper scorned the convenient piety of Tammany Hall figures and made a special target of Jersey City Mayor Frank Hague. In January 1938 Day informed readers: "We have a special interest in Jersey City because the city is over 75 percent Catholic." Hague was embroiled in an often-violent campaign to prevent the CIO from mobilizing workers in a thoroughly anti-union environment. *The Catholic Worker* charged that Hague was abetting communism by discrediting

Church teachings through his actions and questioned "whether Jersey City is still in the United States." [15]

That same month, as if to answer their own question, Catholic Workers John Cort and George Donahue made an incursion across the Hudson. There they enjoyed a memorable exchange with a pair of Jersey City policemen intent on enforcing Mayor Hague's highly unconstitutional "anti-littering" ordinance, which authorized the arrest of anyone in possession of a leaflet that could potentially end up on the ground:

> Cop: You can't distribute that stuff here. You're littering the street.
>
> Donahue: Number one, the Supreme Court has ruled that your anti-littering ordinance is unconstitutional. Number Two, we can't help it if people drop things on the street. If anybody is littering the street, they're littering the street.
>
> Cop: Yeah, but you're the first cause of their littering.

"He kept repeating that phrase 'first cause,'" Cort wrote. "It began to sound like a discussion of metaphysics."

> Cort: If you're going to talk about first causes, then God is the real first cause because God made man.
>
> Second cop (figuring to expose our Catholic pose):
>
> Why did God make man?
>
> Cort (letting him have it straight from the Baltimore Cathechism): God made man to know Him and love Him and serve Him and be happy with Him forever in heaven.
>
> Third cop: That's funny. I thought God made man to break the law so we could have a job." [16]

The incident showed not only that Jersey City cops maintained their sense of humor but that a common vocabulary linked urban Catholics: realists and radicals, "cradle" Catholics and converts. Catholics in the urban Middle Atlantic grew comfortable with internecine conflict so long as it did not impinge on the fundamentals of Catholic doctrine. Dorothy Day often said that she would close down her movement at a moment's notice should Cardinal Spellman request it, which was highly unlikely given his recognition of the movement's prestige and spiritual authority. The Catholic Worker movement was radical because it was radically Catholic and deeply grounded in the Church's teachings and traditions. At the same time, it was part of a broader "movement culture" among whose goals was a severing of the tight connection between the Church and entrenched political machines.

Sometimes internal critiques hit even closer to home. The Association of Catholic Trade Unionists (ACTU), a Catholic Worker offshoot, enraged Spellman in 1949 by its support of a gravediggers strike at archdiocesan cemeteries in New York. Spellman conscripted his seminarians to dig graves, a show of strength that backfired in a changing political environment. Servicemen returning from Europe and Asia found themselves less willing to endure business as usual in the ethnic precincts of the Middle Atlantic cities. Italian Americans rebelled against Tammany Hall in New York and the Hague regime in Jersey City, with Carmine De Sapio ending the Irish dominance of Tammany and John V. Kenny—an opportunistic Irish politician who forged a coalition with Italian and Polish Americans—ending 32 years of Hague rule over the Hudson's west bank in 1949.

Dockworkers of all nationalities rebelled against the corrupt regime of the International Longshoremen's Association "life-President," Joseph P. Ryan. A series of wildcat strikes, beginning in 1945, led to Ryan's downfall from a powerful position bolstered by his close ties with the chaplain of the Port of New York, Msgr. John J. O'Donnell, an archdiocesan powerbroker. Though Ryan cited communist infiltration of the union as the cause of his woes, the rank and file rebels in the ILA were overwhelmingly Catholic and were backed first by the ACTU and later by a Jesuit labor priest, John M. Corridan, working out of the Xavier Labor School in Manhattan's Chelsea neighborhood.

Catholic labor schools were a Middle Atlantic phenomenon that quickly spread across the nation: the first such school was established at St. Joseph's College in Philadelphia in 1935, followed by Xavier and a school at Crown Heights in Brooklyn. Labor schools sought to promote labor-management harmony through application of the social encyclicals to the workplace. In practice the schools provided Catholic working people with opportunities for advancement in the labor movement by honing adult students' skills in public speaking and parliamentary procedure. The most prominent labor priest in Philadelphia, the Jesuit Dennis Comey, became the official mediator of the Port district and enjoyed great success in the 1940s and 1950s as a mediator between labor, management, and local government.

The situation on the New York-New Jersey waterfront was much more contentious and pitted reformers such as John Corridan against the devoutly Catholic union leadership and even more prominent Catholic waterfront entrepreneurs. The struggle was immortalized in the classic 1954 film *On the Waterfront*, whose author, Budd Schulberg, later described Corridan—with much justification—as a forerunner of liberation theologians. But Corridan, no less than Comey and other labor priests in the region, saw his role primarily as mediator between competing forces because the world worked that way. Christian realism was his guiding philosophy, just as it reflected the ethos of urban Catholic Middle Atlantic culture. Corridan became a crusader only after concluding the system was totally out of balance.

Post-War Anxieties

These post-war struggles *within* Catholic communities of the Middle Atlantic belie the standard narrative of suburbanization, by which an urban-immigrant style of Catholicism yields virtually overnight to a homogenized, post-ethnic pastoral retreat. Catholics were certainly very well represented in the suburban experiments that blossomed in the potato fields of eastern Long Island and meadows of South Jersey (no fewer than three Levittown communities arose in the New York-Philadelphia areas). Remarkably little is known about the religious migration to suburbia, especially compared with the rich scholarship of the earlier migration of Catholics from Europe to the cities of the Middle Atlantic. The prevailing assumption is that suburban Catholics became inhabitants of what might be called "Will Herberg's America."

Herberg, the popular sociologist of religion and author of an extraordinarily influential 1955 study, *Protestant-Catholic-Jew*, argued that the communal and theological distinctiveness that had separated Catholics and Jews from each other—and both from the dominant American Protestantism—was supplanted after World War II by a bland religiosity of the "American Way of Life" tailored to new social circumstances. Though Herberg did not treat suburbanization in any depth, *Protestant-Catholic-Jew* helped shaped the understanding of American religion in an era of "de-ethnicization."

While many Catholics fled to suburbia in the postwar decade, a larger number remained behind in core cities or older, inner-ring suburbs; the transition to suburban Catholicism was gradual and played out over five decades. If Catholics stayed longer than members of other religious traditions, devotion to parishes was a key reason. As the historian John McGreevy demonstrated in *Parish Boundaries* (1996), urban Catholics tended to view the parish neighborhood as sacred space with a church at its heart. Since parishes were under the jurisdiction of diocesan authorities, they could not simply move to new suburbs even had parishioners so desired. Protestant and Jewish congregations are free to transplant themselves; Catholic parishes are not. This meant that Catholics would find themselves on the front lines of the post-war "urban crisis," particularly civil rights struggles over housing and integrated schools for waves of African-American migrants from the South. Unlike European Americans, African-American Catholics were deeply wary of the "national" parish model—whether *de facto* or *de jure*—recognizing that in their case it was tantamount to enforced segregation.

Philadelphia was a primary frontier in the struggle for racial justice, a struggle that exposed underlying tensions within American Catholicism. Nowhere did Catholics more strongly identify themselves as citizens of parish neighborhoods than in Philadelphia. In the late 1930s James Maguire, a Jesuit assigned to an enormous North Philadelphia parish, created the Gesu Parish Neighborhood Improvement Association "to keep and bring into the parish respectable home-owners and tenants and to prevent the further influx of undesirables into the neighborhood." Maguire's thinly veiled racism conflicted directly with the burgeoning interracial apostolate promoted by his fellow Jesuit, John LaFarge of New York, as well as by a small number of white Gesu parishioners, includ-ing Anna McGarry, who helped organize the Philadelphia Catholic Interracial Council in the 1940s. As John McGreevy argues, the conflict in Philadelphia revealed the existence of two distinctly Catholic "moral languages," one that equated the faith with "tightly knit, homogenous parishes and schools," another that exposed "the bigotry implicit in such narrow definitions of community."[17]

This was not an abstract issue. "For the first time in our history we Catholics find ourselves fully involved in America's perennial problem," explained John McDermott of the Philadelphia Catholic Housing Council in 1959. "In city after city in the North today, Catholics constitute far and away the largest single group. Thus it is that race relations in these cities to an increasing degree is a matter of white Catholic-Negro relations." When violence erupted in Philadelphia's Folcroft neighborhood after an African-American family tried to move there in 1963, members of the Interracial Council pressured the highly conserva-tive Cardinal John Krol to establish an Archdiocesan Commission on Human Relations. Issues of housing, neighborhood, and race came to define the "urban crisis" of the 1960s and 1970s. The effects on parish life were incalculable, as many questioned for the first time the legitimacy of territorial notions of sacred space. In the 1960s Catholics in the Middle Atlantic began to redefine their understanding of Christian community.[18]

The role of the John F. Kennedy administration in advancing the cause of civil rights and a broader social-justice agenda is well known, but the centrality of Kennedy brother-in-law Sargent Shriver has often been overlooked. Where the Boston-bred Kennedy was always sensitive to the political liabilities of his Catholicism, Shriver was an extraordinarily devout "public Catholic" in the tradition of his Maryland ancestors. Shriver's paternal grandfather was a former seminary classmate and close friend of Baltimore's Cardinal Gibbons and the young Shriver served as an altar boy at Masses celebrated by Gibbons at the Shriver family's summer home in rural Maryland. Imbued with the spirit of the papal social encyclicals, Shriver invited Dorothy Day to speak at Yale during his senior year in 1938, and he went on to direct the Chicago branch of the Catholic Interracial Council, inspired by the example of a family friend, John LaFarge, S.J.

By the time he married Eunice Kennedy in 1953, Shriver was well established as a leading Catholic activist. His leadership of the Peace Corps under John F. Kennedy, and later of the War on Poverty in the Lyndon B. Johnson administration, was deeply grounded in the traditions of Catholic social thought and in the self-confident strain of public Catholicism pioneered in colonial Maryland. Shriver, like so many Catholic public figures, was also deeply influenced by the Second Vatican Council (1962-1964), whose key documents called on Catholics to embrace the aspirations and sufferings of the entire world, including the non-Christian world. Eunice and Sargent Shriver extended this impulse to include the cognitively disabled. The precursor to the Special Olympics was launched in the backyard of the Shriver's Maryland home in 1962. Sargent Shriver was highly emblematic of a moment in American Catholic history when adherence to Church teachings and commitment to social justice were mutually reinforcing and unimpeded by concerns over the place of religion in public life.[19]

The Catholic idealism represented by Sargent Shriver also shaped movements for better relations between white and Latino Catholics of all colors in the cities of the Middle Atlantic. In 1940 New York City was home to a small Puerto Rican community, but by 1955 Puerto Ricans made up fully one-quarter of Catholics in the archdiocese. Church leaders proved incapable of responding to this challenge until the early 1950s, when a young European-bred priest named Ivan Illich decided to tailor his ministry to the needs of Puerto Ricans in the Washington Heights parish he served.

Illich established employment agencies for adults and camps for children while also attending to the spiritual needs of his congregation in their own language. Illich was culturally isolated from the overwhelmingly Irish-American clergy of the New York Archdiocese, but he found a talented and loyal champion in Joseph P. Fitzpatrick, a young, Harvard-trained Jesuit sociologist with his own interest in issues of human migration, an interest that blossomed when the renowned Harvard historian Oscar Handlin urged him to get in touch with his Irish immigrant background.

Illich and Fitzpatrick convinced Cardinal Spellman to speak at the first *Fiesta de San Juan*, sponsored by the archdiocese and held on Fordham University's Bronx campus in June 1956. Police officials expected no more than 5,000 attendees, but 35,000 people swarmed onto Fordham's football field on the day of the *Fiesta*. When at the height of the celebration a *piñata* was broken open by Spellman and members of the crowd surged forward, startled police officers whisked Spellman from the scene, fearing for his safety. Spellman was delighted by the publicity the event generated and Ivan Illich's stature in the archdiocese soared. Made a monsignor at age 29, in 1961 Illich founded—with Spellman's blessing—the Center for Intercultural Formation in Cuernavaca, Mexico. The Center was envisioned as a site for the "de-Yankeefication" of priests in ministry to Latino Americans.[20] While many of the Center's goals went unmet (and Illich eventually left the priesthood), it was a symbol of the Church's intensive if belated recognition of the demographic revolution underway in New York and the region.

The federal Immigration Reform Act of 1965 led to even more profound demographic changes in Middle Atlantic Catholicism. The end of a quota system favoring immigration from countries already well represented in the region made it possible for people from Africa, Asia, and Latin America to gain entry into the United States. The Middle Atlantic region became, with southern California, the most ethnically diverse in the nation. Hudson County, New Jersey, once the redoubt of Irish and Italian Americans, gave rise to a Latino majority by the 1990s. Within this Latino population there was also extraordinary diversity, with the Cuban Americans who had been present in Union City and West New York and the Puerto Ricans long established in Jersey City now joined by large communities of immigrants from Ecuador, Guatemala, and Mexico, among many other countries. Jersey City is also home to a very large and deeply Catholic Filipino community that worships alongside Korean Americans at St. Aloysius Church on West Side Avenue. Similarly diverse parishes are now found in urban centers throughout the region.

The Church no longer designates parishes as "national" or "ethnic," but encourages cooperation among groups within parishes. In practice this means that a given parish might offer separate masses in Tagalog, Korean, and English, among other languages, depending on the communities present. Many "new" immigrants settle almost immediately in parishes viewed as "suburban," though this designation can be highly misleading in the Middle Atlantic, where older suburbs often link urban communities (in the manner, for example, that Union, Roselle, and Hillside, New Jersey, link the cities of Newark and Elizabeth). Some recent immigrants quickly settle into the exurban areas associated with the phenomenon known as "urban sprawl," though this concept too is experienced differently in the Middle Atlantic than, say, the Midwest, where the contrast between "urban" and "suburban" is often sharper.

The vitality newcomers bring to the Church in the region exists alongside a sense of precipitous decline experienced by many older Catholics now inelegantly designated as "European Americans." As the urban ethnic communities that constituted the "first immigrant church" (1840s-1940s) began to disperse in the 1950s and 1960s, many Catholics continued to return to the "old neighborhood" to worship on special occasions if not for weekly Mass. For example, the ongoing vitality of the annual parish *festa* described in Robert Orsi's classic study *The Madonna of 115th Street* (1985) is attributed in part to the devotion of Italian-American returnees to the East Harlem neighborhood each July. A larger number of "white ethnic" Catholics in the region, however, shifted their allegiance to newer parishes, often created in the postwar decades. Appearances notwithstanding, many such parishes in the Middle Atlantic scarcely resemble the "suburban" houses of worship frequently caricatured in the literature of popular sociology. St. Ambrose parish of the diocese of Metuchen, New Jersey, is located in the "suburban" community of Old Bridge, but it was established in the 1960s largely by recent migrants from the Bronx, including a large number of men working in the building trades (many built elevators in Manhattan skyscrapers). The Bronx flavor of St. Ambrose persists to this day.

The "liminality" of Middle Atlantic Catholic life in the 1960s and 1970s—poised awkwardly between urban ethnic tradition and the liberating potential of social mobility—was treated in some remarkable literary works of the period, from Tom McHale's *Principato* (1970), set in South Philadelphia, to Mary Gordon's *Final Payments* (1978), whose characters are rooted in Queens, New York. These works and others treated characters uneasily poised between the inheritance of ethnic "tribalism" and the ambivalent "freedom" represented by geographical, social, and sexual mobility. This "in-between" quality of Middle Atlantic Catholic life also applied to its relationship with the more "tribal" Catholicism of the New England region on the one hand, and the more "acculturated" version found in many parts of the Midwest. New England society was so stratified, anti-Catholicism so deeply embedded, and Irish, Italian, Portuguese, and French-Canadian immigrants so numerous and so heavily concentrated in urban areas that Catholic tribalism was virtually inevitable.

In the Midwest, where German Catholics battled Irish bishops over the alleged "Americanism" of the latter, the Catholicism that developed was never "un-American" at all. The desire to retain linguistic and cultural traditions simply confirmed the insight of the historian R. Laurence Moore: "The foreigner was free to make his own claims about what America should become."

German Catholics lived alongside German Protestants in cities, small towns and rural communities of the Midwest. Since Midwestern Catholicism was always both an urban and a rural phenomenon, suburbanization represented less a new frontier than a form of linkage that filled in spaces between city and country. Though the Midwest certainly holds its share of "culture warriors" among the hierarchy (with the diocese of Lincoln, Nebraska, providing the most striking contemporary example), in general, Catholicism in that region has featured a more "irenic" quality than that found in the Middle Atlantic. At the same time, however, Middle Atlantic Catholicism has remained sufficiently engaged with the broader culture—albeit often at war with it—to resist the separatist tendencies that have periodically flared up. The emerging field of American Catholic studies draws much of its energy from the experiences of Middle Atlantic scholars, raised during the lengthy postwar era of Catholic transformation and committed to their religious tradition while deeply attracted to a form of cultural pluralism that Middle Atlantic Catholics helped create decades ago.[21]

"Difference" on the Ropes

A one-sided model of suburban Catholic flight and urban decline has grown so prevalent in recent years that the sight of Polish-American Catholics protesting the "ethnic cleansing" of a downtown Jersey City parish in 2001 must have startled many observers. The pickets outside Our Lady of Czestochowa Church, in the Gammontown neighborhood, were outraged that the pastor had decided to eliminate a weekly Polish-language Mass at the church. The mostly elderly protesters complained that in the rush to welcome upscale newcomers to the neighborhood—many of whom work in financial services firms that had relocated across the river from Manhattan—the spiritual roots of the parish had been violated. The fact that the parish's historic abbreviation "OLC" now stood for Our Lady's Church on the Waterfront suggested that their grievance was not without foundation. The pastor explained that the number of worshippers had dwindled in recent years and that a Polish Mass was still available in another Jersey City parish.

The reaction of OLC's older parishioners—though not always accompanied by picket signs—was replayed at numerous parishes in 2004 after the Newark Archdiocese announced that as many as 25 parishes in Jersey City and elsewhere would be closed for financial reasons. The archdiocese had already closed a high school in East Orange on very short notice in the spring of 2003, a school that served a primarily African-American student body from lower-income neighborhoods of Essex County. Leaders of the archdiocese did not seem to comprehend the depth of the connection to these parishes and schools felt by the descendants of the Catholics who built them. Other edicts handed down by the archdiocese, including a ban on eulogies delivered by family members at funeral Masses, struck many as insensitive to family and ethnic traditions that were such an integral part of the Catholic experience in the region. When Archbishop John Myers suggested that Catholics supporting abortion rights no longer receive Holy Communion, State Senator Bernard Kenny of Hoboken—a deeply devout Catholic—announced that he was leaving to join the Episcopal Church. Kenny's painful defection powerfully symbolized the deep rupture within the Church.[22]

In the wake of the sex abuse scandal that began in 2002, the closing of schools and parishes was certain to aggravate the disaffection of many Catholics with the institutional church and its leaders. While dioceses of the Middle Atlantic may not have suffered as badly or received as much attention as the Boston Archdiocese, the effects of the scandal are deeply felt and ongoing. In Philadelphia in particular the fallout from the scandal continues to unfold as high-level diocesan administrators face scrutiny for decisions made during the regime of former Cardinal Anthony Bevilaqua.

Other dioceses, particularly Metuchen, New Jersey, under the leadership of Bishop Paul Bootkoski, have earned high praise from abuse victims and their advocates. (Metuchen, covering the counties of Middlesex, Somerset, Hunterdon, and Warren, is the only new diocese created in the Middle Atlantic since 1980.) The nation's first memorial to sex abuse victims was dedicated in April 2004 at St. Joseph's Church in Mendham, New Jersey, in the diocese of Paterson. A 400-pound basalt millstone was installed on the grounds of the church by the current pastor, Msgr. Kenneth Lasch, to commemorate more than a dozen victims of Rev. James Hanley, who was assigned to St. Joseph's in the 1970s and 1980s. The millstone recalls the passage from the Gospel according to Matthew in which Jesus asserts that whoever harms children would be better off "to have a millstone hung around his neck and [be] thrown into the depth of the sea."[23]

Msgr. Lasch evoked a tradition of Middle Atlantic Catholicism in which the realities of suffering and conflict were acknowledged and confronted. The current Church leadership in the region does not generally recognize that this long tradition is a source of strength, not weakness. Many prominent bishops currently serving in the region were sent there from other parts of the country and do not share the experience of their constituents. Ideological rigidity has come to be equated with orthodoxy to the *magisterium*, the universal Church's teaching authority.

But there is little question that a decision to bar John Kerry from attendance at the Al Smith dinner violated the Catholic spirit embodied by Smith himself. Smith's Catholicism was grounded in a practical spirituality shaped by the cultural diversity of his upbringing. As the historian John McGreevy succinctly explains, "Smith developed his ideas in concert with an eclectic mix of Democratic reformers, not Fordham Jesuits." His response to anti-Catholic critics in 1928 was crafted by Father Francis P. Duffy, the most popular priest in New York, a man who, according to the historian Thomas Shelley, moved "effortlessly between the literati and the longshoremen." Like Smith, Duffy was deeply admired by people of all faiths. Smith's position was true to his own experience and convictions.[24]

More than five decades later another Catholic governor of New York State, Mario Cuomo, addressed an issue Smith was never obliged to face. Speaking at the University of Notre Dame in September 1984, Cuomo asserted that "as a Catholic, I have accepted certain answers as the right ones for myself and my family," including a belief that abortion is morally wrong. Yet Cuomo went on to argue that "the Catholic who holds political office in a pluralistic democracy.... bears special responsibility...to help create conditions...where everyone who chooses may hold beliefs different from specifically Catholic ones—sometimes even contradictory to them."[25]

The theological legitimacy of this position has been and will continue to be deeply contested, but there is no doubt that Cuomo's views were authentically grounded in his early days in Ozone Park, Queens, where an Italian-American immigrant community defined itself as part of a multi-ethnic, multi-religious metropolis. The celebration of this diversity became a constitutive element of Catholic spirituality in places like Ozone Park. A subsequent Catholic Republican mayor of New York City, Rudolph Giuliani, shared this spiritual worldview with Cuomo. In the hours after the attacks of September 11, 2001, Giuliani insisted that New Yorkers would demonstrate respect for members of all religious traditions precisely by virtue of being authentic New Yorkers, which is a medium through which Giuliani expresses his fidelity to his brand of urban Catholicism.

The tension between exemplars of this tradition and church leaders in the Middle Atlantic is real, and is most likely to endure. In 2004 John Kerry carried all the heavily Catholic states of the Middle Atlantic despite the clear if unofficial opposition of most of the region's leading prelates. Kerry was, however, singularly unimpressive in his handling of the "Catholic issue," which by 2004 entailed not his fitness to run for president as a Catholic but his ability to ground his positions in a sensibility that is recognizably Catholic, if not to bishops then at least to a substantial portion of the Church community. Kerry failed badly on this score, not only because he seemed untutored in Church teachings but also, perhaps, because he failed to demonstrate a grounding in any *regional* forms of Catholic identity. Unlike his hero, John F. Kennedy, Kerry's links to New England Catholicism were tenuous. He also lacked grounding in the multi-ethnic politics of the Middle Atlantic that lent credibility—in the minds of many—to the less-than-officially Catholic views of Cuomo, Giuliani, and many other Catholic politicians in the region.

The tensions might yield new creative syntheses but only if diversity of opinion is recognized as a vital element of the Catholic legacy to the Middle Atlantic region. It seems clear that there is a *sensus fidelium*, a sense of the faithful in the region that is grounded in the politics and culture of urban immigrant experience. Keeping faith with this tradition has always been a challenge, but it has produced some of the most significant figures and movements in American Catholic history, including the radically Christian witness offered by the brothers Berrigan: Daniel, a New York Jesuit poet and peace activist, and his brother Philip, a former Josephite priest who, with his wife, Elizabeth McAlister, founded Baltimore's

Jonah House in 1973. Jonah House was a peacemaking community in a neighbor-hood beset by poverty and violence, and served as a model for dozens of other communities in Middle Atlantic cities. The Berrigans represented but one of the many varieties of Catholicism found in the region, but their commitment to urban communities was shared by many others.

Catholics in the Middle Atlantic are numerous and vocal, making up more than 40 percent of the population of New York and New Jersey, nearly one-third in Pennsylvania, and one-quarter in Maryland. Even in Delaware, where Catholics constitute but 17 percent of the population, the church is a major force in the Wilmington area, the state's urban center. From the earliest days of European settlement, Catholics in this region have taken their place amid a rapidly chang-ing multiethnic community. Many of the characteristic features of this region, most notably the immigrant neighborhood, were shaped by Catholics who were always engaged in dialogue with those from different backgrounds. If the expe-rience of Catholicism feels different in the urban Middle Atlantic than in other parts of the country, it is in no small measure because the notion of "difference" itself has been understood to represent not a threat but an asset to the church. The institutional church has grown increasingly uncomfortable with expressions of that difference. The future of the church in the region will emerge from the struggle between these conflicting forces.

Endnotes

1. Glazer, Nathan and Moynihan, Daniel Patrick, *Beyond the Melting Pot: The Negroes, Puerto Ricans, Italians and Irish of New York City* (Cambridge, M.I.T. Press, 1963): 275.

2. Moore, R. Laurence, *Religious Outsiders and the Making of Americans* (New York, Oxford University Press): 51.

3. Spalding, Thomas W., "Catholic Church in Maryland," in Glazier, Michael and Shelley, Thomas J., eds., *The Encyclopedia of American Catholic History* (Collegeville, Minn., The Liturgical Press, 1997): 853.

4. Fisher, James T., *Communion of Immigrants: A History of Catholics in America* (New York: Oxford University Press, 2002): 18.

5. Burrows, Edwin G. & Wallace, Mike, *Gotham: A History of New York City to 1898* (New York: Oxford University Press, 1999): 94.

6. Fisher, *Communion of Immigrants*, 43.

7. Morris, Charles R., *American Catholic: The Saints and Sinners Who Built America's Most Powerful Church* (New York: Times Books, 1997): 5.

8. Glazer and Moynihan, *Beyond the Melting Pot*, 276.

9. Spalding, Thomas W., "James Gibbons," in *The Encyclopedia of American Catholic History*, 585.

10. Fisher, *Communion of Immigrants*, 81.

11. Moore, R. Laurence, *Selling God: American Religion in the Marketplace of Culture* (New York: Oxford University Press, 1994): 202.

12. Glazer and Moynihan, *Beyond the Melting Pot*, 246-47; William Kennedy, *O Albany! Improbable City of Political Wizards, Fearless Ethnics, Spectacular Aristocrats, Splendid Nobodies, and Underrated Scoundrels* (New York: Penguin Books, 1983): 276.

13. Morris, *American Catholic*, 170.

14. Morris, *American Catholic*, 167.

15. *Catholic Worker*, January, 1938.

16. Cort, John C., *Dreadful Conversions: The Making of a Catholic Socialist* (New York: Fordham University Press, 2003): 101.

17. McGreevy, John T., *Parish Boundaries: The Catholic Encounter with Race in the Twentieth-Century Urban North* (Chicago: University of Chicago Press, 1996): 260.

18. McGreevy, 132.

19. For Shriver see Stossel, Scott, *Sarge: The Life and Times of Sargent Shriver* (Washington, D.C.: Smithsonian Books, 2004).

20. Gray, Francine du Plessix, *Divine Disobedience; Profiles in Catholic Radicalism* (New York: Alfred A. Knopf, 1970): 241-50.

21. Moore, *Religious Outsiders and the Making of Americans*, 65.

22. *The Star-Ledger* (Newark, New Jersey) May 9 & May 20, 2004.

23. *Star-Ledger*, April 26, 2004

24. Shelley, Thomas J., "'What the Hell is an Encyclical?' Governor Alfred E. Smith, Charles C. Marshall, Esq., and Father Francis P. Duffy," *U.S. Catholic Historian* 15 (Summer, 1997): 94.

25. http://pewforum.org/docs/index.pho?DocID=14.

Chapter Four

Jews—Middle Atlantic and Beyond

Lawrence Grossman

The Jewish communities of the Middle-Atlantic states so predominate within the overall American Jewish population both in numbers and influence that their story is, in many ways, synonymous with that of American Jewry as a whole. This reality, as well as the fact that the other volumes in this series give only limited attention to Jews, dictates this essay's bifocal treatment. While delineating, through one pair of lenses, the dynamics of Middle Atlantic Jewish life, it peers, through the other, at national Jewish trends, noting where the national and regional concur and where they diverge.

Numbers and Regions

In Jewish circles, one of the easiest ways of provoking an argument is to cite a figure for the American Jewish population. Estimates today range from below 5 million to over 7 million, and a particular observer's preference for any number on this continuum often has less to do with any objective knowledge than with relative optimism or pessimism about American Jewish life.

The difficulties in counting the country's Jews are formidable: the U.S. Census does not ask about religion, and thus no government data are available[1]; a large but indeterminate number of Jews consider themselves "secular" rather than "religious" and therefore do not show up on congregational membership lists; and the percentage of Jews in the general population is so tiny (around 2 percent) that the standard telephone survey procedure, random digit dialing, is not cost-effective outside the largest Jewish communities.

Perhaps most vexing is the absence of any consensus on who is a Jew. Definitions run the gamut from the traditional formulation that requires a Jewish mother or conversion, to the common rule of thumb that considers Jewish self-identification sufficient, to the broader inclusion of people born Jewish who no longer identify as such, and even of non-Jews living in Jewish households.

Bearing these caveats in mind, the consensus among experts—at least those with no evident axes to grind—is that there are between 5 and 6 million Jews in the United States.[2]

In striking contrast to our fuzzy knowledge of the national total, the geographic distribution of American Jews is clear, and it differs markedly from that of the American population as a whole. While only a little over 16 percent of Americans live in the Middle-Atlantic region, some 45 to 50 percent of American Jews do—about 2,676,000 people: 1,657,000 in New York, 485,000 in New Jersey, 282,000 in Pennsylvania, 213,000 in Maryland, 27,735 in the District of Columbia, and 13,500 in Delaware. New York is the state with the most Jews in the country, New Jersey ranks fourth, Pennsylvania fifth, and Maryland eighth.[3]

This disproportionate concentration of Jews in the region means that the Jewish share of the Middle Atlantic population, 5.77 percent, is nearly three times as high as the percentage of Jews in the overall American population. In New York, Jews constitute 8.7 percent of the total; in New Jersey, 5.7 percent; in the District of Columbia, 4.5 percent; in Maryland, 4 percent; in Pennsylvania, 2.3 percent; and in Delaware, 1.7.

Although the 2000–01 National Jewish Population Survey (NJPS) utilized the U.S. Census division of the country into regions and thus subsumed much of the Middle Atlantic territory in the "Northeast" along with New England, its finding that "Northeastern" Jews score higher on almost all measures of Jewish identification surely holds—if not more so—for Middle Atlantic Jews. These measures are: having at least half of one's closest friends Jews; attending a Passover seder; lighting Shabbat and Hanukkah candles; fasting on Yom Kippur; keeping a kosher home; having visited Israel; and contributing money to a Jewish cause. However, Northeastern Jews are somewhat less likely than Jews in some other regions to belong to a synagogue or to other Jewish organizations, undoubtedly because the density of Jewish population in the Northeastern communities makes such formal membership less necessary for the establishment of Jewish connections.[4]

For some 200 years American Jews have tended to congregate in the Northeast, both because that was where most immigrants landed and because the region's dynamic economy provided jobs and upward mobility. Nevertheless, three key changes have taken place since World War II. First, the Middle Atlantic region has lost some of its Jewish demographic dominance as Jews have become more dispersed around the country. Second, Middle Atlantic Jews have increasingly tended to live in large metropolitan areas. And third, within those metropolitan areas Jews have been moving beyond city limits to the suburbs.

The demographic predominance of the Middle Atlantic region was most pronounced in the first half of the twentieth century. In the 1930s, some 70 percent of

American Jews lived there, most of them recent immigrants from Eastern Europe and their children. Since World War II, migration to the Sun Belt—particularly California and Florida—has cut into Middle Atlantic hegemony, so that today the Jewish communities of Los Angeles, Miami-Ft. Lauderdale, San Francisco, and West Palm Beach-Boca Raton also rate among the top 10 Jewish urban concentrations.[5] The heavy representation of Jews from the Northeast who have retired to Florida has made the Jewish community there, some 620,000 strong, into something of an offshoot of Middle Atlantic Jewry. In contrast, Jewish life on the West Coast (there are close to a million Jews in California, 131,000 in Texas, 81,500 in Arizona, 77,000 in Nevada, 73,000 in Colorado, 32,000 in Oregon, and 43,000 in Washington) has been gradually developing a separate cultural style, which is reflected in its communal institutions. Western Jews tend to be younger, less Jewishly connected, and more likely to be married to or living with non-Jews than their Eastern counterparts.[6]

Jews today are even more disproportionately represented in the Middle Atlantic urban centers (cities and suburbs combined) than in the region as a whole. Of the country's 10 metropolitan areas with the highest Jewish concentrations, four are Middle Atlantic. The New York (City) Metropolitan Area alone, including the city's New York, New Jersey, Connecticut, and Pennsylvania suburbs, is home to a third of American Jews, some 2 million people, and Jews make up almost 10 percent of the total population. The Philadelphia-Wilmington (Del.)-Atlantic City (N.J.) area contains the fourth largest concentration of Jews, a total of 285,000. Washington, D.C. and its suburbs come in eighth with 215,000 Jews, and Baltimore tenth with 106,000. Over 41 percent of America's Jews reside in these four metropolitan areas.[7]

These four great Jewish communities, in turn, differ significantly from one another. New York and Baltimore, for example, contain the largest concentrations of Orthodox Jews in the country, while Washington Jewry's relatively secular and highly intermarried profile resembles Jewish communities in the American West.

As the largest urban centers attracted rising numbers of Jews over the last 60 years, what had been substantial Jewish communities in a number of medium-sized Middle Atlantic cities have shrunk as these cities, which had thrived as manufacturing and industrial centers, went into economic decline. Examples are Newark and Jersey City, New Jersey; Buffalo and Syracuse, New York; and Pittsburgh and Scranton, Pennsylvania. Also, many Jewish communities of some hundred or so people in small towns that were still vibrant six and seven decades ago have disappeared, some leaving only a cemetery and empty synagogue building behind.[8] The same can be said of defunct Jewish farming communities, the best known located in southern New Jersey in and around Vineland. American Jews founded these, along with a Jewish agricultural school in Doylestown, Pennsylvania, amid great fanfare at the turn of the twentieth century to disprove the contention that Jews were congenital city dwellers, incapable of working the land.[9]

The net movement from city to suburb that has been going on since the mid-twentieth century is strikingly illustrated in a 2002 demographic study of Jews in the New York City area. For the first time in well over a century there were fewer than a million Jews—972,000—living in the city. And yet the number of Jews in the New York area—the city's five boroughs plus neighboring Westchester, Nassau, and Suffolk counties (the latter two constituting Long Island) had barely changed at all since the previous survey done in 1991, dropping just 1 percent from 1,420,000 to 1,412,000. While the city's Jewish population went down 5 percent, that of the three suburbs rose 12 percent, so that suburbanites now make up some 30 percent of the Jewish population of the region. Had the New York study included the city's other suburbs as well—those north of Westchester, in New Jersey, and in Connecticut—the percentage would have been even higher.[10]

Institutional Concentration

Over 44 percent of American synagogues are located in the Middle Atlantic region (New York—995 synagogues, over 26 percent of the national total; New Jersey—331, over 9 percent; Pennsylvania—197, over 5 percent; Maryland—107, some 2.8 percent; Delaware—7, less than .02 percent), a figure virtually identical to the area's share of the country's Jewish population. The four largest Middle Atlantic Jewish metropolitan areas—New York City, Philadelphia, Washington, D.C., and Baltimore, are home to over 40 percent of the country's synagogues. Six of the 10 counties with the largest numbers of synagogues are in the region, and all of them are within the New York metropolitan area: Kings (Brooklyn), Queens, New York (Manhattan), Nassau, Westchester, and Bergen in northern New Jersey. The Orthodox branch of Judaism is particularly strong in the region, as more than half of the nation's Orthodox synagogues are there.

Institutionally, the Middle Atlantic region is considerably more significant for American Jewish life even than its high share of the Jewish population and of synagogues.[11] There exists no recognized hierarchy of authority within American Jewry, and a plethora of national and local voluntary organizations, large and small—religious, philanthropic, cultural, social, and political—operate within it. The national agencies are heavily concentrated in the Middle Atlantic region. Of those dealing with community relations, 27 out of 29 have Middle Atlantic headquarters. Of Israel-related organizations (many of them set up to raise money for specific Israeli institutions), 85 out of 88 are Middle Atlantic. And of the Jewish religious and educational bodies, 52 out of 61 are located there. Organizations dedicated to Jewish culture (many of them Holocaust memorials) are spread somewhat more evenly around the country, 39 in the Middle Atlantic region and 19 elsewhere.

National Jewish agencies that engage in community-relations work and/or combat anti-Semitism are almost all headquartered in New York City, the "capital" of Jewish America. (The sole exception, the Simon Wiesenthal Center in Los Angeles, which evolved from a Holocaust memorial museum into a human-rights and anti-discrimination advocacy organization, opened a New York branch in 2004.) In recent years, as many of these New York-based groups have sought to influence public policy and interact with representatives of foreign governments, they have established Washington offices as well.

All three of the major national community relations/defense agencies—the American Jewish Committee, American Jewish Congress, and Anti-Defamation League—maintain well-staffed offices in both New York and Washington, as well as smaller field offices in other communities around the country. The three most important umbrella (coordinating) bodies of the American Jewish community are New York-based and also maintain a presence in the nation's capital. These are the Conference of Presidents of Major American Jewish Organizations, which represents 52 national agencies largely on matters relating to Israel and the Middle East; United Jewish Communities (UJC, formerly the Council of Jewish Federations), which seeks—not always successfully—to coordinate the allocations to Jewish domestic and overseas causes of monies collected by Jewish philanthropic federations in local communities; and the Jewish Council for Public Affairs (JCPA, formerly the National Jewish Community Relations Advisory Council), which tries (again, with mixed results) to develop consensus positions on domestic and international issues of concern to American Jews for advocacy use by local Jewish community-relations agencies.

The key institutions of the three largest denominations of American Judaism are in New York City. This was not always the case. The first branch of Judaism to organize nationally was Reform, in the late nineteenth century, which spread rapidly in the Midwest and South, where many recent Jewish immigrants from Central Europe had settled. Reform's leader was Rabbi Isaac Mayer Wise of Cincinnati, who founded the Union of American Hebrew Congregations (UAHC, in 2003 renamed the Union for Reform Judaism, or URJ) in 1873; Hebrew Union College (HUC), a rabbinical seminary, in 1875; and the Central Conference of American Rabbis (CCAR), in 1889, all in his hometown.

In the twentieth century, however, the anachronism of basing the country's largest Jewish denomination in what had become something of a Jewish backwater was evident. By mid-century the UAHC and CCAR had moved to New York City. HUC, meanwhile, merged with the non-denominational Jewish Institute of Religion in New York, the latter becoming the East Coast branch of the Reform seminary. The current president of HUC-JIR, Rabbi David Ellenson, struck the final blow for Middle Atlantic supremacy when, upon taking office, he established his permanent residence in New York City.[12]

The center of gravity of Conservative and Orthodox Judaism has always been Middle Atlantic. The Conservative rabbinical training school, the Jewish Theological Seminary, has been a fixture of New York City Jewish life since its founding in 1886, and the movement's congregational body, the United Synagogue of Conservative Judaism, and its rabbinical organization, the Rabbinical Assembly, are located there as well.

The major synagogue groups of American Orthodoxy—the Union of Orthodox Jewish Congregations of America (UOJCA), the National Council of Young Israel, and Agudath Israel of America—are all based in New York City, as are its rabbinical organizations, the most important being the Rabbinical Council of America. Yeshiva University, whose rabbinical seminary, undergraduate colleges, and graduate schools have to a large extent shaped American Orthodox Judaism, is in New York. A number of other important Orthodox rabbinical schools of a more sectarian nature (their curricula include no secular studies) are located in the region. Among them are Beth Medrash Govoha in Lakewood, New Jersey, perhaps the largest such institution in the world, in which thousands of male students devote full-time attention to the study of Jewish texts, and the Ner Israel Rabbinical College in Baltimore, which has profoundly affected Jewish life in that city.

Hasidim, followers of the pietistic Orthodox movement that began in the Ukraine in the eighteenth century, began coming in large numbers to the United States after the Nazi destruction of their European communities in World War II, the bulk of them settling in the New York area. The two most important Hasidic groups are based in Brooklyn, New York—Satmar, which has as little as possible to do with other Jews and denies the legitimacy of the secular State of Israel, and Lubavitch, also known also as Chabad, which engages in extensive outreach to Jews all over the world and whose continued allegiance to its deceased leader, Rabbi Menachem Mendel Schneerson, has drawn criticism from some who consider the movement a messianic cult. There are also a number of Hasidic communities in the suburbs north of New York City, some of them offshoots of Brooklyn-based groups, such as Kiryas Joel in Orange County, made up of Satmar adherents.

Two relatively small Jewish religious streams are headquartered in Philadelphia. One is Reconstructionism, a naturalistic, nontheistic reinterpretation of the Jewish experience developed by the theologian Mordecai Kaplan in the early twentieth century, which has a seminary, rabbinical organization, and congregational organization there. The other Philadelphia-based group is Jewish Renewal, which has attracted considerable attention in recent years for its stress on spirituality, music, and meditation. It also maintains a retreat center, Eilat Hayim, in the Catskill Mountains in New York State.

The establishment in 2000 of the Center for Jewish History, in New York City, underscored the Middle Atlantic region's Jewish cultural preeminence. Describing itself as the "Jewish Library of Congress," it brought together under one roof the American Jewish Historical Society, previously located on the Brandeis University campus near Boston, and four independent New York organizations: the YIVO Institute for Jewish Research (devoted to the cultural heritage of Yiddish-speaking, East European Jewry), the Leo Baeck Institute (focusing on the history of German Jews), the American Sephardi Federation (dealing with Jewish communities of Iberian origin), and the Yeshiva University Museum. The new center joined the venerable Jewish Museum, founded in New York City by the Jewish Theological Seminary in 1904, as twin stars in the Jewish cultural constellation. The Jewish community of Philadelphia has also maintained a longstanding interest in Jewish culture, as evidenced by the ongoing work of the Jewish Publication Society, based in that city, which has been producing and distributing books of Jewish interest since 1888, and the much newer National Museum of American Jewish History, founded on the occasion of the nation's bicentennial in 1976. Hillel, which services Jewish college students on hundreds of campuses around the country, is headquartered in Washington.

The most politically effective American Jewish organization is the American Israel Public Affairs Committee, commonly known by its acronym AIPAC. Located in Washington, D.C., with convenient access to the U.S. administration and Congress, it is the primary pro-Israel lobby in the country, with grass-root members in every state and congressional district. As noted above, the New York-based national community-relations organizations, the major Jewish religious branches, and UJC—the network of philanthropic federations—all maintain Washington offices that seek to promote the groups' legislative priorities. Also based in the capital are the National Jewish Democratic Council and the Republican Jewish Coalition, which engage in outreach to Jewish voters on behalf of the two major parties while at the same time apprising party leadership of Jewish concerns.

Of great symbolic importance for many Americans, Jews and non-Jews alike, is the United States Holocaust Memorial Museum, which is federally chartered and located near the National Mall in Washington. First proposed by the Carter Administration in 1980 and opened for visitors in 1993, its creation and location signify the central role that the memory of the Nazi Holocaust plays in American Jewish life and the clout that the Jewish community wields in national politics. The museum attracts large numbers of visitors, most of them non-Jewish tourists, who, according to all accounts, come away profoundly affected by the exhibits. The museum describes its mission as not only teaching about the Nazi Holocaust—which took place, after all, thousands of miles away—but also "to inspire visitors to contemplate their moral responsibilities as citizens of a democratic nation."

Jewish communities across the country publish newspapers, most of them weeklies. Given the significance of the Middle Atlantic region in Jewish life, however, the papers produced there—the *Washington Jewish Week, New York Jewish Week, Baltimore Jewish Times, Philadelphia Jewish Sentinel, New Jersey Jewish News, Forward*, and *Jewish Press* (the latter two, one secular-leftist, the other rightist-Orthodox, are published in New York and distributed across the country)—are far more influential nationally than those appearing elsewhere. The Jewish Telegraphic Agency, the news service that provides much of the material that appears in the Jewish press, is headquartered in New York City. Furthermore, almost all the major Jewish magazines in America are produced in the region: *B'nai B'rith International Jewish Monthly* and *Moment* in Washington; *Commentary, Congress Monthly, Hadassah Magazine*, and *Midstream* in New York.

Newcomers

The great majority of Jews living in the Middle Atlantic region are descendants of two waves of immigration from Eastern and Central Europe. The first consisted of the 2 million Jews, primarily from Russia (including much of what had been Poland), Romania, and the Hapsburg Empire, who entered the United States between the 1880s and 1914, the bulk of whom settled in or near their Middle Atlantic ports of embarkation. This migration was largely cut off by World War I and the restrictive immigration laws adopted in the 1920s. The second wave was made up of refugees from, and survivors of, the Holocaust, amounting to some 300,000 Jews; these too tended to settle in the region.

There are also significant Jewish ethnic and cultural minorities in the Middle Atlantic Jewish community. The most important of these arrived from the former Soviet Union, beginning in the 1970s, when American Jewish protest movements and U.S. government pressure induced the Soviet authorities to allow some Jews to leave. In the 1980s the flow increased, and with the downfall of communism the battle for free immigration was won. American Jewish organizations put considerable effort into finding homes and jobs for the newcomers, but decades of living in an officially atheistic and, for all practical purposes, anti-Semitic society, in isolation from world Jewry, has made them very difficult to integrate into American Jewish life.

While the fact that most of the Jews from the former Soviet Union lived in New York City has been widely acknowledged for years, the size of this community became apparent only with the release of the 2002 survey of New York Jews. It found 92,000 Russian-speaking households in the greater New York area, with a total of 202,000 Jews living in them. Within the city itself (excluding the suburbs) about one-fifth of all Jews were Russian-speaking, 62 percent of them in Brooklyn (where they made up 27 percent of all Jews) and another 19 percent in Queens (where they were 21 percent of all Jews). These Jews are, on the whole, far more likely to live in poverty than other New York Jews: while 16 percent of all Jewish households are "poor," the figure for Russian-speaking households is 53 percent; for Jews over age 65 the gap is far greater—13 percent of all Jewish seniors are "poor" as compared to 91 percent of the Russian-speakers. The newcomers also differ in political orientation from most other New York Jews. Bringing with them bad memories of the socialist "utopia," they tend to favor conservative politics, not the liberalism endemic to much of "old" New York Jewry.[13]

Another Jewish subcommunity consists of former Israelis. Of the roughly 144,000 adult Israelis living in the United States in 1990, some 22,000 lived in New York (the largest community of Israelis was apparently in Los Angeles).[14] They are relatively young, many coming after compulsory army service to further their education, or to enjoy better employment opportunities than are available at home. Like the Russians but for entirely different reasons, they do not fit easily into the New York Jewish community. Coming from a Hebrew-speaking land where the calendar, public-school system, and other givens of everyday life are Jewish by default, they are unfamiliar with the need to make overt choices about affiliation in a voluntaristic Jewish community such as the United States. Furthermore, many Israelis come with the intention of returning to the homeland. Even as the prospect of return grows more unlikely with the passing years, the sense of being in America only temporarily remains an obstacle to full participation in the American Jewish community.

Other smaller groups of Jews stem from predominantly Muslim countries. With the ouster of the Shah in Iran, almost all the remaining Jews in that country fled, many to the United States. There are concentrations of Iranian Jews in Queens, in New York City, and in Great Neck, on Long Island. Syrian Jews tend to live in Brooklyn and Deal, New Jersey. Coming as they do from a cultural background far different from the established Jewish community, few are involved in the mainstream institutions of Jewish life, and tend to restrict their Jewish activity to their own ethnic enclaves. Jews from Muslim lands practice the Sephardi rite—as opposed to the Ashkenazi practices of Jews of Central and East European origin—and therefore maintain their own synagogues and rabbis. Indeed, the religious customs of these Sephardi Jews differ in minor ways from each other, depending on country of origin. Thus there is an Afghani synagogue in Queens, and, not far away, a congregation of Iraqi Jews that only came to public attention with the outbreak of the U.S.-led war on Iraq.

The Jewish Uniqueness of America

The key to understanding American Jewish life, both in its national and Middle Atlantic manifestations, is the fact that America has afforded Jews as individuals, and Judaism as a religion, an unprecedented degree of freedom and equality. Jews, a small minority amid an overwhelmingly Christian population, attribute their economic, social, and cultural success to this particularly American way of life. Since the loss of Jewish sovereignty in Palestine some two millennia ago and the dispersal of Jews throughout the world, Jewish communities have existed, and often thrived, as minorities in many places. But never, before the establishment of the colonies that would become the United States, were they equal citizens anywhere, nor was their religion granted anything more than toleration. America thus constitutes a novel experience in Jewish history.

The seedbed for the revolutionary new status of Jewish equality in America lay in the Middle Atlantic region. To be sure, the novel dispensation did not emerge full-blown with the arrival of the earliest colonists. England had expelled its Jews in 1290, and when its first colonies were planted in the New World in the early seventeenth century, Jews were still not allowed to live legally in the mother country. This situation would not change until the 1650s, when Jews began drifting back into England, with the tacit approval of Lord Protector Oliver Cromwell, a reversal of policy that continued under the Stuart Restoration and after.[15]

The first English colony in the Middle Atlantic region, Maryland, founded in 1634, banned Jews and anyone else who "shall deny our Saviour Jesus Christ to be the son of God, or shall deny the holy Trinity." (Maryland, in fact, would be among the last of the states of the American republic to grant Jews equality, including the right to hold state office, in 1826, and only after a protracted political struggle.)[16]

The precedent for full Jewish freedom in America came not in an English colony, but in the Middle Atlantic colony founded by the Dutch in 1624, New Amsterdam, now New York. Upon achieving its independence from the Spanish Hapsburgs in the late sixteenth century, the Netherlands had become a haven for Jewish refugees fleeing the Inquisition. The Calvinist Dutch republic granted a degree of toleration (though not full equality) to these Jews, a policy motivated, in part, by the contribution that Jewish business acumen was thought likely to make toward the enrichment of the country. The relatively comfortable position of Dutch Jewry would turn out to be the key to ensuring Jewish rights in the New World.

In early September 1654 a boatload of 23 Jews, almost all with names indicating Sephardic (Iberian) roots, landed at the tip of Manhattan Island in New Amsterdam. While individual itinerant Jews had previously visited the colony and perhaps other European settlements on the Atlantic coast as well, these newcomers were the first group of Jews to request the right to live in the area of one of the colonies that would later become the United States.

They were refugees from Recife, a Dutch colony in Brazil that had been captured by the Portuguese. While the Netherlands provided Jews religious toleration, Portugal, over a century earlier, had outlawed the practice of Judaism and, somewhat later, instituted the Inquisition both at home and in its colonies. This tribunal could condemn to death Jewish converts to Christianity who reverted to their former faith—a designation that would fit a number of the 23. Although historians have not been able to piece together the exact details of how these Jews found their way to New Amsterdam, the purpose of these refugees was clear: to live once again under tolerant Dutch rule.

The governor of the colony at the time, however, Pieter Stuyvesant, was something of a religious bigot who envisioned New Amsterdam as a purely Dutch Reformed community. He requested permission from the Dutch West India Company, which directed colonial affairs from its headquarters in Holland, to allow him to expel "such hateful enemies and blasphemers of the name of Christ," who were, in addition, indigent, and likely to request support from the public coffers during the coming winter. The company rebuffed Stuyvesant. Noting that these Jews had given patriotic service to the Dutch cause in the unsuccessful defense of Brazil and that a number of Dutch Jewish merchants were stockholders of the company, the directors ordered Stuyvesant to let the Jews stay on condition that they take responsibility for the needs of their poor members.[17]

Governor Stuyvesant continued to place roadblocks in the way of the Jews to prevent their assumption of full civic recognition ("burgher rights") and their freedom to engage in certain trades and professions. Repeatedly, the Jews, their numbers augmented by new arrivals, appealed over the governor's head to the company directors in order to achieve their goals. One of Stuyvesant's letters to the company, warning that the incremental accumulation of Jewish rights might lead to a demand for the right to public worship (instead of the status quo, unobtrusive Jewish services in a private home), proved prescient. "By giving them liberty," the governor cautioned, "we cannot refuse the Lutherans and the Papists."[18] Indeed, concessions granted to Jews for pragmatic and political reasons carried a far broader implication—freedom of religion for all. New York would become that great cosmopolitan city where people of all religions—and none—would rub elbows, evoking the American vision of equality and democracy begetting prosperity.

The British seizure of New Amsterdam in 1664—a decade after the arrival of the 23 Jews—enshrined the principle of tolerance. The agreement the British reached with Stuyvesant on surrendering the colony guaranteed freedom of conscience to everyone, although public worship was legally restricted to Christians. But late-seventeenth-century city maps indicate the existence of a synagogue, presumably located in a rented house, and in 1731 the community, calling itself Shearith Israel (Remnant of Israel), erected its own building. Located today—after several moves—on Manhattan's Central Park West, it is the oldest continuously functioning Jewish congregation in North America.

The religious and economic freedom and geographic mobility enjoyed by New York Jews contrasted markedly with the situation in much of Europe, where Jews were often still confined to ghettos and severely restricted in how they could make a living. Other Jewish communities developed along the Eastern Seaboard during the eighteenth century—in neighboring Philadelphia, in Newport, Rhode Island, and, in the South, in Charleston and Savannah—where Jews also had religious and economic freedom. But New York remained unique in also affording Jews political equality. Jews voted there and were eligible to be elected to office throughout the eighteenth century. At the time of the American Revolution, in fact, New York was the only colony with no restrictions of Jewish voting and office-holding. Elsewhere, even in Rhode Island and Pennsylvania, whose founders espoused the principle of religious tolerance, office holding, and sometimes voting, were confined to Christians (in some states, just Protestants). Only after the Revolution would other states gradually emulate New York and modify their constitutions to eliminate political bias against non-Christians.

The federal government established under the Constitution of 1787—written in Philadelphia and originally based, it should be recalled, in New York—included no Christian phraseology and barred any religious test for holding office. It thus brought into existence, at least on the federal level, "a government where all Religious societies are on an Equal footing," as requested in a letter to the Constitutional Convention from Jonas Phillips, a leading member of the Philadelphia Jewish community.[19] The First Amendment, ratified in 1791, barred Congress from legislating "an establishment of religion" or prohibiting its "free exercise." President George Washington, in his famous 1790 letter to the Jews of Newport, Rhode Island, enunciated clearly what was new about the status of Jews in the American republic:

> It is now no more that toleration is spoken of as if it were the indulgence of one class of people that another enjoyed the exercise of their inherent natural rights, for happily, the Government of the United States, which gives to bigotry no sanction, to persecution no assistance, requires only that they who live under its protection should demean themselves as good citizens in giving it on all occasions their effectual support.[20]

Jewish Americans fully appreciated their good fortune, and Jewish references to America as a "new Jerusalem" became commonplace. To be sure, legal equality did not automatically dispel the popular prejudice against Jews that was part and parcel of premodern Christian culture. Ever since, the ostensibly unbounded vistas open before Jews in the United States have coexisted with social and religious antagonisms directed at Jews, and these have waxed and waned over time. The potential for outbreaks of Jew hatred has never been far from the consciousness even of the most successful American Jews, a fact that explains why so much Jewish organizational energy is taken up with monitoring and countering anti-Semitic manifestations. The fact remains, though, that there has never been anything approaching an anti-Semitic political party in the United States, Jewish civic equality has never been threatened, and today anti-Semitism is at an all-time low in the country.[21]

And yet the same unprecedented freedom that America offered Jews also created an unprecedented challenge. Under conditions of full civic and religious equality, with neither physical ghettoes nor legal barriers keeping Jews out of any area of life, could a tiny Jewish minority in an overwhelmingly Christian nation maintain Judaism? American cultural influences would surely erode the parochial religious traditions these Jews brought with them from the Old World, such as synagogue attendance; maintaining Saturday as the day of rest; eating only kosher food; regularly studying Jewish texts; providing children a Jewish education; and rearing new Jewish families to extend the community's life into the future.

In America, where choice of religion was voluntary, Jews could opt out with ease, the road made even smoother by the very paucity of anti-Semitism. The relatively few potential Jewish marriage partners available in America before the late nineteenth century made marriage to a non-Jew highly likely either with or without conversion to the majority faith, a process that would accelerate as each generation of Jewish immigrants found its way into the American mainstream. And even without any overt act of renunciation—intermarriage or conversion—under conditions of American freedom a Jew could simply melt into the majority.

The Jewish Religion

Judaism is recognized in the commonplace tripartite division of "Catholic, Protestant, Jew" as a bona fide and legitimate American religion—one-third of American religion, in fact, a far greater proportion than its meager numbers warrant. Yet it is not just an alternative religion to Christianity, but a different kind of religion. The differences must be appreciated in order to understand the dynamics of American Jewish life in the Middle Atlantic region and beyond.

Unlike Christianity, which, in all of its variations, presents a theology of salvation for all mankind, Judaism has a clear ethnic/national dimension. Premodern

Judaism, in fact, did not distinguish between the concepts we know today as "religion" and "ethnicity." American Jews, then, tend to see themselves as part of a Jewish "family" that extends both temporally—back to the Bible and forward to the end of time—and geographically, spread over the globe. That is why so many of their concerns today, having to do with the welfare of Jewish communities abroad and especially with the survival and well-being of the State of Israel, look to outsiders as matters of secular, not religious, significance. That is why a 41-percent plurality of a national sample of Jews in 2002, given a list of items and asked which "do you consider most important to your Jewish identity," answered "being part of the Jewish people." Only 13 percent cited "religious observance."[22] While the phenomenon of ethnic churches is not unknown among Christians, these consist of believers with a national or regional orientation transplanted from the Old World, and lose their distinctiveness within a few generations; in none is religion viewed as coextensive with ethnicity, as in Judaism.

Also, theology is far less important in Judaism than Christianity, a much greater emphasis being given to the fulfillment of Jewish law and ethics. That is why the distinction between "born again" Christians and others, a staple of the Protestant evangelical experience in America, is quite foreign to Jews. Divisions among Jews tend to rest, instead, upon differences in religious practice. In premodern times these might be variant customs in the order of the prayer service. Since the eighteenth century, disagreements over which traditional religious practices—if any—were still binding have become the major bone of contention, often serving as surrogates for deeper social and cultural cleavages over how far Jews should go in adapting their traditional way of life to contemporary society.

Jews, united by a common sense of peoplehood and not riven by deep theological fissures, rarely use the Christian term "denominations" to indicate their differences, preferring instead to call them "branches" or "streams."

The first of the streams, Reform, developed in early-nineteenth-century Germany under the influence—as the name indicates—of Protestant Christianity. Much as Martin Luther's Reformation sought to restore what it believed to be "original" Christianity, Reform saw as its mission the purging from Jewish practice what it considered medieval accretions, and returning to Biblical Judaism, by which it meant the preference of the Hebrew prophets for moral behavior over ritual. Reform Judaism spread rapidly in the United States with the immigration of Jews from Central Europe in the nineteenth century. The most liberal expression of Judaism, both religiously and politically, Reform has no ritual requirements. Nevertheless, religious practice has made something of a comeback in recent decades as many Reform Jews have found personal meaning in such traditions as the kosher food restrictions, Sabbath rest, and the study of sacred texts; this is especially true of Reform congregations in the Middle Atlantic region. Reform

Judaism espouses abortion rights, gender equality, and gay rights—many of its rabbis will perform commitment ceremonies for gays and lesbians.

Although the Central Conference of American Rabbis, the Reform rabbinical organization, is on record against the performance of marriages between Jews and non-Jews, the rabbis of the movement enjoy complete autonomy. Many officiate at such marriages either with or without pledges about how the children will be raised, and some also co-officiate together with non-Jewish clergy. Around 1980 Reform dropped the traditional definition of Jewish identity as passed down through the mother, and declared that anyone with one Jewish parent, mother or father, might be considered Jewish. Reform's openness to mixed-religion families—often termed "outreach"—has swelled its membership, but has also strained relations with the more traditional branches that will not accept children of non-Jewish mothers as Jews.

Orthodox Judaism, the second branch to emerge, arose to combat Reform. Originally a term of opprobrium in the mouths of the Reformers, "Orthodoxy" quickly became the banner for those Jews in Europe determined to preserve Jewish tradition. They were, in fact, a heterogeneous lot, ranging from those, like the Hasidim, who reject any contact with modern culture, to the so-called Modern Orthodox, who espouse a synthesis between Western culture and strict Jewish practice.

Unlike Reform, Orthodoxy did not strongly influence American Judaism until the late twentieth century. For one thing, virtually no one thought that the Orthodox way of life had a future in a modern, democratic society; it was viewed as medieval, old-world, unaesthetic. Furthermore, its leaders were underrepresented in the United States since they, both laymen and rabbis, were loath to emigrate from the centers of traditional Jewish life to the New World lest their children be lost to alien influences. Only the bloody manifestations of anti-Semitism, culminating in the Holocaust, essentially forced these people to flee for America. Orthodox influence within American Jewry has been climbing since the 1960s largely due to a strong system of private day schools and academies of higher Jewish learning. These have not only succeeded in imparting serious Jewish education but have also insulated its young people, to some extent, from the assimilatory pressure of the American environment. The Orthodox form of Judaism has also benefited from the new appreciation for religious tradition in America that is associated with the Christian right.

Conservative Judaism evolved in late-nineteenth- and early-twentieth-century America among Jews eager to retain the tradition, but in modernized form. Its intellectual leaders valued the scientific study of Jewish texts and believed that a historical understanding of Judaism's development might guide the future pace and direction of change in Jewish law. On the lay level, a Conservative congregation afforded its members a traditional but decorous Hebrew worship service with English translation, mixed-gender seating in contrast to Orthodox segregation of men and women, and a liberal interpretation of Jewish law. Conservative Judaism appealed to the children and grandchildren of Eastern European immigrants. It enjoyed a boom period after World War II, outstripping Reform and becoming the largest branch of Judaism in the United States, largely because it embodied, more than its competitors, the ethnic folk religion of American Jews.

Beginning in the 1960s, however, the contradictions inherent in a movement dedicated to both tradition and change became evident. A campaign to ordain women, though ultimately victorious, led to defections from the Conservative fold, and the current pressure for eliminating all barriers to the equality of gays is likely to succeed as well, generating more defections. The 2000–01 NJPS reported a precipitous decline in the strength of the Conservative branch: among the 4.3 million Jews who had religious or communal affiliations to the community, 33 percent said they were Conservative, down a full 10 percentage points from 1990. The movement had lost its place as the strongest of the streams, replaced by Reform, whose 39 percent share was up from 35 percent a decade earlier. Release of these numbers has evoked predictions from both Orthodox and Reform leaders of the imminent demise of Conservative Judaism.

Conservative spokesmen acknowledge a morale problem but indignantly reject the doomsday scenario. Nevertheless, the movement's decline clearly indicates the erosion of American Judaism's moderate religious center and the consequent strengthening of its extremes. On the right, Orthodoxy—which most observers had relegated to a slow death a few decades earlier—was thriving, its share of affiliated Jews up from 16 to 21 percent during the 1990s. And on the left, it was not so much the Reform increase that was significant, but an impressive jump in the proportion of Jews unidentified with any branch of the faith.

The national rise in Orthodox identification was surely greatest in the Middle Atlantic region, though since local community surveys measure denominational affiliation as a proportion of all Jews, the numbers come out lower than those in NJPS 2000–01, where they are percentages of the affiliated only. In the metropolis of New York and its suburbs, the Orthodox made up 19 percent of all Jews in 2002, up from 13 percent in 1991; 37 percent of Jews in the borough of Brooklyn are Orthodox, as are some 20 percent of those in Queens and the Bronx. Baltimore was home to the second-largest Orthodox community, percentage-wise, in the country, 17 percent of the total in 1999. And the third largest, consisting of 12 percent of the Jewish total, was in Bergen County, New Jersey, close to New York City. Other pockets of Orthodox strength were Ocean County, New Jersey, and Orange County, New York. Ocean, which includes the city of

Lakewood, had a Jewish population of 29,000 in 2001, a huge increase over the 11,500 previously reported—a gain largely due to the presence of a major yeshivah there. Orange County is the home of Kiryas Joel, an entirely Hasidic community, and the Jewish population in 2001 was 19,000, a 4,000 increase over previous estimates.[23]

Two factors magnify Orthodox strength in the Middle Atlantic region even beyond these numbers. First, the religious requirements of the Orthodox—synagogues within walking distance, convenient access to stores selling kosher products, Jewish day schools nearby—meant that they would tend to concentrate in specific neighborhoods, and there they might constitute 50 percent or more of the residents. Second, Orthodox Jews, on average, tend to be far more involved in Jewish activity of all kinds—religious, social, philanthropic, educational—than other Jews, and therefore have a disproportionate impact on Jewish life.

The Orthodox resurgence has affected Middle Atlantic Jewry in many ways. There has been a proliferation of Jewish day schools and kosher eating establishments.[24] Many of the national Jewish organizations that are headquartered in New York and Washington have done away with Saturday meetings to avoid offense to their Sabbath-observing members; serve only kosher food at their events; and close their offices on all Jewish holidays. Professional staff positions within these agencies have increasingly been filled by young Orthodox men and women, both because Orthodoxy provides the largest pool of committed and knowledgeable applicants and because those doing the hiring do not share the anti-Orthodox prejudices that animated their predecessors in previous decades. It has also not gone unnoticed that large public events sponsored by the Jewish community, such as the annual parade for Israel down Fifth Avenue in New York City, the meetings of AIPAC (the primary pro-Israel lobby) with political figures, and the mass rally for Israel that drew thousands to Washington, D.C., on April 15, 2002, have been attended by large numbers of Orthodox activists, who often constitute a majority of the participants.[25]

The new prominence of the Orthodox element has brought with it a heightened Orthodox sense of triumphalism as well, creating tensions with other Jews. One common complaint is that Orthodox families send their children to private Jewish day schools rather than the public schools, and yet use their numbers to gain representation on local school boards, which they then exploit to benefit those day schools. Another—which Orthodox Jews vehemently deny—is that the Orthodox treat other members of the faith as if they were not authentic Jews, making them feel guilty for keeping their businesses open and driving on the Sabbath, and discouraging their children from playing with Jewish boys and girls who do not attend day schools. On several college campuses in the Middle Atlantic region the representation of Orthodox students is so high and their Jewish activity so intensive, that complaints have been raised by non-Orthodox students who feel excluded from the Jewish campus community.

Unlike the more liberal pattern of many of their predecessors a generation ago, Orthodox rabbis today will not participate in joint programs with their Reform and Conservative counterparts, a policy that the Orthodox justify on the grounds that they do not wish to suggest that the other movements are legitimate. It is no surprise that this argument enrages the non-Orthodox. In certain neighborhoods, existing non-Orthodox Jewish communities have attempted to discourage Orthodox "invasions." [26]

Even more remarkable than the growth of Orthodoxy has been the jump in the absolute number and percentage of Jews not identifying with any of the religious streams. In 1990, 80 percent of those with at least one Jewish parent considered themselves Jews by religion, and 20 percent did not. By 2001, only 68 percent considered themselves Jews by religion (a loss of over 400,000), and 32 percent did not. The two major factors in this transformation were the rise in marriage between Jews and non-Jews and the secularization of the Jewish community. Furthermore, Jews were, on the whole, less "religious" than members of any other religion: more likely to respond "none" when asked about their religion; more likely to think of themselves as "secular"; less likely to belong to a house of worship; and less likely to believe in God. Indeed—amazingly—a higher proportion of Americans claiming "no religion" tended to believe that God performs miracles (78 percent) than Jews who said they were Jewish by religion (67 percent). [27]

The 2002 survey of Jews in greater New York shows how deeply Jewish movement away from the religious stream has affected the largest Jewish community in the country, the bellwether of the Middle Atlantic region. The 10 percent who identified as "nondenominational" or "just Jewish" in 1991 grew to 15 percent in 2002, and the percentage of those describing themselves as "secular" or having "no religion" escalated from 3 percent to 10 percent. Thus those not identifying with a religious stream almost doubled in the course of the decade, from 13 percent to 25 percent. [28]

It would be wrong, however, to assume that the lives of Jews unidentified with one of the religious movements or who call themselves secular are devoid of Jewish substance. In New York, for example, the steep rise in these categories has gone hand in hand with slightly higher rates of performance of certain Jewish rituals. [29] Many American Jews, like other Americans, are eager for "self-fulfillment" and have increasingly privatized their religious behavior, so that even an unaffiliated or self-styled "secular" Jew may consider him or herself "spiritual," and express that feeling by maintaining a kosher home or lighting Sabbath candles. Indeed, this is true even among Jews who identify with one of the movements: many reject the right of any outside authority—their own rabbi included—to dictate the right way to practice Judaism, and insist that whatever their own consciences dictate is Judaism—for them.[30]

Another manifestation of this individualized, antiestablishment Jewish experience is the vogue of mysticism. Although the current fascination with Kabbalah (the Jewish mystical tradition)—or some semblance of it—originated on the West Coast and is closely associated with Hollywood stars, Jewish and non-Jewish (Roseanne, Madonna, Britney Spears, etc.), it has made great strides in the Middle Atlantic region. Beside independent Kabbalah "centers" that offer classes and meditation sessions, many synagogues have introduced music and chanting with mystical associations into their liturgy so as to attract the large number of young people who do not generally attend standard services.[31]

This redefinition of American Judaism in terms of personal experience clearly threatens the traditional ethnic dimension of Jewish identification, and has been condemned within the community on precisely such grounds. Loss of a sense of Jewish peoplehood, the argument goes, leaves precious little of Jewish substance, and a generic "spirituality" in a country where Jews are vastly outnumbered by adherents of other faiths is likely to lead to mass defection from the Jewish fold. Others, however, argue that finding self-fulfillment in any form of Judaism constitutes bona fide Jewish identification, and, indeed, that the discovery of personal meaning in Judaism by more and more people may be the key to ensuring the Jewish future in America.

Politics

The political role of Middle Atlantic Jews has been much in the news recently. Many critics of the Bush administration's controversial war in Iraq ascribed it to the influence of "neoconservative," primarily Jewish, policymakers and intellectuals in Washington and New York on the non-Jewish president, vice president, secretary of state, secretary of defense, and national security advisor. The most prominent bête noire for the war's opponents has been one of the Jews, then-Deputy Secretary of Defense Paul Wolfowitz (currently president of the World Bank).

The critics deride not only the Iraq policies, but also the broader global strategy of which it is a part—using American might to spread democracy, primarily in the Arab and Muslim world. Since this would have the effect of improving the security of the State of Israel, some have suggested that American foreign policy is being conducted in the interest of Israel. So far has the fascination with the Jewish-neoconservative nexus gone that elaborate intellectual genealogies have been constructed to trace the current "hawks" either to the communist revolutionary leader Leon Trotsky (a Jew born Lev Bronstein) or to the Jewish, German-born, University of Chicago political philosopher Leo Strauss.[32] Such fascination with the Jewish role in American policy today is reminiscent of similar assessments of Franklin D. Roosevelt's New Deal, called by some of its critics the "Jew Deal" because of the allegedly disproportionate place of liberal Jews in that administration.

A balance sheet of the Jewish position on the war would note that many of its critics are also Jews, MIT's Noam Chomsky being only the best known.[33] Furthermore, opinion polls taken in the weeks leading up to the beginning of the Iraq war in March 2003 showed a consistent pattern of higher levels of opposition in the Jewish community than among Americans as a whole. This was one reason why Jewish organizations were very cautious about expressing support for war before it began.

Part of the widespread fascination with Jewish political involvement is the undoubted fact that Jews wield more clout than their sheer numbers would dictate. For one thing, Jews tend to live in states with large numbers of electoral votes, where close elections can determine the national outcome (exhibit A: Florida, 2000). In addition, Jews "are more likely than other Americans to vote, contribute to campaigns, and embrace social activism."[34] Some reasons suggested for this are high levels of education among Jews, their comparative affluence and therefore leisure to volunteer time, and their diverse social networks that are useful for political activity.

Jewish involvement in political fund-raising has apparently grown in recent years. Ed Rendell, the Jewish Pennsylvanian who served as chairman of Democratic National Committee from 1999 through 2001 (between stints as mayor of Philadelphia and governor of Pennsylvania), immediately succeeding another Jew in that post, Steven Grossman, who held it from 1997 to 1999. Both of them tread a path already laid out by Robert Strauss, committee chair from 1972 to 1977.

The Republicans began serious cultivation of Jewish money in 1980; their finance chairman in 2000 was Jewish; Mel Sembler raised an estimated $7 million from Jews for the Bush campaign. Other Jews chaired Team 100, Republican Eagles, and GOPAC that year, all fund-raising arms of the Republican National Committee.

Jews are represented in the U.S. Congress far out of their proportion in the general population. In 2005, 11 of the 100 senators were Jewish, nine of them Democrats. Interestingly, only three of them represented Middle-Atlantic states (Arlen Specter of Pennsylvania—one of only two Republicans—Charles Schumer of New York, and Frank Lautenberg of New Jersey). Both California senators are Jewish women, Barbara Boxer and Dianne Feinstein. Two other members are from states with relatively substantial Jewish communities, Joseph Lieberman of Connecticut and Carl Levin of Michigan. The rest are from states with few Jews:

Russell Feingold and Herb Kohl of Wisconsin, Ron Wyden of Oregon, and Norm Coleman (the other Republican) of Minnesota.[35] It should be added that the rising incidence of Jewish-Christian marriage means that a non-Jewish lawmaker might very well have Jews in his family: Paul Sarbanes of Maryland is a case in point; in late 2003, the Greek Orthodox senator was a proud guest at his granddaughter's bat mitzvah.[36]

There are 26 Jews in the U.S. House of Representatives; 24 are Democrats, one a Republican, and the other an Independent. Eight were elected from Middle Atlantic constituencies—six from New York State and one each from New Jersey and Maryland. The state sending the largest contingent of representatives is California, with eight. Two Jewish state governors were elected in 2002, the first Jews to hold the title since 1994. One was Ed Rendell, the former Democratic mayor of Philadelphia, elected governor of Pennsylvania; the other was Linda Lingle, the Republican governor of Hawaii. Three Middle Atlantic states have had Jewish governors previously: New York—Herbert Lehman, 1933–42; Maryland—Marvin Mandel, 1969–79; and Pennsylvania—Milton Shapp, 1971–79.

The only Jewish mayor of a major Middle Atlantic city is Michael Bloomberg of New York. He is the third Jew to be mayor of the metropolis, after Abraham Beame (1974–77) and Ed Koch (1978–89). Perhaps the most visible Jew in New York State politics is State Assembly Speaker Sheldon Silver, an Orthodox Jew who represents the Lower East Side.[37]

The days when there was supposed to be a Jewish "seat" on the U.S. Supreme Court are long gone. Two of the nine justices today are Jewish, and the minimal public attention that fact has received indicates how integrated Jews have become into American public life. Both have deep connections with the Middle Atlantic region. Ruth Bader Ginsburg, a native of Brooklyn, New York, attended Cornell University and Columbia University Law School, taught law at Rutgers and Columbia, and served on the U.S. Circuit Court of Appeals for the District of Columbia from 1980 to 1993, when she was elevated to the Supreme Court. Justice Stephen Breyer, though born and bred on the West Coast, spent much of the 1960s and 1970s in Washington, D.C., in a variety of government posts.

The prominence of Jews in American political life is a relatively new phenomenon, its beginnings discernible only in the late nineteenth century. The experience of Jews in their countries of origin was that of political outsiders, and there was a long tradition in Jewish circles to view government with suspicion (in the words of the Rabbi in "Fiddler on the Roof," when asked if there was a prayer for the Tzar, "Of course there is. 'May God bless and keep the Tzar—far away from us!'").

The small Jewish communities after the American Revolution tended to back the Jeffersonian Republican Party, and then Andrew Jackson's Democrats, seeing them as more friendly to (white) minorities than the opposition. Many Jews moved into the new Republican Party beginning in the 1850s. The large waves of Jewish immigration from Eastern Europe beginning in the 1880s brought Jewish socialists and other political radicals; "only a fraction of American Jews have been radicals," one historian notes, "but a conspicuous number of radicals have been Jews..."[38]

The first Jew elected to the U.S. House of Representatives from the Lower East Side of New York was Meyer London, a Socialist, who served from 1915 to 1923. In the presidential election of 1920, the Socialist candidate, Eugene V. Debs (a non-Jew), won 38 percent of the Jewish vote, double that of the Democratic candidate, James Cox and just five points behind Warren Harding, the victorious Republican.

The much discussed Jewish embrace of the Democratic Party in presidential elections began in 1928, when Alfred E. Smith, who had garnered strong Jewish support in his four successful campaigns for governor of New York, captured 72 percent of the national Jewish vote in a losing cause. That same year Franklin D. Roosevelt succeeded Smith as New York governor, defeating a Jewish Republican with the help of most of the Jewish vote. In his four presidential-election victories, Roosevelt garnered huge national Jewish majorities—percentages of 82 in 1932, 85 in 1936, and 90 in 1940 and 1944. Since then, the only presidential election in which the Democratic candidate has polled less than 60 percent was 1980, when Jimmy Carter, in losing his race for reelection, got 45 percent of the Jewish vote—a plurality nonetheless, as the victorious Ronald Reagan captured 39 percent and Independent John Anderson 15 percent. In the election of 2000, Al Gore won 79 percent of the Jewish vote and George W. Bush 19 percent.[39] (In 2004, Bush received 25 percent of the Jewish vote, according to exit polls.)

In state elections Jews are more open to voting Republican, if the candidate is perceived to be politically liberal. In the Middle Atlantic region, Governor George Pataki won 37 percent of the Jewish vote in New York in 1998, probably the best showing for a Republican candidate in the state in eight decades, and when he breezed through to reelection in 2002 that percentage was undoubtedly higher, perhaps a majority.[40] Jacob K. Javits, a liberal Jewish Republican, received only 19 percent of the Jewish vote in his first election to the U.S. Senate in 1956, but in his three subsequent reelections his Jewish percentage was 60 and over. Interestingly, Republican Rick Lazio, a virtual unknown, got 45 percent of the Jewish vote in his losing bid for a New York Senate seat in 2000, as against 53 percent for the winner, Democrat Hillary Rodham Clinton. In New York City, Republican Mayor Rudy Giuliani consistently raised the level of his Jewish support, from 60 percent in his losing race in 1989 to 65 in his 1993 victory and 72 in his 1997 reelection. In Philadelphia, Jewish Republican Sam Katz gained 82 percent of the Jewish vote in 1999 in his race for mayor against the victorious Democrat, John Street. In 2003, however, Katz's Jewish percentage declined drastically as Street won a second term.[41]

The liberal tendencies of Jewish voters and their heavy Democratic percentages in national elections have been scrutinized intensively. They do not match the patterns of other ethnic and religious groups, which tend toward greater conservatism as average income rises. In Milton Himmelfarb's classic formulation, Jews earn like Episcopalians but vote like Puerto Ricans. Surveys over the years indicate that Jews understand their political liberalism as an expression of their Jewishness, a phenomenon easily understandable in light of the highly secular content of American Judaism. "Asked explicitly about the qualities that most strongly define their own Jewish identity, Jews are four times as likely to mention a commitment to social equality as they are to choose either support for Israel or religious involvement."[42]

Whether or not Judaism dictates liberal politics—or any other political agenda—can be left for rabbis and theologians to debate. What is indisputable is the intimate connection between the process of Jewish emancipation in Europe and Jewish liberalism: The right—conservatives, monarchists, the churches—opposed equality for Jews, while the left—liberals, democrats, socialists, anti-clericals—tended to support it. To this day, the assumption that conservatives, especially those seriously espousing Christianity, are anti-Semitic is widespread in the Jewish community. In 2002, 39 percent of American Jews believed that "many" or "most" people associated with the Religious Right were anti-Semitic, as opposed to only 11 percent of Jews who felt that way about mainstream Protestants.[43]

When the New York-based national Jewish organizations and their Washington counterparts advocate a legislative agenda remarkably similar to that of the Democratic Party, they are reflecting the views of their members. Not only do most Jews support economic and social policies that benefit lower-income groups, but, at least since the end of World War II, they have also strongly backed the civil rights of all minority groups—racial, cultural, and sexual. This posture is grounded in a universalistic ethic presumed to be part of Jewish teaching, but also upon a very particularistic perspective: that Jews, a tiny minority with a history of persecution, are most safe when the rights of *all* minorities are protected and the autonomy of every individual unfettered.

Jews have been more likely than other Americans to support racial equality. To be sure, the Jewish organizational establishment in New York and Washington that found it easy to override the hesitations of the small Jewish communities in the South in the 1950s developed some doubts when the civil rights movement came to Northern cities in the late 1960s. But even such events as the Ocean

Hill-Brownsville affair of 1968 that pitted a predominantly Jewish teachers union against militant New York blacks did not shake the underlying Jewish commitment to racial equality. In 2000, while about one-fifth of both Jews and non-Jews said they favored affirmative action for blacks, 53 percent of Jews denied the assertion that "most blacks" receiving welfare payments could get along without it, as opposed to just 34 percent of non-Jews.[44]

Jews tend to align themselves with the American Civil Liberties Union stance on lifestyle issues and privacy rights. They heavily favor a woman's right to an abortion and homosexual rights—including, now, marriage. The disparities between Jewish and non-Jewish opinion on these issues are in fact startling: 75 percent of Jews are pro-choice as against 36 percent of non-Jews, while 57 percent of Jews favor the legalization of gay marriage as compared to 26 percent of non-Jews.[45]

The paradigmatic political cause for the Middle-Atlantic Jewish establishment has been separation of church and state. The American Jewish Congress's establishment of its Commission on Law and Social Action in 1945 was the opening of what would turn out to be a highly successful Jewish-led legal campaign to construe the First Amendment's "no establishment of religion" clause in the broadest possible terms. Members of a minority faith, Jews had previously chafed at such impositions of the majority Christian religion as Sunday "blue laws" and Bible readings in the public schools. Now, however, under the energetic leadership of AJCongress and Leo Pfeffer, its lead attorney, the organized Jewish community used litigation as a tool to remove the influence of religion (read: Christianity) from government.

Ironically, the Jewish organizations stayed out of the key case that first applied the First Amendment to the states, *Everson v. Board of Education*, a New Jersey case decided by the U.S. Supreme Court that involved state subsidies for school-bus transportation to parochial schools. In 1948, when the case was decided, Jews were still somewhat leery about sticking their necks out to offend the Catholic Church. But, led by Pfeffer, the Jewish organizations entered many church-state cases thereafter with amicus briefs. To a great extent due to Jewish exertions, the Supreme Court declared unconstitutional "release-time" programs in which public-school students were allowed out of school early to participate in religious classes. Even more pathbreaking—and controversial—was Leo Pfeffer's role in *Engel v. Vitale*, a lawsuit challenging the constitutionality of New York State's nondenominational prayer for voluntary recitation in the public schools, and *Abington v. Schempp*, a case originating in Philadelphia that challenged Bible readings in the schools. In both cases, the first decided in 1962 and the second in 1963, the U.S. Supreme Court upheld the principle of strict separation, to the delight of the Jewish organizations and the despair of many Christians.[46]

While Supreme Court jurisprudence has grown considerably less friendly toward the extreme separationist position since then, the mainstream of the Jewish community has not. Asked by pollsters in 2000 whether "there should be a high wall of separation between church and state," 88 percent of Jews responded affirmatively as compared to 45 percent of non-Jews. And while 70 percent of non-Jews would favor a constitutional amendment allowing public-school prayer, only 14 percent of Jews agree. [47]

For decades, there have been predictions that the persistently anomalous liberalism of American Jews was about to collapse, and, as is the case in other Western countries, Jews would begin turning conservative. Especially in presidential election seasons, Republicans eagerly read the tea leaves to spot Jewish trends in their direction.

To be sure, a sturdy minority of American Jews diverge from the liberal consensus. They are most visible in the form of Jewish neoconservatives, led by politically involved intellectuals such as Norman Podhoretz, Irving Kristol, and their younger counterparts who edit and write for magazines like the New York-based *Commentary* and the Washington-based *The Public Interest* and *The Weekly Standard.* These people tend to be former liberals who moved rightward in reaction to what they saw as radical and isolationist proclivities in the Democratic Party since the 1970s. Another, quite different segment of American Jewry that has turned in a conservative direction consists of Orthodox Jews, also largely based in the Jewish communities of the Middle Atlantic region. Although still adhering to the old economic progressivism of New Deal liberalism, a good number of Orthodox Jews, objecting on moral and religious grounds to the contemporary liberal social agenda—abortion, gay marriage, etc.—and preferring, as well, a more hawkish foreign policy, vote Republican.[48]

But defections to Republicanism and conservatism have not made a serious dent in the Jewish liberal phalanx. In 2004, Republican operatives launched an aggressive campaign in the Jewish community, expecting that President Bush's strong stand against terrorism and support for Israel would yield significant political dividends—a jump, they hoped, from the 19 percent of Jews who voted for him in 2000 to over 30 percent. This did not materialize: exit polls indicated that some 25 percent of Jews voted Republican in the presidential election of 2004, certainly a gain, but of disappointing proportions. Bush did enjoy comfortable majorities within two Jewish subgroups: immigrants from the former Soviet Union, and the religiously Orthodox—in the case of the latter, paralleling a similar dichotomy in the Christian electorate, where regular churchgoers were far more likely than others to vote Republican. As Orthodox Jews, with their relatively large families and minimal rate of religious defection, come to make up a larger proportion of the Jewish community, the Republicans might eventually reap substantial benefits at the ballot box.[49]

"Jewish" Issues: Anti-Semitism and Israel

Aside from the standard liberal (or, for a minority of Jews, conservative) agenda, the Jewish organizations headquartered in New York and Washington focus on two issue of particular Jewish concern, defense against manifestations of anti-Semitism, and support for the State of Israel.

New York City has always been the home base for American Jewish defense against anti-Semitism. To be sure, the New York Jewish leadership muted its outrage when, in the most famous instance of American anti-Semitism, Leo Frank, a Brooklyn-born Jew living in Georgia, was convicted in 1913—on dubious evidence—of murdering a young female employee, and then lynched after the governor commuted his death sentence. That Jewish reticence was grounded in an unwillingness to give southern anti-Semites an excuse to charge a "plot" by powerful New York Jews to get Frank off—a charge they made anyway.[50] The Anti-Defamation League (ADL) was formed in the wake of the Frank case by Jews who wanted to mount a more aggressive stand against anti-Semitism. It, along with the American Jewish Committee and the American Jewish Congress, has used a variety of means to address the problem: reducing prejudice through education and the media, supporting legislation against "hate crimes," bringing lawsuits against businesses and institutions that discriminate, and improving the conditions of the underprivileged so as to counter what some believe to be the "root causes" of Jew-hatred.

Meanwhile, on the assumption that the teachings of the Christian churches were the most likely source of anti-Jewish sentiment, Jewish leaders in New York City allied with some liberal Protestants in 1923 to create a Commission on Good Will Between Jews and Christians, which became the National Conference of Christians and Jews five years later (its current name is National Conference for Community and Justice). Through its exertions, New York City established the first "Brotherhood Week" in the country in 1934. All of this occurred at a time of pervasive quotas that severely limited Jewish entry into elite universities, certain professions, and exclusive neighborhoods both in the New York area and elsewhere.

This situation changed dramatically after World War II, as barriers to Jewish advancement fell and attitudes toward Jews, as measured in opinion polls, turned more positive. To be sure, hostility toward Jews still exists, but it tends to be confined to fringe groups located at the political extremes. The nomination of Sen. Joseph Lieberman, a Jew, for vice president by the Democratic Party in 2000 and the campaign that followed confirmed that anti-Semitism was now a matter of minor importance. The party's assumption that a Jew on the ticket would not lose votes turned out to be correct; in fact, most observers believe Lieberman's candidacy was a net plus for the Democrats.

American Jews, however, still worry about anti-Semitism. In 2002, 29 percent considered it a "very serious problem" and 66 percent "somewhat of a problem." Furthermore, 44 percent believed that anti-Semitism was likely to increase in the United States over the next several years. Two years after the Lieberman campaign, 44 percent of Jews disagreed with the statement that "virtually all positions of influence in the United States are open to Jews," and 66 percent thought that anti-Semitism constituted a greater threat to American Jewish life than intermarriage (31 percent cited intermarriage as the greater threat).[51]

How can this high level of anxiety at a time when Jews are more secure in America than ever before—and more than anywhere else in the world—be explained? The upsurge of anti-Semitic incidents in Europe and the Muslim world in recent years certainly is part of the answer, as evidenced by the popularity of several new books on what is alleged to be a new global wave of anti-Semitism. The Nazi Holocaust, after all, happened only six decades ago, and it signifies, to many Jews, that a society with a democratic constitution and equal rights—Weimar Germany—can turn totalitarian and anti-Semitic.

Jewish sensitivities about anti-Semitism were on public (perhaps too public) display in the recent controversy over Mel Gibson's 2004 film *The Passion of the Christ*. For months, as the movie went through production and editing, reports that it included traditionally negative Christian stereotypes about Jews and blamed Jews rather than the Roman authorities for the crucifixion of Jesus worried Jewish leaders. And Gibson's refusal to invite Jewish representatives to the showings of rough-cut versions that he organized for Christian leaders intensified their suspicions. The loudest words of warning came, predictably, from New York Jews, in particular Abraham Foxman, executive director of the ADL, and Frank Rich of the *New York Times*. Gibson seemed to relish their attacks (according to Foxman and Rich, he deliberately provoked them), and they certainly helped give the film enough publicity or notoriety to gross millions.

A generation ago, in the mid-1960s, the New York-based Jewish organizations had lobbied for and lauded the Catholic Church's Vatican II statement that not all Jews in Jesus' time, nor Jews today, were responsible for the crucifixion. Now, they felt genuinely threatened by the movie's apparently pre-Vatican-II emphasis on demonizing Jews, and betrayed by the silence or acquiescence of leading Catholic and Protestant church leaders, many of them veterans in the field of interreligious dialogue. The East Coast Jewish leaders had become used to associating with liberal Christians and secular Bible scholars who viewed the negative portrayals of Jews in the Gospels as late historical distortions. They seemed unaware that millions of Christians—especially in the South and West, and therefore invisible when viewed from the Anti-Defamation League's offices in Manhattan—took the New Testament literally.

In fact the Jewish attacks on the film were largely a Middle Atlantic phenomenon. Those national organizations with branches elsewhere in the country, where Jews regularly came face to face with Christian fundamentalists, found such local chapters extremely reluctant to criticize the movie as anti-Semitic. And while the Jewish newspapers—and the secular media—in the East excoriated the film and its producer while lionizing the Anti-Defamation League, their counterparts in Los Angeles took a much more relaxed stand. Familiar with the ways of Hollywood, they saw *The Passion of the Christ* as just another money-making venture, and the efforts of the New York organizations to pin the anti-Semitic label on it as one more example of Eastern arrogance and ignorance that boomeranged by swelling the movie's profits. On the cover of its March 5, 2004 issue, the *Jewish Journal of Los Angeles* showed Mel Gibson, wearing a tuxedo and holding two Oscars, over the caption, "*Passion* Sweeps Oscars, Gibson Hires ADL to Promote Sequel."

Supporting Israel ranks along with fighting anti-Semitism as a bottom-line "Jewish" issue, and the national Jewish organizations in Washington and New York devote considerable resources to both. Indeed, the two are sometimes not easy to distinguish. Many Jews carefully scrutinize statements critical of Israeli policies—especially in the media—for evidence of anti-Semitic bias, and sometimes claim to find it.

American Jewish interest in the Zionist enterprise and Israel has waxed and waned over the last century. In a sense, the 2 million East European Jews who came to the United States rather than Palestine from 1881 through 1914 opted against participating in the realization of the Zionist dream, and Zionism did not become a major force in American Jewish life until the 1930s, when the Nazi threat to the millions of Jews in Europe underlined the need for a Jewish homeland. American Jews played a key role in convincing the Truman administration to back the creation of Israel in 1948; there are even historians who suggest that Truman decided to recognize the Jewish state in order to shore up Jewish political support in New York in advance of the 1948 election. There was another surge of American Jewish interest in Israel in the weeks leading up to the Six-Day War of 1967, when the threats of Arab leaders conjured up fears of a second Holocaust; American Jews raised $240 million for Israel in 1967 and bought $190 million in Israel bonds. Israel's stunning victory made ensuring its continued success a top priority for American Jews.

The two most important Jewish organizations dealing with Israel are AIPAC, widely considered the second most potent lobbying group in Washington (the National Rifle Association is the first), and the Conference of Presidents of Major American Jewish Organizations, based in New York. AIPAC generally takes the line that Israeli policies—whatever they are at any particular time—are in the best interests of the United States. AIPAC's clout rests in convincing political figures that this is true, as well as in the unstated assumption that members of congress up for reelection are likely to benefit from Jewish campaign contributions if they have good records on Israel. The Conference of Presidents is made up of over 50 Jewish organizations that reflect a wide spectrum of opinion, from hawkish groups that believe Prime Minister Ariel Sharon has "sold out" the Zionist dream, to peace groups that still believe the Oslo Accords a valid basis for a settlement. The Conference makes policy by consensus, which, in practice, generally lines up, like AIPAC, in support of Israeli government policy.

Polling data seem to indicate a slow but steady erosion of Jewish interest in Israeli matters. This distancing is due, in large part, to a decline in strong Jewish identification of all kinds in many sectors of the community, and also to a growing realization of the intractable nature of the Arab-Israeli conflict. Jewish leaders have found that on a number of college campuses many Jewish students are apathetic about Israel, some participating in pro-Palestinian rallies. Not surprisingly, enthusiasm for Israel is noticeably higher in the Middle Atlantic region, where Jewish consciousness is strongest, than among Jews elsewhere. Nationally, 73 percent of Jews say they feel "close" to Israel, and the same percentage say that "caring about Israel is a very important part of my being a Jew." In New York, a different picture emerges (even though the wording of the question differs slightly): the survival of Israel is "very important" to 92 percent of Jews. Jews in the "Northeast" census region are more likely to visit Israel than other American Jews, 39 percent claiming to have been there, four percentage points higher than Southern Jews (older Jews in South Florida constituting most of these visitors), and 10 percentage points higher than Jewish communities in the Midwest and West.[52]

Gary Rosenblatt, editor of the *New York Jewish Week*, has eloquently portrayed the growing geographical disparity within American Jewry over Israel. Told that the *Jewish Journal of Los Angeles* was heavily criticized for running an anti-Arafat cartoon that was, according to the critics, "too harsh and critical of the Palestinians," Rosenblatt was sure that his New York paper "would have been praised" for running that cartoon. "One constant" in the 10 years Rosenblatt had been editing the *Jewish Week*, he wrote, "is that most of the letters we get are about Israel and are tilted strongly to the right." And he wondered whether the "national Jewish leaders" in Washington and New York appreciated just how differently Jews in other regions of the country viewed the Middle East.[53]

Ironically, those national Jewish leaders in the Middle Atlantic region relied heavily on Christian evangelicals in the South and West to rally pro-Israel sentiment on Capitol Hill and in the White House, the very Christians, as noted above, who were most enthusiastic about the allegedly anti-Semitic *Passion of the Christ*.

Culture

The actor Marlon Brando, in a 1996 television interview, claimed that "per capita, Jews have contributed more to American—the best of American—culture than any other single group." And he went on, "if it weren't for the Jews, we wouldn't have music. If it weren't for the Jews, we wouldn't have much theater. We wouldn't have, oddly enough, Broadway and Tin Pan Alley and all the standards that were written by Jews, all the songs you love to sing." In the post-World War II era, one historian has noted, "Jews taught Americans how to dance (Arthur Murray), how to behave (Dear Abby and Ann Landers), how to dress (Ralph Lauren), what to read (Irving Howe, Alfred Kazin, and Lionel Trilling), and what to sing (Barry Manilow and Barbra Streisand)."[54] Aside from the two advice-givers (sisters born and raised in the Midwest), all of the aforementioned Jews came from New York City.

That Jews, Middle Atlantic or otherwise, would play any role at all in shaping American "high" culture would have been inconceivable before World War II. Formal or informal quotas kept the number of Jewish students down in prestigious Middle Atlantic universities like Columbia and Princeton, and very few Jews could hope to join the faculty—especially in fields like English and history, where a white Anglo-Saxon cultural upbringing was considered a prerequisite. The exclusionary pattern broke down in the postwar years, and by the mid-1970s Jews averaged more years of schooling (14) than any other religious group, and constituted one-fifth of the faculties at elite universities—a quarter at Ivy League institutions. In 1980, Michael Sovern assumed the presidency of Columbia, the first Jew to head an Ivy League school. That made news, but seven years later, by the time Harold T. Shapiro became president of Princeton, the idea of Jewish presidents had become so commonplace that his religion was hardly mentioned.

Listing the large number of Jews, most of them children of immigrants born in the Middle Atlantic region, who have distinguished themselves in the various academic disciplines would yield a truly astonishing catalog. Of the 200 people generally acknowledged to be the most important intellectuals in the country in 1974, fully half were Jewish. A 1977 survey indicated that 27 percent of Nobel Prize winners raised in the United States were Jews. Some were culture heroes, like Dr. Jonas Salk, who, along with another New York Jew, Alfred Sabin, conquered the scourge of polio. Literary critics Alfred Kazin, Lionel Trilling, and, today, Harold Bloom and Stanley Fish, have transformed the way books are read and understood. Among American historians—over 20 percent of whom were Jewish by 1970—Richard Hofstadter, Richard B. Morris, and Bernard Bailyn are three names among many who have shaped our view of the nation's past. In the social sciences, where anti-Jewish bias had always been milder, mentioning economists

Paul Samuelson, Simon Kuznets, and Milton Friedman, and sociologists David Riesman, Nathan Glazer, and Daniel Bell does not even scratch the surface.

In the realm of fiction, most of the great American Jewish writers have been Middle Atlantic, and much of their work reflects that background. The line goes from New Yorkers Abraham Cahan (himself an immigrant), to Henry Roth, Phillip Roth (Newark, New Jersey), Bernard Malamud, Chaim Potok, Cynthia Ozick, and Elie Wiesel, another immigrant. The only major exception—and it certainly is major—is Saul Bellow, the Chicagoan who became the first American Jew to win the Nobel Prize for literature.

The world of Broadway has been "inescapably Jewish."[55] There were Oscar Hammerstein (only his father was Jewish), Lorenz Hart, George and Ira Gershwin, and Stephen Sondheim, for example, but the saga of Irving Berlin is in a class by itself. This Jewish immigrant boy from the Lower East Side intuited the essence of American sentiment so accurately that he was able to create such classics as "Alexander's Ragtime Band," "God Bless America," "A White Christmas," and "Easter Parade." (When "God Bless America" was first played at Ebbets Field in 1939, the spectators "rose and removed their hats, as though hearing what Francis Scott Key should have written.")[56]

The place of Middle Atlantic Jews in American film and broadcasting has been central.[57] It was in the heavily Jewish Lower East Side of New York that movie theaters (then called "nickelodeons") got their start. Although Hollywood, which became the motion picture capital in the 1920s, was in California, the movers and shakers of the industry, the "moguls," were almost all Middle Atlantic (mostly New York) Jews—Marcus Loew, Adolph Zukor, William Fox, Carl Laemmle, Samuel Goldwyn, Louis B. Mayer, and, more recently, Harry and Jack Warner, and David O. Selznick. (The only non-Jew who fit into this rarefied company was Darryl Zanuck). So identified were Jews with the early motion picture industry that superstar Charlie Chaplin, a non-Jew, was assumed to be Jewish. The first "talking" picture, of course, was *The Jazz Singer* (1927), in which Al Jolson portrayed the son of a Lower East Side cantor who must choose between following in his father's footsteps or entering the new world of jazz music, precisely the "tradition vs. modernity" dilemma that stood, and still stands, at the heart of the American Jewish experience. To be sure, the widespread and justified identification of Jews with the industry drew the attention of anti-Semites, and the left-wing political orientation of many Hollywood personalities, Jews prominent among them, eventually led to congressional hearings and the blacklists.

Radio broadcasting, which came into its own during the 1930s, also had a strong Jewish presence. William Paley (CBS) and David Sarnoff (NBC) were leading executives, and the fact that many of the series aired on radio were produced in New York enabled Jewish performers based in the Middle Atlantic region—such as Jack Benny, Gertrude Berg ("The Goldbergs"), George Burns, Fanny Brice, and Eddie Cantor—to achieve national reputations. The Marx brothers, New York born, revolutionized American comedy both on the movie screen and on radio.

"The Goldbergs," depicting a fictional Jewish family in the Bronx, New York, crossed over from radio to television after World War II. "Your Show of Shows," starring the Jewish comedian Sid Caesar, which NBC television carried from 1950 to 1954, and, in different incarnations ran till 1958, was a major hit, featuring the jokes of a stable of New York Jewish writers, some of whom would achieve fame later on their own—Carl Reiner, Mel Brooks, and Woody Allen, among others. Probably out of sensitivity to charges of excessive Jewish control of the networks, the executives kept noticeably "Jewish" characters from appearing on TV for years (except for "The Goldbergs"). The taboo was broken by the fictional Rhoda Morgenstern, born in the Bronx—played by the non-Jewish Valerie Harper—who first appeared in the *Mary Tyler Moore Show* in the early 1970s and starred in her own situation comedy, *Rhoda*, from 1974 to 1978.

American popular culture has become so saturated with media-generated "Jewish" humor—of Middle Atlantic, specifically New York, origin—that it is no longer easy to tell "Jewish" and "American" apart. Hence the debates over whether *Seinfeld*, the immensely popular television sitcom that takes place on the Upper West Side of Manhattan, whose characters are not identified as Jews, and where references to anything Jewish are few and far between, is "Jewish" because of the nature of the humor and the personalities of the characters.[58]

Postscript

The hijackers of four airplanes on September 11, 2001, targeted the Middle Atlantic region: they crashed two planes into the World Trade Center in Lower Manhattan, one into the Pentagon in Washington, and the fourth, apparently intended either for the White House or the Capitol, fell in a Pennsylvania field. The perpetrators clearly intended to strike at the most visible symbols of American influence in the world—New York, center of American enterprise and culture, and Washington, center of American power.

The region, as we have seen, is also the primary locus of Jewish life for the most influential community of Jews in the world. Mohammed Atta, the 9/11 ringleader, understood this. At the trial in Hamburg, Germany, of Mounir el Motassadeq, an alleged accomplice of Atta, Shahid Nickels, another member of the cell, said that Atta "was convinced that 'the Jews' are determined to achieve world domination. He considered New York City to be the center of world Jewry, which was, in his opinion, Enemy Number One." Furthermore, testified Nickels, the group that planned 9/11 "were convinced that Jews control the American government as well as the media and the economy of the United States."[59]

But it did not take 9/11 to convince Middle Atlantic Jews—or their coreligionists elsewhere—that their fate was inextricably bound up with the future of America.

Endnotes

1. U.S. Census Bureau, *Statistical Abstract of the United States 2003*, p. 68, has 6,155,000 as the number of Jews in the country, and its source is the *American Jewish Year Book*, published by the American Jewish Committee. The relevant *Year Book* article, in turn, derived the number by adding up estimates, some of uncertain reliability, provided by local Jewish communities.

2. The recent National Jewish Population Survey conducted by United Jewish Communities (NJPS 2000–01) came up with a figure of 5.2 million American Jews, but some demographers believe this to be an undercount. This NJPS and its two predecessors are available online at www.jewishdatabank.org/index.cfm.

3. California ranks second, Florida third, Massachusetts sixth, and Illinois seventh. The figure for the District of Columbia does not include areas within Maryland and Virginia.

4. For details see NJPS 2000–01, p. 8.

5. Los Angeles is the second largest Jewish metropolitan concentration (668,000), Miami-Ft. Lauderdale third (331,000), San Francisco seventh (218,000), and West Palm Beach-Boca Raton eighth (167,000). Rounding out the top ten are the fifth and sixth largest communities, Chicago (265,000) and Boston (254,000). The far-reaching implications of American Jewish geographic mobility are set out in Sidney Goldstein and Alice Goldstein, *Jews on the Move: Implications for Jewish Identity* (Albany: State University of New York Press, 1996).

6. See, for example, Ami Eden, "West Coast Seen Flexing Muscle," *Forward*, January 18, 2002. For useful tables comparing different Jewish communities see Ira M. Sheskin, *How Jewish Communities Differ: Variations in the Findings of Local Jewish Population Studies* (New York: North American Jewish Data Bank, 2001).

7. *American Jewish Year Book 2003*, p. 162, updated on the basis of a new, as yet unpublished study of Washington reported in Eric Fingerhut, "Unmoored on the Potomac—Study: Jews in area less connected than elsewhere," *Washington Jewish Week Online edition*, February 12, 2004.

8. The first step in the process is dispensing with the services of a rabbi: "There will be no more full-time, practicing rabbis in Fayette County, when Rabbi Sion David retires from Uniontown's Temple Israel...." *Jewish Chronicle* (Pittsburgh), June 19, 2003.

9. On the small-town communities see *We Call This Place Home: Jewish Life in Maryland's Small Towns* (Baltimore: Jewish Museum of Maryland, 2002), especially Lee Shai Weissbach's wide-ranging essay, "The Jewish History of Small-Town America," pp. 11–25. On the New Jersey farming communities see Joseph Brandes, *Immigrants to Freedom: Jewish Communities in Rural New Jersey since 1882* (Philadelphia: Jewish Publication Society, 1971), and Gertrude Dubrovsky, *The Land Was Theirs: Jewish Farmers in the Garden State* (Tuscaloosa and London: University of Alabama Press, 1992).

10. UJA-Federation of New York, *The Jewish Community Study of New York: 2002 Highlights*, p. 17. A study of the Pittsburgh Jewish community, also conducted in 2002, found that 37 percent of Jews lived in the suburbs. These and other local community studies referred to below are available on the same Web site as the NJPS, www.jewishdatabank.org/index.cfm.

11. The discussion of Jewish institutional life that follows is culled from the listings in *American Jewish Year Book 2003*, pp. 615–707.

12. The same path from Midwest to Middle Atlantic has been taken more recently by Secular Humanist Judaism, a movement initiated in the 1960s in a Detroit suburb that removed all references to God and celebrates Jewish cultural values; in 2003 its Center for Cultural Judaism relocated to New York.

13. *Jewish Community Study of New York 2002*, pp. 27–30, 48; Adam Dickter, "'Healthy' Political Change," *New York Jewish Week*, June 27, 2003. Some leaders of the Russian-speaking community believe that there are more Jews from the former Soviet Union in New York than indicated in the survey. Walter Ruby, "Big Undercount in New Survey, Russians Claim," ibid.

14. Gold, Steven J., *The Israeli Diaspora* (Seattle: University of Washington Press, 2002), pp. 24–25. Information on Israelis from the 2002 New York study has not yet been released.

15. Despite the exertions of historians, no documentary evidence has yet been uncovered tying Cromwell's government to any decision about admitting Jews. To this day the expulsion order of 1290 has never been officially revoked, a fact that does not disturb the 300,000 Jews who reside in Great Britain as full and equal citizens, a status gradually attained in the 19th century.

16. Fein, Isaac M., *The Making of an American Jewish Community: The History of Baltimore Jewry from 1773 to 1920* (Philadelphia: Jewish Publication

Society, 1971), pp. 4–8, 25–36.

17. Mendes-Flohr, Paul and Reinharz, Jehuda, ed., *The Jew in the Modern World: A Documentary History* (New York: Oxford University Press, 1995), pp. 452–53.

18. Ibid., pp. 453–54.

19. Cited in Sarna, Jonathan D. and Dalin, David G., *Religion and State in the American Jewish Experience* (South Bend: University of Notre Dame Press, 1997), p. 73.

20. *Jew in the Modern World*, pp. 458–59.

21. Dinnerstein, Leonard, *Antisemitism in America* (New York: Oxford University Press, 1994).

22. Coming in second was "a commitment to social justice" with 21 percent. *2002 Annual Survey of American Jewish Opinion* (New York: The American Jewish Committee, 2003), p. 8.

23. *American Jewish Year Book 2002*, p. 249.

24. Levy, Faygie, "More Jews Find an Outlet in Day-School Education," *Jewish Exponent* (Philadelphia), September 18, 2003; Runyan, Joshua, "Attention Kosher Shoppers: Feel Free To Dunk!" Ibid., November 26, 2003; Dorfman, Dan, "Kosher Eateries Thrive in Gotham," *New York Sun*, October 29, 2003. For 15 years there has even been an annual kosher food show, "Kosherfest," at the Javits Center in New York City.

25. Besser, James D., "Capitol Gains," *Baltimore Jewish Times*, December 5, 2003, focuses on Orthodox groups that have their own lobbyists in Washington. For a portrayal of an upscale Orthodox synagogue near Washington that is home to a good number of prominent academics and government officials, see Alana Newhouse, "An Orthodox Powerhouse in D.C. Suburb," *Forward*, January 10, 2003.

26. *American Jewish Year Book 2003*, p. 131. The communal impact of the growth of Orthodoxy is incisively portrayed by Samuel Freedman in *Jew vs. Jew: The Struggle for the Soul of American Jewry* (New York: Simon and Schuster, 2000).

27. Mayer, Egon, Kosmin, Barry, and Keysar, Ariela, *American Jewish Identity Survey 2001*, pp. 20, 9, 36, available at www.gc.cuny.edu/studies/studies_index.htm.

28. *Jewish Community Study of New York*, p. 31.

19. Ibid., p. 39.

30. Cohen, Steven M. and Eisen, Arnold M., *The Jew Within: Self, Family, and Community in America* (Bloomington: Indiana University Press, 2001).

31. See, for example, Stone, Adam, "Spiritual Paths," *Baltimore Jewish Times,* July 4, 2003.

32. Berger, Matthew, "Some Say U.S. Is Fighting Israel's War," Jewish Telegraphic Agency Daily Report, March 11, 2003; Atlas, James, "A Classicist's Legacy: New Empire Builders," *New York Times,* May 4, 2003; William Pfaff, "The Long Reach of Leo Strauss," *International Herald Tribune,* May 15, 2003. One left-wing publication went so far as to list the names of prominent architects and supporters of administration policy, with black marks in front of the "Jewish" names. Lasn, Kalle, "Why Won't Anyone Say they Are Jewish?" *Adbusters,* March-April 2004, www.adbusters.or/magazine/52/articles/jewish.html.

33. Rosenberg, Mica, "'You Don't Have To Be Anti-Israel To Be Anti-War': Jews Join D.C. Rally," Jewish Telegraphic Agency Daily Report, January 21, 2003. Eli Pariser, who organized the first series of national antiwar protests after September 11, 2001, and also led rallies against the Iraq war, "descends on his father's side from Zionist Jews...." Both his parents protested the Vietnam War. Packer, George, "Smart-Mobbing the War," *New York Times Magazine,* March 9, 2003, p. 48.

34. Greenberg, Anna and Wald, Kenneth D., "Still Liberal After All These Years? The Contemporary Political Behavior of American Jews," in Maisel, L. Sandy and Forman, Ira N., eds., *Jews in American Politics* (Lanham: Rowan and Littlefield, 2001), p. 188.

35. Coleman's seat has been held by Jews since 1978 (he was preceded in it by Rudy Boschwitz and the late Paul Wellstone), this in a state where Jews make up less than 1 percent of the population.

36. Stone, Adam, "Stephanie's Simchah," *Baltimore Jewish Times,* October 10, 2003. Five of the contenders for the 2004 Democratic presidential nomination had Jewish family connections: Joseph Lieberman was a Jew; John Kerry had Jewish grandparents; Gen. Wesley Clark, a Jewish grandfather; Howard Dean, a Jewish wife; and Dennis Kucinich, a Jewish girlfriend (the couple ate only "kosher vegan").

37. On the speaker see McKinley, Jr., James C., "Silver Is an Albany Strongman, and It's Not Because He's Flashy," *New York Times,* February 11, 2003.

38. Whitfield, Stephen J., "Famished for Justice: The Jew as Radical," Maisel and Forman, eds., *Jews in American Politics,* p. 214.

39. Forman, Ira N., "The Politics of Minority Consciousness: The Historical Voting Behavior of American Jews," ibid., p. 153.

40. Kessler, E.J., "After Pataki's Win, Miffed N.Y. Dems Call on Party To

Rebuild Jewish Base," *Forward,* December 6, 2002.

41. Runyan, Joshua, "No Contest: Street Topples Katz, *Jewish Exponent* (Philadelphia), November 6, 2003; Runyan, "Street Reigns Where Katz Once Ruled," ibid., November 13, 2003.

42. Greenberg and Wald, ibid., p. 162.

43. *2002 Annual Survey of American Jewish Opinion,* p. 9. The figure for the Religious Right was second only to that for Muslims: 57 percent of Jews considered many or most of them anti-Semitic.

44. The pivotal role of the national Jewish organizations in post-World War II liberalism is spelled out in Stuart Svonkin, *Jews Against Prejudice: American Jews and the Fight for Civil Liberties* (New York: Columbia University Press, 1997). Jewish involvement in the civil rights struggle and the complicated evolution of black-Jewish relations are covered in Friedman, Murray, *What Went Wrong? The Creation and Collapse of the Black-Jewish Alliance* (New York: The Free Press, 1995). The situation in New York City is covered by Sleeper, James in *The Closest of Strangers: Liberalism and the Politics of Race in New York* (New York: W.W. Norton: 1990). The 2000 numbers are in Greenberg and Wald, "Still Liberal After all These Years?" p. 183.

45. For data on attitudes toward abortion and homosexuality see Greenberg and Wald, "Still Liberal After All These Years?" pp. 177–78. It may or may not be significant that the first notice of a gay "commitment ceremony" published in the *New York Times* (Sept. 1, 2002) was for two Jewish men.

46. On this topic see the comprehensive study by Ivers, Gregg, *To Build a Wall: American Jews and the Separation of Church and State* (Charlottesville: University Press of Virginia, 1995).

47. Greenberg and Wald, "Still Liberal After All These Years?" p. 180.

48. In an event that drew some media attention, on November 9, 2003, Pennsylvania Senator Rick Santorum, a leading figure on the Republican right, keynoted a major dinner of the Union of Orthodox Jewish Congregations in New York City.

49. Lefkowitz, Jay, "The Election and the Jewish Vote," *Commentary,* Feb. 2005, pp. 61–65.

50. Dinnerstein, Leonard, *The Leo Frank Case* (New York: Columbia University Press, 1968).

51. *2002 Annual Survey of American Jewish Opinion,* pp. 8, 9. As evident from the tables on p. 15, these numbers have held steady at least since 1997.

52. *2002 Annual Survey of American Jewish Opinion,* p. 2; *Jewish Community Study of New York 2002,* p. 33; *NJPS 2000–01,* p. 12.

53. Rosenblatt, Gary, "New York State of Mind," *New York Jewish Week,* June 27, 2003.

54. Whitfield, Stephen J. , *In Search of American Jewish Culture* (Hanover and London: Brandeis University Press, 1999), pp. xi–xii; Shapiro, Edward, *A Time for Healing: American Jewry since World War II* (Baltimore and London: Johns Hopkins University Press, 1992), p. 29.

55. Whitfield, *In Search of American Jewish Culture,* p. 61.

56. Ibid., p. 98.

57. The material in this section is derived from Gabler, Neal, *An Empire of Their Own: How the Jews Invented Hollywood* (New York: Crown, 1988) and J. Hoberman and Jeffrey Shandler, *Entertaining America: Jews, Movies, and Broadcasting* (Princeton: Princeton University Press and The Jewish Museum, 2003).

58. Weinstein, Natalie, "Is 'Seinfeld' Jewish? Experts Seek Cultural Definitions," *Jewish Bulletin of Northern California,* May 24, 1996; Elber, Lynn, "Seinfeld's Jewishness," *Nando Times News,* http://archive.nandotimes.com/nt/special/seinfeld08.html.

59. Eggers, Christian, a reporter for Reuters, took notes of the testimony. See http://pnews.org/art/10art/ROOT.shtml

CHAPTER FIVE

RELIGIONS OF IMMIGRANTS
IN THE MIDDLE ATLANTIC STATES

Wendy Cadge

Flushing, a neighborhood in the borough of Queens, in New York City, is one of the most ethnically and religiously diverse areas in the United States. A walk through Flushing on a warm spring day reveals the languages, foods, dress, cultures, and customs of people born in parts of Africa, Asia, Central and South America, and Europe. More than 40 houses of worship exist on and around Bowne Street in the heart of Flushing, and on a usual weekend thousands of people gather to worship at the Hindu temple, Muslim mosques, Buddhist temples, and numerous Christian churches in the square mile around Bowne Street.[1]

In other areas of New York state, smaller-scale versions of this religious diversity are evident in Schenectady, where Guyanese immigrants, with the mayor's assistance, recently moved their Hindu temple into a building that was formerly a Catholic church, and in the region around Poughkeepsie, where the number of families involved with the Hindu Samaj has increased by 150 since it opened in 1997 and the number of Muslim mosques has multiplied.[2]

In the Allentown-Bethlehem area of Pennsylvania, a two-hour drive southwest of New York City, a Hindu temple, two Muslim mosques, a Buddhist temple, and a number of Catholic churches serving Puerto Rican, Mexican, and Central-American immigrants, many of whom moved to the area from New York City, thrive in an area with a population of 600,000.

Religious diversity in the developing United States first took shape in Pennsylvania, New York, and other Middle-Atlantic colonies in the eighteenth and nineteenth centuries, and today the Middle Atlantic region remains unique in the degree of religious difference contained within its borders. As in most of the United States, religion in the Middle Atlantic states of New York,

New Jersey, Pennsylvania, Delaware, and Maryland, and in Washington, D.C., has been reshaped over the past 40 years by immigration, particularly from Asia and Latin America. New immigrants, many of whom arrived in the United States through the gateway cities of New York and Washington, D.C., brought their cultures and customs to the region as well as a wide range of religious traditions. Some joined existing Christian, particularly Catholic, churches while others built Hindu, Buddhist, Christian, and Muslim religious centers through which they gather, worship, and become engaged in American public life.

This chapter focuses on the religions of immigrants who arrived in the Middle Atlantic states after changes to the immigration laws in 1965 and describes how these immigrants became involved in American public life in and through their religious organizations and traditions.

This public involvement normally began when immigrants gathered and rented or purchased a building where they could practice their religion, thereby making their first religious mark on American soil. From these early organizations, immigrants have developed complex religious and ethnic centers through which they continue to practice their religious traditions, offer social services and support for newer immigrants, do outreach to non-immigrants, and hear sermons and teachings about their involvement in American politics.

In some cases, like in Flushing, immigrants and native-born Americans have come to worship side by side with little interaction or conflict, while in other cases the easy interactions between immigrants and native-born people in different religious traditions that some argue characterize the Middle Atlantic region have been more difficult to achieve.

History and Demography

The Immigration Act of 1965 dramatically altered immigration to the Middle Atlantic region, and the country as a whole, by ending country-of-origin quotas in U.S. immigration and diversifying the ethnic and religious backgrounds of immigrants. Millions of immigrants have entered the United States since 1965, with the majority from Latin America and Asia, rather than Europe, where previous generations of immigrants were born.[3]

The 2000 U.S. Census counted 31.1 million foreign-born people in the United States, 11.1 percent of the total U.S. population and an increase of 57 percent, or 11.3 million people, since 1990. In 2000, the majority of foreign-born people living in the United States were born in Latin America (52 percent) followed by Asia (26 percent).[4] Immigrants were not spread evenly throughout the United States in 2000, as is evident in **Figure 5.1**. With the exception of the Pacific region, immigrants comprised a larger proportion of resi-

Figure 5.1   Percentage of foreign-born people
in the United States by region
(U.S. Census 2000, 1990, 1980, 1970)

	United States	New England	Middle Atlantic	South	Midwest	Southern Crossroads	Mountain West	Pacific Northwest	Pacific
1970	4.7	7.9	7.8	2	3.5	1.8	2.9	4.0	8.7
1980	6.2	7.8	9.0	4	3.8	3.8	4.1	5.1	14.8
1990	7.9	7.9	10.5	4.7	3.7	5.6	4.9	5.9	21.0
2000	11.1	9.8	14	7.6	5.7	9.1	8.8	9.4	25.3

dents in the Middle-Atlantic states (14 percent, approximately 6.5 million people) than in any other region of the country. As in the country as a whole, the majority of immigrants in the Middle-Atlantic states, as can be seen in **Figure 5.2** (page 136), were born in Latin America (44 percent) followed by Asia (26.4 percent), Europe (23.4 percent), Africa (4.2 percent), North America (1.5 percent), and Oceania (.2 percent).

Within the Middle Atlantic region, as evident in **Figure 5.3** (page 137), New York had the largest proportion of immigrants in 2000, followed by New Jersey, Washington, D.C., Maryland, Delaware, and Pennsylvania. In New York, immigrants comprised 20.4 percent of the state's population while in Pennsylvania they comprised just 4.1 percent. New York and Washington have historically been home to large numbers of immigrants, in part because many immigrants arrive in New York City and Washington as their first point of contact in the United States. Outside of New York City and Washington, large numbers of immigrants also live in other larger and smaller cities in the region. Between 1990 and 2000, Delaware was the state in the region that experienced the largest percentage change (a 101.6 percent increase) in the number of immigrants in residence as large numbers of Latin Americans, particularly Guatemalans and Mexicans who had been working in agriculture on the East Coast moved to the Delmarva peninsula to work in the poultry processing industry.[5]

The U.S. Census gathers detailed data about the country of origin and demographics of foreign-born residents but does not gather any information about the religious beliefs and memberships of foreign- or native-born Americans, making the religious behaviors of the American public difficult to describe concisely. Nationally representative surveys that do ask questions about religion are most often conducted in English and rarely include enough foreign-born residents to draw meaningful conclusions. Researchers only began to study the religions of post-1965 immigrants around 1990, and most of their research to date has been focused on case studies rather than larger surveys.

Figure 5.2   Region of Origin for Immigrants in the Mid-Atlantic States, 2000

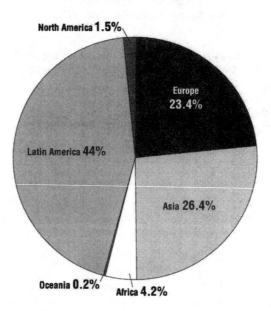

The best demographic information currently available about the religious beliefs and practices of post-1965 immigrants was gathered in the pilot project for the New Immigrant Survey, a nationally representative survey of immigrants living in the United States that is in the process of being conducted.[6] This pilot study shows that the majority (two-thirds) of immigrants in the United States are Christian and 42 percent of immigrants are Catholic.[7] Information from the New Immigrant Survey about the Middle Atlantic states generally follows the national patterns, showing that the majority of new immigrants in the region are Catholic (34 percent) followed by Protestant (17 percent), no religion (15 percent), Muslim (12 percent), Hindu (6 percent), Jewish (5 percent), Orthodox Christian (5 percent) and Buddhist (4 percent).[8] Rather than de-Christianizing the United States, the sociologist R. Stephen Warner and others argue, new immigrants in the Middle Atlantic and nationally are de-Europeanizing American Christianity.[9] While about 17 percent of immigrants nationally identify with non-Christian or Jewish religions, in comparison to about 4 percent of native-born people, the number of Christians among new immigrants cannot be over-emphasized.

The large number of Christians among post-1965 immigrants to the United States is explained by a number of factors including immigration to the United States from predominantly Christian countries, the selection of Christians among different religious groups in a country for migration, and large-scale

Figure 5.3   Percentage of foreign-born people
in the Middle-Atlantic states, 1970-2000
(U.S. Census 2000)

	DE	D.C.	MD	NJ	NY	PA
1970	2.9	4.4	3.2	8.9	11.6	3.8
1980	3.2	6.4	4.6	13.6	10.3	3.4
1990	3.3	9.7	6.6	12.5	15.9	3.1
2000	5.7	12.9	9.8	17.5	20.4	4.1

conversions to Christianity within some ethnic groups shortly after arrival in the United States.

First, Mexico, an overwhelmingly Christian country, sends more immigrants to the United States than any other country. There were approximately 9.2 million Mexican-born people in the United States in 2000.[10] Second, in some countries, more Christians than people in other religious traditions migrate to the United States. In South Korea, for example, one quarter of the population is Christian and one quarter is Buddhist. Nearly half of Koreans who immigrate to the States, however, are Christian, coming from the more urban, educated, and less settled sector of Koreans.[11] A similar pattern is evident among Vietnamese immigrants, a great number of whom are Catholic. Finally, some immigrants, particularly those from mainland China, report having no religion when they arrive in the States. Many are quickly introduced to Protestant churches and convert, leading researchers to estimate that Christianity is the largest religion among Chinese immigrants in the United States.[12]

Public Presences

Once they arrive, many immigrants to the Middle Atlantic states quickly become involved in American life. Much like among native-born people, religion serves as a port of entry for many immigrants, leading them to first become involved in American life through religious organizations. By joining existing religious organizations and creating new ones, post-1965 immigrants in the Middle Atlantic states have become a part of American public life, contributing their own unique strands to the American religious tapestry in the process.

As Will Herberg argued in his now classic *Protestant-Catholic-Jew*, religion has been and remains central to the lives of first-generation immigrants. While Herberg expected immigrants or their children to eventually give up their language, nationality, and manners of life, they were not expected to give up their religions; "...not only was he [the immigrant] expected to retain his old religion…but such was the shape of America that it was largely in and through his religion that he or rather his children and grandchildren, found an identifiable place in American life."[13] Religion has been and remains a vibrant form of identification for first-generation immigrants in this country and a powerful basis of group formation through which many immigrants in the Middle Atlantic region have become participants in broader American life and society.

The first step for many immigrants in this process is becoming part of a religious organization. Christians, especially Catholics, have tended to join churches and parishes, which often change or amend their practices slightly so that recent immigrants feel comfortable and at home. St. Cecilia's Roman Catholic Church in East Harlem, the spiritual home of a number of Mexican, Puerto Rican, Ecuadorean, and Filipino immigrants in the city, for example, has created spaces inside the church for shrines for the saints traditionally associated with their home countries. In the 1990s, Mexican immigrants first created a shrine for their patron saint, the Virgin of Guadalupe. Since then shrines for St. Martin de Porres, the Virgin of Providence, the Virgin of Cisne, and others have been created, and related feasts have been celebrated there and at other Catholic churches in the area.[14]

In addition to Catholic churches, immigrants join churches in other religious traditions. In the Washington, D.C. area, Africans and African influences are seeping into many area worship services as large numbers of Africans, about half of whom are Christian, have arrived in the area since the early 1990s. In Prince George's County, Maryland, for example, hundreds of African and Caribbean immigrants attend St. John's Episcopal Church, bringing their music and other cultural traditions with them. St. John's was a small church with a shrinking congregation until the mid-1990s, when immigrants from Nigeria, Sierra Leone, Ghana, Liberia, and the Caribbean began to attend. Today about 100 immigrants from Nigeria attend the Igbo-language service, and all but one person in church leadership is an African immigrant.[15]

Other immigrants, particularly Buddhists, Hindus, and Muslims, have started new religious organizations since arriving in the United States. Although there is certainly no one form of religious organization, many of these new religious centers start with a group of lay people first meeting in a rented house or apartment for religious services and then planning and fundraising to purchase a building or land for construction.

Wat Mongkoltempunee, a Thai Buddhist temple in the suburbs of Philadelphia, for example, began in the mid-1980s when Thai immigrants in the area grew tired of traveling to New York and Washington, D.C. to celebrate Buddhist holidays. They gathered funds to purchase land and a building and invited monks from Thailand to come to the United States to lead the new temple. They eventually purchased a small house on a larger piece of property in Bensalem, Pennsylvania, where they worshipped for eight years while constructing a much larger Thai-style Buddhist temple that was completed in 1994. Today 50 to 60 people attend the temple on Sundays for weekly gatherings and several hundred attend the festivals held eight times each year.[16]

Rather than constructing new buildings, some immigrant religious organizations move into existing buildings, often ones previously used by other religious congregations. A large number of Vietnamese Buddhists were resettled to Fort Indiantown Gap, near Harrisburg, Pennsylvania, in the late 1970s and 1980s, where they gathered to worship in a rented apartment until their numbers increased and parking became a serious problem. In 1993, they gathered donations and purchased their current temple, a building that was formerly a United Methodist church. The building now has a white sign in front of it that reads, "Buddhist Association of Pennsylvania Phap Hoa Temple." Similarly, the Garfield Hindu Mandir temple in Garfield, New Jersey, is currently housed in a building that was formerly a Jewish synagogue and still has stained glass windows with Jewish images and symbols. Other religious centers exist in buildings that were formerly schools and community centers. And the Hindu Temple Society of South Jersey is located in a building that was formerly a warehouse.[17]

While some immigrants have joined or created new religious organizations in the Middle Atlantic states with few obstacles or problems, others have faced numerous challenges in the process. When the monks and founders of Thai Buddhist temple Wat Mongkoltempunee first located a piece of land to purchase for their temple and approached the county zoning board to see about the necessary zoning changes, scores of angry residents protested and the Thais withdrew their application.[18] Similarly, when the Hindu American Religious Institute (HARI) temple, formed in the Harrisburg area in the early 1970s, decided to purchase a piece of land on which to build a temple more accessible to Hindus in the area, local residents protested at the local zoning board meeting. Many were afraid that the HARI temple was related to the Hari-Krishna movement and did not want an Indian temple in the area. In response, the HARI community gave up on this first piece of property and located a second piece of land in New Cumberland, Pennsylvania. Before approaching the local zoning board, members of the HARI community went door to door in the neighborhood where they hoped to purchase land, talking with local residents about their religion and their hope of building a temple, and making it clear that they had no connection to the Hari-Krishna movement. No one protested and the piece of land was purchased and the building constructed, opening on July 4, 1986, with Hindus from New York, Harrisburg, Lancaster, Pittsburgh, Allentown, Baltimore, and Washington, D.C. in attendance.[19] This example points to the extra work immigrant members of non-Christian religious traditions often do to become accepted in the United States, work that might make them more outward looking than Christian religious groups.

The challenges immigrants face in starting new religious centers are not restricted to zoning and the construction of buildings, however, but also relate to their practices. These types of conflicts were evident most dramatically in the lengthy battle fought in federal court between members of the Gujarati Indian community and the township of Edison, New Jersey, about whether and how they could celebrate the Hindu Navrati festival in the township. In the end the festival was permitted without many of the restrictions about the ending time of the festival and other issues that the township sought to impose.[20] In addition to conflicts between religious organizations and the towns and cities in which they are located, there are also numerous examples of conflicts within immigrant religious organizations, particularly around leadership and elections. For example, in 1994 a conflict between Sikhs at a temple in Queens about temple elections spilled onto the sidewalk and the police were summoned.[21]

As evident in the examples described here, the religious organizations joined and started by immigrants in the Middle Atlantic states range widely. Some, like the Shiva Mandir community shrine, in a storefront in Jersey City, are visited regularly but include no specific worshipping community, while others, like Wat Thai Washington, D.C. in Silver Spring, Maryland, have a core of weekly attendees and hold festivals several times a year, led by six or more monks and attended by hundreds of people and sometimes visiting dignitaries.

Some are attended primarily by people from the same ethnic background while others include a mix of people. The Harrisburg Chinese Alliance Church in Harrisburg, Pennsylvania, for example, includes people from China, Taiwan, Hong Kong, Malaysia, Indonesia, and Vietnam, and services are held in English, Mandarin, and Cantonese.[22] Pan-Asian churches are a common adaptation in the United States when individual groups of Asians do not have the resources necessary to start their own houses of worship.

Some religious centers hold regular daily or weekly gatherings while others are much more informal, offering ceremonies whenever people drop by rather than at specific times planned beforehand. Some centers, like Catholic churches in particular, are also formally linked to large transnational organizations, while others are a part of larger U.S.-based organizations or exist more independently. The religious centers that immigrants attend regularly for worship are complemented by related new businesses (i.e., Hindu summer camps, Halal butcher shops that prepare meat according to Islamic law, and other services, like the chapel for Hindu ceremonies created at the Garden State Crematory) that support religious beliefs and practices.

Sociologists who study the religious organizations started and attended by immigrants since 1965 have focused primarily on places where immigrants regularly gather in face-to-face meetings for worship. Calling these organizations "congregations," R. Stephen Warner, Helen Rose Ebaugh, Janet Saltzman Chafetz, and other sociologists argue that regardless of how religious gathering and worship were organized in their home countries, new immigrants' religious centers in the United States are largely structured and function as congregations in which participation and membership are voluntary and the identity of the group is based on the people who gather rather than the space or territory they occupy.[23]

While some centers draw people mostly from their local neighborhoods like parishes, others occupy particular niches and are attended by people who travel long distances to be there. People tend to gather at these centers once a week, normally on a Saturday or Sunday, for worship and celebration, under the leadership of people who increasing resemble clergy or other religious professionals. Lay people tend to be more involved in leadership positions and day-to-day operations than they were in their home countries. Many centers serve as both religious centers and community centers, in which educational, cultural, social service, and political gatherings are held. In addition to religious services, secular ethnic holidays are celebrated at many centers, and English as a Second Language and citizenship classes are offered, job listings are posted, and secular recreation takes places.

The specific forms immigrants' religious organizations take, of course, vary and depend on characteristics of the environment in which the group is started, as well as the group's goals and priorities. Broad structural factors related to the economy of the area, the residential patterns of different immigrant groups, the demographic profile of the neighborhood in which the religious center is located, and the demographic profiles of practitioners, all have an obvious influence. Additionally, whether the group is Christian or part of a minority religious tradition is important, as is whether practitioners were members of minority or majority religious groups in their home countries and what other resources they have at their disposal. The presence or absence of other religious organizations in the tradition in the new location is also an important factors, as are the specific way in which it has traveled (with or apart from religious leaders, for example) and the continuity of its possible links to the home country. In addition to these environmental, historical, and organizational issues, the teachings around which new religious organizations are formed are also critically important to understanding how they adapt in the Middle Atlantic states and the United States more broadly.

In her study of one of the country's oldest immigrant Muslim mosques, located in Brooklyn, the sociologist Rogaia Mustafa Abusharaf describes how the mosque was founded in 1928 by a wealthy Moroccan immigrant and has since developed into a largely Yemeni ethnic religious institution. As it developed, the mosque adopted a congregational form by creating governing structures via membership and an elected board of directors, and by professionalizing the clergy. In the process, the mosque's own identity became clear as Muslim immigrants struggled to adapt their faith to a new environment while maintaining the distinctive attributes of both their tradition and their culture. As the mosque developed and Muslims adapted and adjusted, Abusharaf argues, they become "more aware of their distinctive identity in contrast with other groups."[24]

More recent research further illustrates how congregational forms nurture the differences between the norms of behavior within particular religious traditions and broader society. A mosque in Washington, D.C., described by the political scientist Michael Foley, teaches distinctly Islamic standards of dress for women in the mosque and distinct notions of family and childrearing. Marriage classes at the mosque are well attended and begin by differentiating between Islamic and Western notions of marriage.[25] Both of these examples show how religious adaptation takes place as organizational forms and individuals' roles inside and outside of their religious center are negotiated and renegotiated.

Within the Hindu tradition, a wide range of organizations have started and been adapted in the Middle Atlantic states, particularly in central New Jersey, where many Hindu Indians live. *Satsangs,* or regular devotional meetings, are held in people's homes as well as *bala vihars,* or gatherings to teach children.[26] In addition, numerous temples and shrines exist and have opened in recent years as places that teach Hindu traditions as well as Indian cultures and languages. In north-central New Jersey, an ISKCON (International Society for Krishna Consciousness) temple has been housed in a two-story colonial house for over 20 years. Several members live in the house and large numbers of people gather on Sunday evenings for worship in congregational-type gatherings.[27]

Temples in India do not normally have such gatherings and two temples in the Middle Atlantic region, the Maha Vallabha Ganapati Devasthanam, or "Ganesha Temple," in Flushing and the Sri Venkateswara Temple, in Pittsburgh. follow these more traditional models, though they do make some efforts to create community along ethnic lines.[28] In the 1980s another temple was started in Bridgewater, New Jersey, after a number of professional Hindu Indians moved to the area and wanted to have a temple nearby that would teach traditional Hindu religious practices and values to their children.[29] These different Hindu organizations vary in the degrees to which they emphasize individual and communal practices and the extent to which they replicate, amend, or create new models of Hindu religious organization in the United States.

In Muslim and Hindu organizations in the United States, as well as in religious organizations started by immigrants in other religious traditions, negotiations about the roles and responsibilities of women and men take place, often in ways different from immigrants' home countries. In their research about the religious organizations of immigrants in Houston, Helen Rose Ebaugh and Janet Saltzman Chafetz found that women's access to leadership positions within organizations is increasing, both as the number of such positions increases in the United States and as women gain educational and employment experience that leads them to want such roles. Women's access to these roles in Houston was indirectly related to men's desires to fill them.[30] Systematic research about gender in immigrants' religious organizations in the Middle Atlantic states has yet to be completed, though there is evidence both of more and less change. Research about second-generation Korean-American Christians in the New Jersey suburbs shows that many do not believe women are suited for leadership positions, while evidence from first-generation Thai Buddhists in the area shows women occupying more leadership positions than they did in Thailand.[31] Religion, generation, length of time in the United States, and other demographic and contextual factors, all influence the gender dynamics in new-immigrant religious organizations across the region.

Public Involvements

Through their participation in religious organizations, many immigrants also become more involved in public life through their centers' outreach efforts to immigrants and native-born Americans alike. Many of the religious organizations immigrants create or are involved with are multi-functional, and include religious, educational, cultural, social service, and political activities and events. Based on his interviews with Korean head pastors in New York City, for example, the sociologist Pyong Gap Min argues that Korean-Christian churches serve multiple purposes, such as providing fellowship for Korean immigrants, maintaining Korean cultural traditions, and providing social services for church members and the Korean community more broadly.[32] Bethel Korean Presbyterian Church in Ellicott City, Maryland, for example, provides weekly worship, Korean-language classes, and other programs for first-, second-, and third-generation Koreans. Recently, the church hosted a concert attended by almost 700 people that raised money for a help line for Korean immigrants.[33]

Many immigrant religious centers provide social services for recent immigrants, making them particularly welcoming institutions, especially for immigrants who face difficult situations in the United States. Many churches offer food, clothing, and other kinds of financial and material assistance to recent immigrants, as well as legal counsel and access to medical care and housing. Many of the religious centers in New York's Chinatown that serve recent, mostly undocumented, immigrants from Fuzhou on China's southeast coast, for example, act as "safe harbors" by providing the social networks, information, emotional and often financial and legal support needed to survive in the United States.[34] In Silver Spring, Maryland, members of the Muslim community planned to open a free health-care clinic staffed by Muslim doctors for low-income Muslims in the Washington, D.C. area.[35]

In another example, St. Bernard's Catholic Church in Prince George's County in Maryland, started in the 1950s among working-class Catholics, now primarily serves Mexicans, providing them with religious as well as social services. Described as a "one-stop social service center," it is a place where priests and lay volunteers help congregants complete immigration documents, translate for them with doctors and landlords, and offer referrals to free local medical clinics, immigration service centers, local consular officials, and county agencies. The church distributes much of the $15,000 it donates annually in charity to its own members to help them pay their rent and buy food, medicine, and other necessities.[36] Other Catholic churches in the region do the same, offering workshops to help immigrants with their immigration forms and to help them apply for Temporary Protected Status and political asylum. St. John the Baptist Catholic church in Silver Spring, Maryland, for example, recently held an informational meeting with Indonesian parishioners and a lawyer from Catholic Charities who spoke their language so they could learn the new rules about social registration. Mosques and community groups in the area have also started to hold meetings both to inform their congregants about and to register their public opposition to the U.S. government's new immigration and security laws for Muslim, Arab, and South-Asian residents.[37]

In addition to the practical day-to-day assistance many immigrant churches and religious centers provide their members, higher levels of leadership in some churches and denominations have also lobbied on behalf of immigrants at the state and national levels. Catholic Church officials have openly criticized policies likely to harm immigrants, such as the Illegal Immigration Reform and Responsibility Act and the Welfare Reform Act of 1996, and have repeatedly advocated for immigrants' rights.[38] The National Conference of Catholic Bishops in 2000 passed a resolution calling on federal policymakers to "reexamine our immigration laws and enact legislative and administrative reforms which uphold the basic dignity and human rights of immigrants and preserve the unity of the immigrant family."[39] A number of Christian churches in the region, regardless of the proportion of immigrants in their congregation, have also sponsored and supported refugees, helping them come to the United States and find their way once they arrive.

Many of the religious organizations started by post-1965 immigrants to the United States not only provide support for co-ethnics and other recent immigrants, but also have outreach programs for non-immigrants as well. A number of Buddhist organizations, in particular, have reached out in recent years to non-immigrants interested in Buddhism. The Washington Buddhist Vihara, the first Theravada Buddhist organization in the United States, started in 1966, included Sri Lankan- and American-born Buddhist practitioners from the start. Since its opening, it has included a wide range of immigrants and non-immigrants, leading to some conflicts amidst mostly harmonious relations.[40] Rather than include non-immigrants from the start, the Thai Buddhist temple in Silver Spring, Maryland, started to offer meditation classes in English after it was firmly established, aimed at people in the area interested in learning about Buddhist meditation. For a number of years, an English-speaking Thai monk also traveled regularly from Washington, D.C. to the West Reading area of Pennsylvania to hold meditation classes at a yoga studio for people in the area, at their request.

The leaders and lay people at many Buddhist temples, as well as other immigrant religious centers in the Middle Atlantic region, are also increasingly involved in public life through the formal and informal educational programs they offer for non-believers about their religious traditions. At Wat Mongkoltempunee, in the suburbs of Philadelphia, groups from area colleges and universities regularly visit to learn about Thai Buddhism. Especially since September 11, Muslim mosques and organizations across the region and the country have sponsored many talks and programs about Islam. In 2004, for instance, the Islamic Center of Pittsburgh sponsored open houses at public libraries in the area, hosted open houses at their mosque, and offered Introduction to Islam classes.[41] And the leaders of the Islamic Society of Monmouth County in Middletown, New Jersey, have regularly given talks at other religious centers and in secular settings to help the broader public understand the Muslim faith.[42]

Organizations in each of these religious traditions teach about and encourage immigrant practitioners to be involved in American public life in different ways. While some do not explicitly encourage immigrants to make their opinions known, to vote, or to think about broader public issues, others do; the extent to which they focus on outreach and education to different constituencies, as opposed to public advocacy, varies by location and tradition. The extent to which practitioners are encouraged to focus on political issues in their home countries, as opposed to the United States, also varies.

At some Thai Buddhist temples absentee ballots are available for Thai citizens, and newspapers from Thailand are readily available and read. At other centers, like the Islamic Cultural Center mosque in New York City, announcements are made encouraging people to register and to vote in the United States. "As the election comes, our constitutional rights and religious rights are being trampled on," the executive director of the New York branch of the Council on American-Islamic Relations said over the intercom one Friday before the 2004 elections, in a mixture of English and Arabic. "We don't have clout. And so it is very important for all of us, God willing, to register."[43]

A Few Examples

The diversity of immigrants and the kinds of religious organizations they belong to and create in the Middle Atlantic states makes overarching generalizations about religion and the public presence and involvements of immigrants in the region difficult to sustain. It is helpful, therefore, to examine a few examples in detail to illustrate more fully the range of ways members of specific religious and ethnic groups come to be involved in American public life in and through their religious organizations in the region.

The political crisis, subsequent civil war, and economic conditions in El Salvador led residents of that country to begin migrating to the United States in the 1970s. Early immigrants were concentrated on the West Coast, but since the 1980s increasing numbers have arrived and stayed in Washington, D.C., the only city in the United States in which Salvadorans currently comprise the majority of Latino residents.[44] Recent Salvadoran immigrants to Washington, D.C. are involved in Catholic and evangelical churches in the region, as described by the sociologist Cecilia Menjivar. Clergy and lay people at both Catholic and evangelical churches in the city support Salvadoran church members by providing assistance with immigration issues, legal counsel, and other challenges, though Catholic churches have many more formal programs than do evangelical churches.

The Catholic churches Salvadorans attend tend to promote a "communitarian ethic," Menjivar explains, through which attention is focused on what can collectively be done to improve immigrants' situations. Rather than focusing just on Salvadorans, Catholic churches tend to work with Latinos of different ethnicities, as well as other immigrants and native-born Catholics in the United States and around the world. By reaching out to their ethnically diverse membership, Catholic priests and leaders in the region attempt to build coalitions and to bring their faith into dialogue with broader public issues that affect parishioners' day-to-day lives and immigrants' integration into broader American society.

Catholic priests in Washington, D.C. bring their faith into dialogue with broader public issues by involving themselves in social issues and by speaking about these issues in their church services. During the riots in 1991 between Latinos and police in the city's Mount Pleasant neighborhood, for example,

Catholic priests and other church leaders tried to ease the tensions by holding community meetings in one of the area's churches. More recently, Salvadoran priests have delivered homilies during Mass about pressing social issues. A few days before President Clinton was to sign the welfare reform bill into law, for example, Salvadoran priests in the city urged congregants to use their religious and spiritual beliefs to reflect on and come to their own opinions about the issue. In these and other examples, Cecilia Menjivar shows how Catholic leaders in the city encourage immigrant and native-born parishioners to use their religious beliefs as tools for social mobilization and action.

In contrast to the pan-ethnic models advanced in the Washington area's multi-cultural Catholic parishes, many evangelical churches Salvadorans attend are more homogenous, often started by new immigrants themselves, and have tended to advocate more individual responses and involvements in public life. Rather than working to form coalitions or supporting programs that assist immigrants and others in their communities, evangelical pastors have tended to emphasize prayer, church rituals, and individual salvation. Like evangelical Christians across the United States, the evangelical Salvadorans Menjivar describes tend to have the strongest connections with others in the church, making the church the most important institution in their lives. Evangelical Salvadorans tend to believe that the individual salvation at the heart of the evangelical message is most beneficial to them rather than broader social actions in the world. Despite these differences, Menjivar argues that both evangelical and Catholic Salvadorans in the city find that their churches help and support them, and believe this is an important component of the churches' missions.[45]

Based on early information from a study of a dozen immigrant religious organizations in Washington, D.C., the political scientist Michael Foley found that, as in the Salvadoran case, Catholic and mainline Protestant congregations tend to be more involved in public life than conservative Christian congregations. These differences may be related to specific church teachings or to the amount of time different churches ask church members to devote to church activities. The small sample also suggests that religious organizations that include immigrant groups with more pressing social and political issues are more engaged in public life than others.[46]

In another example, many Chinese immigrants in the Middle Atlantic region belong to conservative Protestant churches and tend to be involved in public life more indirectly than the immigrant Catholics described above. The majority of Chinese immigrants in the United States are Christian, though large numbers are Buddhist or claim no religion. Many converted to Christianity after arriving in the United States, the sociologist Fenggang Yang argues, as a result of their immigration experiences, the absoluteness of conservative Protestantism, and conservative Christianity's social-ethical values. Some belong to Chinese Christian churches while others attend more ethnically mixed, often Asian-American, churches.[47] Recent counts suggest that there are at least 20 Chinese Protestant churches in Washington, D.C., the majority independent rather than affiliated with a particular denomination. In his study of the Chinese Christian Church in Washington, D.C., Yang examines how the churches and congregants create three identities—Christian, American, and Chinese—all of which have indirect consequences for public life as practitioners evangelize and assimilate into American life and culture.[48]

In addition to the first-generation immigrant religious centers described here, many second-generation immigrant centers and second-generation immigrants themselves are also involved in public life in and through their churches. In her study of a multi-ethnic church and a church attended largely by second-generation Korean-Americans in suburban New Jersey, the sociologist Elaine Howard Ecklund found that second-generation Americans at both churches believe it is important to be involved in their communities, particularly non-Korean communities; but they define these communities in different ways. Those in the second-generation Korean church, for example, use evangelical Christianity to talk about their own positions as model minorities in the United States and to distance themselves from impoverished ethnic minorities in the area where they volunteer, while those in the multi-ethnic church use evangelical Christianity to argue for their place as ethnic minorities. Despite their best intentions, this kind of civic participation does not always go smoothly, however. In one instance, members of the second-generation Korean church went to volunteer at a local youth shelter but had trouble gaining entry because the people running the shelter did not think the Korean Americans would be able to readily identify with its largely African-American and Latino youth.[49]

First- and second-generation immigrants in the Middle Atlantic states who are not Christians and do not live in large cities like Washington, D.C. and New York are also present and involved in public life in and through their religious centers in ways often unnoticed by researchers. The Muslim Community Association in Utica, New York, an hour west of Albany, for example, opened the Kemble Street mosque in a former Jehovah's Witnesses Hall in 1994 to serve the largely Muslim Bosnian refugee population relocated to the city. The mosque is currently open for prayers five times a day, provides year-round religious instruction for children, and is looking for a larger building, having outgrown its current facility.[50] In Pittsburgh, several Muslim centers support local immigrants and also provide speakers for area schools, invite non-Muslims in to celebrate Muslim holidays, and otherwise spread the faith.[51] And in Rochester, New York, numerous religious and inter-religious gatherings are held at the Islamic Center for Rochester under the guidance of Imam Dr. Mohammed Shafiq.[52]

It is not only in Flushing that different religious centers exist in close proximity to one another. The Presbyterian Korean Church in the Allentown-Bethlehem area sits across the street from the Islamic Center of the Lehigh Valley, and the Al Ahad Islamic Center for Shiite Muslims in the area is less than a quarter of a mile from Jordan United Church of Christ, attended largely by native-born Americans.[53]

Conclusions

Like the early colonists to the region, immigrants who arrived in the Middle Atlantic states since the 1960s have shaped and reshaped the region's religious geography through their presence, centers, and public involvements. In 2000, a larger proportion of residents in the Middle Atlantic states were immigrants than in almost any other region of the country, and the religious diversity they brought to the region marks it as unique. Catholic immigrants from Central and South America reshaped many parishes with their national shrines, saints, festivals and religious practices, while Buddhists, Muslims, Hindus, and members of other religious traditions built their own organizations in both rural and urban areas. From the multiple religious centers along Bowne Street in Flushing to individual mosques and temples in Utica and the Allentown-Bethlehem area, recent immigrants, like generations before them, have become part of American public life in and through their religious organizations.

In many instances, and particularly given the range of religious traditions and sheer number of immigrants in the region, a relatively conflict-free religious pluralism has existed in the Middle Atlantic states with little tension or conflict between religious organizations and practitioners. As the journalist Somini Sengupta describes in her description of Bowne Street in Flushing, the most significant point of conflict between religious practitioners there has been about parking rather than the substance of religious traditions or beliefs.[54] In other cases, however, the religious centers and practices of post-1965 immigrants have not been readily welcomed in the Middle Atlantic states making the religious pluralism, as it exists, more conflict-ridden and strained. More detailed research is needed, however, to determine the extent to which the patterns of conflict and consensus described here are unique to the region or characteristic of the United States as a whole.

Regardless of their degrees of conflict or consensus, immigrants' religious centers in the Middle Atlantic region have tended to emphasize religious or national identities, be they American identities or identities in terms of their country of origin, rather than distinctly regional ones. Like the religious centers of native-born people in the region, local rather than regional identities dominate as immigrants and their religious centers take their public places on the American religious landscape. As the religious historian Catherine Albanese states, the "tale [of religion in America] is one of meeting and change."[55] This meeting and change has certainly happened in the Middle Atlantic region, in multiple loud and quiet ways, on the land where American religious pluralism started and continues to expand.

Endnotes

1. R. Scott Hanson examines the history of the area in "City of Gods: Religious Freedom, Immigration, and Pluralism in Flushing, Queens, New York City, 1945—2000." Unpublished Dissertation. University of Chicago (2002). Journalists also report on it; Somini, Sengupta. "A Snapshot of World Faith: On One Queens Block, Many Prayers Are Spoken." *The New York Times*. 7 November 1999, Sec. 1, p. 37.

2. Sarah, Kershaw. "For Schenectady, A Guyanese Strategy; Mayor Goes All Out to Encourage a Wave of Hardworking Immigrants." *The New York Times*. 26 July 2002. Sec. B, p. 1; June 15, 2003, *Poughkeepsie Journal*, Online.

3. For a short overview, see Stephen, Warner R. "Immigration and Religious Communities in the United States," p. 3-34 in R. Stephen Warner and Judith G. Wittner eds. *Gatherings in Diaspora: Religious Communities and the New Immigration*. (Philadelphia: Temple University Press, 1998)

4. Malone, Nolan *et al*. *The Foreign Born Population: 2000*. Census 2000 Brief. (Issue December 2003).

5. Information about percentage change is summarized in Malone *et al*. For information about the growing numbers of Latin Americans in Delaware, see Horowitz, Roger and Miller, Mark J. "Immigrants in the Delmarva Poultry Processing Industry: The Changing Face of Georgetown, Delaware and Environs." (JSRI Research and Publication Series: Occasional Paper No. 37, January 1999).

6. For more information, see http://www.pop.upenn.edu/nis/index.htm.

7. Jasso, Guillermina *et al*. "Exploring the Religious Preference of Recent Immigrants to the United States: Evidence from the New Immigrant Survey

Pilot" p. 217-253 in Haddad, Yvonne Yazbeck, Smith, Jane I., and John L. Esposito eds. *Religion and Immigration: Christian, Jewish, and Muslim Experiences in the United States.* (Walnut Creek: AltaMira Press, 2003).

8. The percentages here represent 325 people in the pilot survey who said they intended to reside in one of the Middle Atlantic states.

9. Warner, R. Stephen. "Religion and New (Post-1965) Immigrants: Some Principles Drawn from Field Research." *American Studies.* 41(2/3), 2000.

10. See Malone *et al.*

11. Warner, R. Stephen. "Coming to America." *Christian Century* 10 February 2004, Vol. 121, No. 3, p. 20-23.

12. Yang, Fenggang. "Religious Diversity among the Chinese in America." p. 71-98 in Min, Pyong Gap and Jung Ha Kim Eds. *Religions in Asian America: Building Faith Communities.* (Walnut Creek: AltaMira Press, 2002).

13. Herberg, Will. *Protestant-Catholic-Jew: An Essay in American Religious Sociology.* Garden City: Doubleday, 1955, p. 40.

14. This particular church is described in Navarro, Mireya. "In Many Churches, Icons Compete for Space." *The New York Times.* 29 May 2002. Sec. B, p. 1.

15. Ly, Phuong. "Churches Adopt African Aura." *Washington Post.* 7 December 2003. p. C01.

16. Cadge, Wendy. *Heartwood: the First Generation of Theravada Buddhism in America.* (Chicago: University of Chicago Press, 2005).

17. Harvard University Pluralism Project Center Profiles. http://www.fas.harvard.edu/~pluralsm/.

18. Swearer, Donald K. "The Worldliness of Buddhism." *Wilson Quarterly* 21 (1999).

19. Harvard University Pluralism Project Center Profiles. http://www.fas.harvard.edu/~pluralsm/.

20. Anand, Vivodh Z.J. "Edison's Navratri: A Report on Religious Conflict in the Community." Harvard University Pluralism Project. http://www.fas.harvard.edu/~pluralsm/.

21. Herszenhorn, David M. "Neighborhood Report: Richmond Hill; Sikh Immigrant Community Experiencing Growing Pains." *The New York Times.* 7 August 1994. Sec. 13, p. 8.

22. Harvard University Pluralism Project Center Profiles. http://www.fas.harvard.edu/~pluralsm/.

23. See Warner, R. Stephen and Wittner, Judith, eds. *Gatherings in Diaspora: Religious Communities and the New Immigration.* (Philadelphia: Temple

University Press, 1998); Ebaugh, Helen Rose and Chafetz, Janet Saltzman. *Religion and the New Immigrants: Continuities and Adaptations in Immigrant Congregations.* (Walnut Creek: AltaMira Press, 2000).

24. Abusharaf, Rogaia Mustafa. "Structural Adaptation in an Immigrant Muslim Congregation in New York." p. 235-264 in Warner, R. Stephen and Wittner, Judith, eds. *Gatherings in Diaspora: Religious Communities and the New Immigration.* (Philadelphia: Temple University Press, 1998).

25. Foley, Michael W. "A Preliminary Report on Religion and New Immigrants." Paper Prepared for the American Political Science Association, 2001.

26. Although not about Hinduism in the Middle Atlantic states, see Kurien, Prema. "Becoming American by Becoming Hindu: Indian Americans Take Their Place at the Multicultural Table" p. 37-70 in Warner, R. Stephen and Wittner, Judith, eds. *Gatherings in Diaspora: Religious Communities and the New Immigration.* (Philadelphia: Temple University Press, 1998).

27. Harvard University Pluralism Project Center Profiles. http://www.fas.harvard.edu/~pluralsm/.

28. Prentiss, Karen Pechilis. "The Pattern of Hinduism and Hindu Temple Building in the U.S." Harvard University Pluralism Project. http://www.fas.harvard.edu/~pluralsm/.

29. Harvard University Pluralism Project Center Profiles. http://www.fas.harvard.edu/~pluralsm/.

30. Ebaugh, Helen Rose and Chafetz, Janet Saltzman. "Agents for Cultural Reproduction and Structural Change: The Ironic Role of Women in Immigrant Religious Institutions. *Social Forces.* Vol. 78, No. 2, p. 585-612, 1999.

31. Alumkal, Anthony. "Preserving Patriarchy: Assimilation, Gender Norms, and Second-Generation Korean American Evangelicals." *Qualitative Sociology* Vol. 22 No. 2, p. 127-140. Cadge, Wendy. "Gendered Religious Organizations: The Case of Theravada Buddhism in America." *Gender and Society.* Forthcoming.

32. Min, Pyong Gap. "The Structure and Social Function of Korean Immigrant Churches in the United States." *International Migration Review.* Vol. 26, No. 4, p. 1370-1394, 1992.

33. Ly, Phuong "Church Offers Haven, Link to Heritage." *The Washington Post.* 20 November 2003. T14.

34. Guest, Kenneth. *God in Chinatown: Religion and Survival in New York's Evolving Immigrant Community.* (New York: New York University Press, 2003).

35. Park, Sarah. "Cultures of Care: Montgomery Groups Launch Separate Ethnic

Care Clinics." *The Washington Post.* 6 August 2002. p. HE01.

36. Aizenman, Nurith C. "As Hispanic Membership Grows, Church Serves a New Need." *The Washington Post.* 18 December 2003. p. T16.

37. Aizenman, Nurith C. "Local Muslims Turn Attention to Civil Rights." *The Washington Post.* 27 March 2003. p. T05.

38. Menjivar, Cecilia. "Religion and Immigration in Comparative Perspective: Catholic and Evangelical Salvadorans in San Francisco, Washington D.C., and Phoenix." *Sociology of Religion.* Vol. 64, No. 1, p. 21-45, 2003.

39. http://www.usccb.org/mrs/reform.htm.

40. Blackburn, Anne. "The Evolution of Sinhalese Buddhist Identity: Reflections on Process ." Senior Thesis, Department of Religion, Swarthmore College, 1987; Fitzpatrick, Bridget. "Diversity in Practice: Placemaking Among Sinhalese and Americans at the Washington Buddhist Vihara." Unpublished Dissertation, American University, 2000.

41. See their webpage: http://www.icp-pgh.org/.

42. Alexander, Andrea. "Growing pains: Shore Muslim community seeks to be understood." *Asbury Park Press.* 30 September 2002.

43. Hauser, Christine. "Getting Out the Muslim Vote." *The New York Times.* 1 March 2003. Sec. B, p. 1.

44. Menjivar, Cecilia. "Religion and Immigration in Comparative Perspective: Catholic and Evangelical Salvadorans in San Francisco, Washington D.C., and Phoenix." *Sociology of Religion.* Vol. 64, No. 1, p. 21-45, 2003.

45. Menjivar, Cecilia. "Religion and Immigration in Comparative Perspective: Catholic and Evangelical Salvadorans in San Francisco, Washington D.C., and Phoenix." *Sociology of Religion.* Vol. 64, No. 1, p. 21-45, 2003.

46. Foley, Michael W. "A Preliminary Report on Religion and New Immigrants." Paper prepared for the American Political Science Association, 2001.

47. Yang, Fenggang. "Religious Diversity among the Chinese in America." p. 71-98 in Min, Pyong Gap and Jung Ha Kim Eds. *Religions in Asian America: Building Faith Communities.* (Walnut Creek: AltaMira Press, 2002).

48. Yang, Fenggang. *Chinese Christians in America: Conversion, Assimilation, and Adhesive Identities.* University Park: Pennsylvania State University Press, 1999.

49. Ecklund, Elaine Howard. "The 'Good' American: Religion and Civic Life for Korean Americans." Unpublished Dissertation, Cornell University, 2004.

50. Chadwick, Melissa. "Utica Muslims seek larger building." 16 March 2004. Uticaod.com.

51. Rodgers-Melnick, Ann. "Muslims reach out to U.S. mainstream." *Pittsburgh Post Gazette*. 10 January 1999.

52. www.rochesterislamiccenter.org.

53. McDermott, Joe. "Range of worship widens in the Valley." *Morning Call*. 22 December 2003. A1.

54. Sengupta, Somini. "A Snapshot of World Faith: On One Queens Block, Many Prayers Are Spoken." *The New York Times*. 7 November 1999, Sec. 1, p. 37.

55. Albanese, Catherine. "Exchanging Selves, Exchanging Souls: Contact, Combination, and American Religious History." p. 200-285 in Thomas Tweed, ed. *Retelling U.S. Religious History*. (Berkeley: University of California Press, 1998).

CONCLUSION

THE PLURALIST IMPERATIVE

Randall Balmer

On September 23, 2001, a scant 12 days after the terrorist attacks of September 11, a variety of political and religious leaders–Catholic, Jewish, Hindu, Muslim, Protestant–participated in a nationally televised event called "A Prayer for America" at Yankee Stadium in the Bronx. When David H. Benke, president of the Atlantic District of the Lutheran Church-Missouri Synod and pastor of St. Peter's Lutheran Church in Brooklyn, approached the dais, he expressed appreciation for the service of remembrance, held "on this field of dreams turned into God's house of prayer." He concluded his prayer with a fairly standard Protestant phrase, "in the precious name of Jesus," and sat down.

Amid the collective grief, participants left well satisfied with the occasion honoring the victims who had perished in the tragedy a dozen days earlier. Robert D. McFadden's account of the event in the next day's *New York Times* noted that the service "gave the devastated families of the victims and others a chance to stand together, weep openly, and reach across religious and cultural lines in an afternoon of shared solace."[1] The article noted the presence of Oprah Winfrey and James Earl Jones, the governor of New York State, and the mayor and former mayors of New York City. Bill Clinton was there, as were Senators Hillary Rodham Clinton and Charles Schumer. McFadden's article mentioned only one cleric by name, Cardinal Edward M. Egan of the Roman Catholic Archdiocese of New York, and McFadden's account waxed elegiac.

"It was the first full day of autumn and a lovely afternoon," he wrote. "Many wept silently as they listened to the speeches, murmured the prayers and sang the anthems and hymns, their faces grim reminders of the lost loved ones, the heroes and the poignant years that were not to be."[2]

If the press took no notice of Benke's presence at the "Prayer for America," the cleric's superiors in the Midwest did, and they were clearly not moved by the poignancy of the occasion. The Lutheran Church-Missouri Synod is one of the most conservative denominations in the nation (although it probably ranks second to the Wisconsin Synod as the most conservative expression of Lutheranism). Benke, who had spent 30 years as a Missouri Synod minister in New York City and been active in ecumenical affairs, soon faced disciplinary charges for participating in a "pagan" event. Denominational officials accused Benke of syncretism. He was brought before his superiors and suspended, although the suspension was eventually reversed on appeal.

While such actions may have been justified elsewhere in the nation, New Yorkers were furious and rallied to Benke's defense. "There is no room on this planet for such anachronistic people," a letter in the New York edition of *Newsday* remarked, referring to Benke's ecclesiastical accusers. The writers went on to applaud diversity, noting that Benke had "participated in good conscience in a service that celebrated the diversity of views, religions and cultures, which has served to make this country the greatest ever to exist on this planet."[3] The whole Benke ordeal "was a sad reminder of how close-minded and petty some religious leaders can be," a letter to *The New York Times* read. "It's disturbing that Pastor Benke's church leaders disapprove of such ecumenical prayer services and may dismiss him from their clergy as a result."[4] Yet another letter took on the tone of regret. "How truly sad that the Lutheran Church-Missouri Synod has chosen to focus on differences rather than shared values," the *Newsday* letter read. "And what an irony that pastors took exception to the minister praying with Jews, among others, when their very religion is founded on the teachings of one of the most—if not, the most—famous practicing Jew in history," referring to Jesus Christ.[5]

The Importance of Institutions

Ecumenical relations may not play well in other parts of the nation, where people with religious sympathies tend to be more conscious of their particularity, but the Middle Atlantic region of the United States remains both a seedbed of ecumenical and interfaith relations as well as a proving ground for religious diversity, just as it was in the colonial period. Although the tenancy of religious groups has diminished considerably in recent decades (more or less coincident with the decline of mainstream Protestantism), the Interchurch Center, in the Morningside Heights neighborhood of Manhattan, serves as the temple of ecumenical and, increasingly, interfaith activity. Despite the fact that several denominations have moved their offices elsewhere in an attempt to reconnect with their constituents, the National Council of Churches maintains its offices in the "God Box," together with a still-impressive range of other religious organizations.

The Middle Atlantic is a region that takes institutions and institutional life seriously, from foundations and hospitals to churches, universities, and museums. The older and more venerable the institution—*The New York Times*, for instance, or the Philadelphia Museum of Art—the more cultural influence it wields. Consider the heft of the Ford Foundation, Princeton and Columbia universities, Memorial Sloane-Kettering Hospital, the *Washington Post*, and the Pew Charitable Trusts. All of these institutions exert an enormous influence in their respective fields, an influence that extends far beyond the Middle Atlantic region.

Is it any wonder, given the plethora of institutions in the region, that the institutional dimensions of religious life remain important in the Middle Atlantic? Protestants elsewhere in the nation may pay little attention to the pronouncements emanating from the Interchurch Center or the machinations of denominational executives, but many Protestants in the Middle Atlantic take notice. While there can be little doubt that the ecumenical movement has cost mainstream Protestant denominations dearly in members, attendance, and giving since the 1960s, the National Council of Churches continues to pursue the chimera of theological conflation and institutional cooperation.[6]

After *Humanae Vitae* (the 1968 encyclical of Pope Paul VI that prohibited artificial means of birth control) undermined the credibility of the Roman Catholic hierarchy in the eyes of many American Catholics, they may no longer obey Church leaders, but a declaration or even a public appearance by Cardinal Edward M. Egan, archbishop of New York, attracts notice in the media. The demographic density of Jews in the Middle Atlantic ensures that the actions of the Jewish Theological Seminary or the American Jewish Committee will be noticed and, more than likely, scrutinized.

The political statements and activities of these various groups will also attract notice, if for no other reason than for the concentration of media in the Middle Atlantic, especially in New York City. The declarations issued in the 1960s by the National Council of Churches on civil rights, poverty, and the war in Vietnam invariably attracted national attention. When Pat Robertson and the Christian Coalition joined forces with Cardinal John O'Connor, the late archbishop of New York, to run a slate of politically conservative candidates for the New York City board of education, the media took notice—and citizens paid attention to the race for the first time in decades. The influence of the pro-Israel lobby in Washington is formidable, and when the American Jewish Committee or the American Israel Political Action Committee (AIPAC) issues a press release or takes a stand on an issue, legislators, the media, and ordinary citizens pay attention.

Politics and Religion

If religious leaders and organizations in the Middle Atlantic take positions on political issues, the reverse is also true: Politicians take stands on religious matters. The most notable example in recent years has been New York Governor

Mario Cuomo's address at the University of Notre Dame on September 13, 1984. "I protect my right to be a Catholic by preserving your right to believe as a Jew, a Protestant, a nonbeliever, or anything else you choose," Cuomo declared. "We know that the price of seeking to force our beliefs on others is that they might someday force theirs on us. This freedom is the fundamental strength of our unique experiment in government."

Cuomo, a devout Roman Catholic and a liberal Democrat, often tangled with Cardinal O'Connor, especially over the issue of abortion. Cuomo repeatedly said that he could not, in good conscience, impose his views as a Catholic personally opposed to abortion on the larger public. Although his position was somewhat disingenuous—Cuomo often cited his religious convictions as the reason he would never sign a law legalizing capital punishment—the Notre Dame speech was recognized almost immediately as a major statement by a thoughtful, devout politician on the proper relationship between church and state, religion and politics, especially coming as it did at the onset of the Age of the Religious Right.

Among African Americans, the line between politics and religion has historically been blurred—due to the fact that, because of the ravages of slavery and the paucity of opportunities for professional advancement, the only avenue for the expression of leadership in the black community was the church, which itself served as an advocate for African-American social concerns. Adam Clayton Powell Jr., pastor of Harlem's Abyssinian Baptist Church and, concurrently, Harlem's representative in Congress from 1945 until 1971, was a controversial figure who was expelled from Congress on February 28, 1967, for misuse of public funds (though the Supreme Court overturned the expulsion two years later). As both a Baptist minister and member of Congress, Powell was an outspoken advocate for civil rights. A more recent example of the commingling of religion and politics is Floyd H. Flake, pastor of the Allen African Methodist Episcopal (AME) church in Jamaica, Queens. Flake won election to Congress in 1986 and served until his resignation on November 17, 1997, to return full-time to his duties as pastor. Other pastors, such as Calvin O. Butts of Abyssinian Baptist Church (Powell's successor after Samuel Proctor), succeed in making their voices heard on social and political matters without holding elective political office.

The most visible African-American preacher in New York politics in recent years has been Al Sharpton. Born in Brooklyn and ordained when not yet 10 years old, in 1963, Sharpton, billed as the "Wonder-boy Preacher," shouted out sermons at the New York World's Fair in 1964. He went on to become active in civil rights causes, including a stint as youth minister for Operation Breadbasket, the organization founded by Jesse Jackson. After two years at Brooklyn College, Sharpton dropped out to become a tour manager for James Brown (Sharpton retains his long, wavy hairstyle as homage to Brown).

The minister came to public attention following an incident in Howard Beach, in Queens, in 1986, when an African-American man was run over by a car while fleeing a mob of white men. The following year he and two other African-American leaders, Alton Maddox and C. Vernon Mason, publicized the case of Tawana Brawley, a black teenager from Wappingers Falls, north of New York City, who claimed that she had been detained, raped, and sodomized for several days by six white police officers. Brawley's story began to disintegrate under scrutiny, and the courts eventually ruled it a hoax, demanding that Sharpton pay damages for slandering one of the officers.

Following the Brawley debacle, Sharpton burnished his reputation as a spokesman for the underdog after a 1991 incident when a Hasidic Jew ran a red light in Crown Heights in Brooklyn and hit a young black child. When a Jewish ambulance arrived on the scene, the emergency medical technicians attended to the lightly injured driver, not the victim, who eventually died. In the inter-ethnic violence that ensued, a Jewish rabbinical student, Yankel Rosenbaum, was stabbed to death. Sharpton preached the funeral for the African-American child, in the course of which he made several anti-Semitic statements, and then led a protest through the streets of Crown Heights, shouting "No justice, no peace."

After Sharpton himself was stabbed while organizing a rally in Bensonhurst, Brooklyn, on January 12, 1999, he became more careful to renounce violence. He organized a remarkably ecumenical "coalition of conscience" to protest the killing of an unarmed Muslim, Amadou Diallo, by New York City police officers on February 4, 1991. In the ensuing weeks, Sharpton mobilized humanitarian organizations, such as Amnesty International, as well as a diverse array of religious leaders, including Baptists such as Calvin Butts, Jews, Muslims, representatives from the Nation of Islam, and an exceedingly reluctant Cardinal O'Connor—reluctant because of the cardinal's close alliance with Rudolph Giuliani, mayor of New York and a Roman Catholic.[7]

Sharpton has sought repeatedly to parlay his name recognition into elective political office. He ran for the Democratic nomination to the U.S. Senate from New York in 1978, 1992, and 1994, and for the mayoral nomination in New York City in 1997. All attempts were unsuccessful, but what began as quixotic candidacies—with Sharpton acting like, and being regarded as, a buffoon—eventually gave him some real stature. Although he has never been able to overcome his relative lack of financing and poor organization, his pithy statements, his rapier wit (especially in debate contexts), and his knack for publicity won him a measure of credibility and even some grudging respect. His long-shot quest for the 2004 Democratic presidential nomination was similarly doomed, but he unquestionably made himself a real presence beyond the confines of Gotham.

Among elected officials, a survey of the region's U.S. senators, many of whom are strongly associated with their respective religious groups, suggests the persistence of the Protestant-Catholic-Jew paradigm in the region. At the opening of the 109th Congress in January 2005, each religious grouping, in fact, claimed three members. The Protestants were Thomas Carper of Delaware (Presbyterian), Jon Corzine of New Jersey (United Church of Christ), and Hillary Rodham Clinton of New York (United Methodist); the Catholics, Barbara Mikulski of Maryland, Joseph Biden of Delaware, and Rick Santorum of Pennsylvania; and the Jews, Chuck Schumer of New York, Frank Lautenberg of New Jersey, and Arlen Specter of Pennsylvania. The only senator who didn't fit the paradigm was the Greek Orthodox Paul S. Sarbanes of Maryland. When Sarbanes announced his decision not to run for re-election in 2006, among the several politicians who stepped forward to express interest in running for the seat was Baptist Kweisi Mfume, a former member of Congress and past president of the National Association for the Advancement of Colored People (NAACP).

Of the region's senators only Santorum is associated with the politics and policies of the Religious Right. His political base is western Pennsylvania, a fact that underscores James Hudnut-Beumler's locating of the demarcation between liberals and conservatives at the Catskill-Pocono line. Reinforcing that point, the region's only other politician with a national profile who maintained close ties with religious conservatives also hailed from the western portion of the region. Jack Kemp, former quarterback for the Buffalo Bills and Republican member of Congress, representing Erie County from 1971 until 1989, assiduously courted the Religious Right during his run for the Republican presidential nomination in 1988 and again as Bob Dole's vice-presidential running mate in 1996.

Despite the persistence of the Protestant-Catholic-Jew paradigm, politicians in the region acknowledge the importance of other religious traditions in a multicultural society, in what former New York City mayor David N. Dinkins described as a "gorgeous mosaic." During their years in the White House, Bill and Hillary Clinton held public events honoring Muslim holidays. Politicians in the Middle Atlantic now recognize the political necessity of connecting with non-Western religions. In 2002, for instance, Delaware's lieutenant governor, its only U.S. Congressman, and one of its two U.S. Senators attended the dedication of the Hindu Temple in Hockessin.

Red State-Blue State

In July 2004, during the run-up to the 2004 presidential election, an article in the *Nation* magazine offered John Kerry some advice on how to appeal to red-state voters, especially evangelical voters. The Democratic candidate was counselled to follow the example of Bill Clinton and attend an evangelical church from time to time, and to underscore the importance of the First Amendment and the separation of church and state "as the best friend that religion in America has ever had." The article also suggested ways to nuance somewhat Kerry's support for abortion rights. "A statement like, 'I have no interest in making abortion illegal; I want to make it unthinkable,' captures the proper distinction between abortion as a legal issue and abortion as a moral issue," the article read. While upholding the principle that "the rights of individual privacy preclude a legal ban on abortion," the piece continued, Americans should be reminded that "abortion is a choice with moral repercussions, albeit a choice to be made by an individual and her conscience, not by the state." Finally, the article suggested ways that the government, through public-service campaigns and in conjunction, perhaps, with religious and citizens groups, could actually discourage abortion, all the while keeping it legal.[8]

Although Kerry tried to soften his stand on abortion in the third presidential debate by saying that his Roman Catholic upbringing led him to believe that abortion itself was wrong, he refused to temper his pro-choice orthodoxy on the issue. As the Democrats were licking their wounds after November 2, 2004, and when polls suggested that "moral issues" decided the outcome of the election, some Democrats, notably Senator Hillary Rodham Clinton of New York, wondered if some alteration might be necessary if Democrats were ever to appeal to red-state voters. In a speech at Albany, New York, on January 24, 2005, Clinton acknowledged that "abortion in many ways represents a sad, even tragic choice to many, many women."

While reiterating her support for keeping abortion legal, she added that she was "pleased to be talking to people who are on the front lines of increasing women's access to quality health care and reducing unwanted pregnancy—an issue we should be able to find common ground on with people on the other side of this debate." Clinton concluded by resolving to "take real action to improve the quality of health care for women and families, to reduce the number of abortions and to build a healthier, brighter more hopeful future for women and girls in our country and around the world."[9]

Clinton's remarks, coming just days after George W. Bush's 2005 inauguration, may have signaled her own ambitions to reach beyond the relative blue-state safety of New York and the Northeast in order to appeal to a broader electorate in anticipation of her own run for the presidency in 2008. Many liberals criticized her speech and the attempts at rapprochement with conservative opponents of abortion. Others at least recognized the significance of the gesture, and, coincident or not, a poll released several weeks after Clinton's Albany speech showed that her popularity had increased and that the percentage of voters who viewed her negatively had fallen.

Whether that kind of overture could succeed, however, was not at all certain, as evidence mounted that the kind of live-and-let-live ethic of the Middle Atlantic was out of step with other parts of the country. For both the 2000 and 2004 presidential elections, the Middle Atlantic—New York, New Jersey, Pennsylvania, Delaware, Maryland, and the District of Columbia—lined up solidly in the blue-state column. In such Democratic strongholds as New York, Maryland, and the District of Columbia, that was hardly noteworthy. But New Jersey and Pennsylvania were classic swing states, and Delaware has traditionally been Republican.

The decisive Democratic majorities throughout the region might be interpreted as evidence that Americans in the Middle Atlantic look for a certain kind of religion in the public square, a kind of modified Protestant-Catholic-Jew paradigm that makes room for new religions and novel forms of religious expression. Multiculturalism and religious diversity flourish in the Middle Atlantic, and, according to an NBC poll, its denizens think that is right and proper. By a significant margin, for example, they (in comparison with the residents of other regions) are *least likely* to believe that religious institutions should remain silent on the issue of civil rights. Religious institutions, therefore, should not only align themselves with the pluralistic proposition—the right of individuals and groups to participate fully in public discourse—but should support it vigorously and vociferously.

At a time when conservative politics and Religious Right rhetoric hold sway over much of the nation, the Middle Atlantic remains stubbornly and determinedly its own self. Why? Clearly, the region's long history of religious and ethnic diversity played an important role in shaping the ethos of the region, from the pluralism of Dutch New York and the school wars of the nineteenth century to the settlement of various Anabaptist groups in Pennsylvania and the unbridled pluralism of places like Queens. This is a region that manages somehow to accommodate both the Hare Krishnas on Manhattan street corners and the Schwenkfelders of Berks County, Pennsylvania, the Bruderhof in the Hudson River valley, and the Hasidim in the Crown Heights neighborhood of Brooklyn. Throughout its history, the region has seemed to show a proclivity for deemphasizing theology and its hard lines of division in favor of something that combines a kind of Old World enclave pluralism—here's the Greek quarter, here's the Armenian, there are the Sicilians, there the Jews, down the street from the Sikhs—with an embrace of American constitutional ideology, an ethic of toleration and freedom of expression inscribed in the First Amendment. An earlier generation referred to this accommodation as "civil religion," a nationalism that transcends the particularities of individual religious traditions to affirm the broader ideals of inclusiveness and pluralism.

In the Middle Atlantic, a region all too familiar with the ravages of ethnic conflict—the English *versus* the Dutch, Catholic *versus* Protestant, Irish *versus* Italians, Jews *versus* African Americans—the pluralist imperative has been forged out of numberless confrontations and tempered by such mediating institutions as schools, government, the media, and (not least) places of worship. Small wonder, then, that institutions remain important in the Middle Atlantic, for they have helped to build and continue to sustain a remarkable measure of comity in the midst of pluralism. Other regions of the nation cannot boast such a history—nor, it appears, would they want to. In an age of hard-right conservatism and Religious Right politics, it's much easier to retreat to some form of religious hegemony— public prayer in public schools, for instance, or posting the Decalogue in public spaces—than to countenance the messy business of pluralism.

The multiculturalism of the Middle Atlantic, however, offers no such luxury, where the people of the region negotiate religious and ethnic boundaries daily. The pluralist imperative of the Middle Atlantic was born amid the Protestant diversity of the seventeenth century, it expanded to include Catholicism in the nineteenth century, and came into its own following World War II in the twentieth century, especially after changes to the immigration laws in 1965. The pluralist imperative persists in the twenty-first century in the Middle Atlantic, and although this once seemed like the American future, it now looks more like a receding past.

Endnotes

1. McFadden, Robert D., "A Nation Challenged: The Service," *New York Times*, September 24, 2001.

2. Ibid.

3. Letter from Duane Bergman and Phil Konigsberg, *New York Newsday*, July 28, 2002.

4. Letter from Lawrence F. Wallace, *New York Times*, February 9, 2002.

5. Letter from Ken Beiner and Francia Reed, *New York Newsday*, July 18, 2002.

6. On the effects of ecumenism, see Balmer, Randall, *Travels Along the Mainline of American Protestantism* (New York: Oxford University Press, 1996).

7. Regarding Sharpton and the Diallo case, see Piotrowski, William K., "The Diallo Killing: Sharpton *Ecumenistes*," *Religion in the News*, Summer 1999.

8. Balmer, Randall, "Election Matters: Kerry and the Evangelicals," *The Nation*, July 5, 2004.

9. Remarks by Senator Hillary Rodham Clinton to the NYS Family Planning Providers, Albany, New York, January 24, 2005.

APPENDIX

In order to provide the best possible empirical basis for understanding the place of religion in each of the religions of the United States, the Religion by Region project contracted to obtain data from three sources: the North American Religion Atlas (NARA); the 2001 American Religious Identification Survey (ARIS); and the 1992, 1996, and 2000 National Surveys of Religion and Politics (NSRP).

NARA For the project, the Polis Center of Indiana University-Purdue University at Indianapolis created an interactive Web site that made it possible to map general demographic and religious data at the national, regional, state-by-state, and county-by-county level. The demographic data were taken from the 2000 census. The primary source for the religious data (congregations, members, and adherents) was the 2000 Religious Congregations and Membership Survey (RCMC) compiled by the Glenmary Research Center. Because a number of religious groups did not participate in the 2000 RCMS—including most Historically African-American Protestant denominations—this dataset was supplemented with data from other sources *for adherents only*. The latter included projections from 1990 RCMC reports, ARIS, and several custom estimates. For a fuller methodological account, go to *http://www.religionatlas.org*.

ARIS The American Religious Identification Survey (ARIS 2001), carried out under the auspices of the Graduate Center of the City University of New York by Barry A. Kosmin, Egon Mayer, and Ariela Keysar, replicates the methodology of the National Survey of Religious Identification (NSRI 1990). As in 1990, the ARIS sample is based on a series of national random digit dialing (RDD) surveys, utilizing ICR, International Communication Research Group in Media, Pennsylvania, national telephone omnibus services. In all, 50,284 U.S. households were successfully interviewed. Within a household, an adult respondent was chosen using the "last birthday method" of random selection. One of the distinguishing features of both ARIS 2001 and NSRI 1990 is that respondents were asked to describe themselves in terms of religion with an open-ended question: "What is your religion, if any?"[1] ARIS 2001 enhanced the topics covered by adding questions concerning religious beliefs and membership as well as religious switching and religious identification of spouses/partners. The ARIS findings have a high level of statistical significance for most large religious groups and key geographical units, such as states. ARIS 2001 detailed methodology can be found in the report on the American Religious Identification Survey 2001 at *www.gc.cuny.edu/studies/aris_index.htm.*

NSRP The National Surveys of Religion and Politics were conducted in 1992, 1996, and 2000 at the Bliss Center at the University of Akron under the direction of John C. Green, supported by grants from the Pew Charitable Trusts.

Together, these three surveys include more than 14,000 cases. Eight items were asked in all three surveys (partisanship, ideology, abortion, gay rights, help for minorities, environmental protection, welfare spending, and national health insurance). The responses on these items were pooled for all three years to produce enough cases for an analysis by region. These data must be viewed with some caution because they represent opinion over an entire decade rather than at one point in time. A more detailed account of how these data were compiled may be obtained from the Bliss Institute.

Endnote

1. In the 1990 NSRI survey, the question wording was: "What is your religion?" In the 2001 ARIS survey, the phrase, "...if any" was added to the question. A subsequent validity check based on cross-samples of 3,000 respondents carried out by ICR in 2002 found no statistical difference in the pattern of responses according to the two wordings.

BIBLIOGRAPHY

Balmer, Randall. *A Perfect Babel of Confusion: Dutch Religion and English Culture in the Middle Colonies*. New York: Oxford University Press, 1989.

Carnes, Tony, and Anna Karpathakis, eds. *New York Glory: Religions in the City*. New York: New York University Press, 2001.

Dolan, Jay P. *The Immigrant Church: New York's Irish and German Catholics, 1815-1865*. Baltimore: Johns Hopkins University Press, 1975.

Fauset, Arthur Huff. *Black Gods of the Metropolis: Negro Religious Cults of the Urban North*. Philadelphia: University of Pennsylvania Press, 1944.

Glazer, Nathan. *Beyond the Melting Pot: The Negroes, Puerto Ricans, Jews, Italians, and Irish of New York City*. 2nd ed. Cambridge, Mass.: M.I.T. Press, 1970.

Hanley, Thomas O'Brien. *Their Rights and Liberties: The Beginnings of Religious and Political Freedom in Maryland*. Chicago: Loyola University Press, 1984.

Harris, Lis. *Holy Days: The World of a Hasidic Family*. New York: Simon & Shuster, 1985.

Jacoby, Tamar, ed. *Reinventing the Melting Pot: The New Immigrants and What It Means to be American*. New York: Basic Books, 2004.

Moore, Deborah Dash. *At Home in America: The Second Generation New York Jews*. New York: Columbia University Press, 1981.

Nolt, Stephen M. *A History of the Amish*. Intercourse, Pa.: Good Books, 1992.

Orsi, Robert Anthony, ed. *Gods of the City: Religion and the American Urban Landscape*. Bloomington and Indianapolis: Indiana University Press, 1999.

_____. *The Madonna of 115th Street: Faith and Community in Italian Harlem, 1880-1950*. New Haven: Yale University Press, 1985.

Taylor, Robert. *The Black Churches of Brooklyn*. New York: Columbia University Press, 1994.

Watts, Jill. *God, Harlem U.S.A.: The Father Divine Story*. Berkeley and Los Angeles: University of California Press, 1992.

INDEX

vidual organizations and political
issues
Johnson, Lyndon, 10, 15, 87

Kennedy, John F., 71, 86, 87, 92
Kenrick, Francis, 10, 18, 75
Kerry, John, 43, 67, 71, 91, 92,
130n36, 160, 161

Lautenberg, Frank, 114, 160
Lieberman, Joseph, 114, 120, 121,
130n36
Leo XIII, 79, 82
Lutherans: beliefs of, 53; Delaware,
33, 35, 53; educational institutions, 53; Evangelical Lutheran
Church of America, 35, 46, 53;
history of, 50, 53; Lutheran
Church-Missouri Synod, 61,
155–56; Maryland, 33, 35, 64–65;
Middle Atlantic region, 35, 41, 46,
53; Midwest, 41; New England,
41; New Jersey, 33, 35; New York
City, 61, 155–56; New York State,
33, 35, 36; Pennsylvania, 33, 35,
36, 53, 67; United States, 35, 41;
Washington, D.C., 33

Maryland: adherents, number of, 35;
demographics, 26, 27, 28, 30, 31;
history of, 10, 11, 16, 31, 32, 33,
46, 51, 73–74; population, 26,
35; Prince George's County, 144;
Silver Spring, 144. See also immigrants; and individual religions and
denominations
McGlynn, Edward, 77–78
McGreevy, John, 85, 86, 91
Mennonites, 9, 10, 41, 55, 68
Methodists: African American, 57;

conservative, 48; Delaware, 32,
35, 37, 63–64; history of, 50;
Maryland, 33, 35, 37; Middle
Atlantic region, 32, 35, 41, 64;
Midwest, 41; New Jersey, 33,
35, 62; New York City, 61; New
York State, 33, 35, 36; Pacific
Northwest, 41; Pennsylvania, 33,
35, 36, 37, 48; South, 41; United
States, 41, 51; Washington, D.C.,
33
methodology, 6–7, 21, 40, 165–66
Middle Atlantic region: adherents,
number of, 35; church membership,
34; comparisons to other regions,
25, 26, 30, 34, 38, 39, 41, 135;
demographics of, 17, 25–26, 27,
30, 31; ecumenism, 156; history of,
9–10, 31, 32, 46–47, 102, 104, 163;
institutionalism, 156–57; intra-
regional differences, 47–48, 66–67,
68, 160; Judeo-Christian tradition
of, 14–15; political ideology in, 40,
43; population, 25, 35; religious
minorities in, 15–16; religious
pluralism in, 9–10, 17, 19–20, 25,
46, 133–34, 149–50, 162, 163;
religious self-identification in, 21,
38; religious toleration, 19–20.
See also Baltimore; Delaware;
immigrants; Maryland; New
Jersey; New York City; New York
State; Pennsylvania; Philadelphia;
Washington, D.C.; and individual
religions and denominations
Midwest, 26, 30. See also immigrants;
and individual religions and
denominations
minority achievement, programs to
encourage. See affirmative action

CONTRIBUTORS

Randall Balmer, professor of American religious history at Barnard College, Columbia University, has taught at Columbia since earning the Ph.D. from Princeton University in 1985. He has been a visiting professor at several universities, including Yale and Northwestern, and at the Columbia Graduate School of Journalism. He has published widely both in scholarly journals and the popular press. He is the author of 10 books, including *Mine Eyes Have Seen the Glory: A Journey into the Evangelical Subculture in America*, which was made into a three-part PBS series.

Wendy Cadge is assistant professor of Sociology at Bowdoin College and a Robert Wood Johnson Foundation Scholar in Health Policy Research at Harvard University. She earned her Ph.D. in sociology from Princeton University in 2002. Her research focuses on religion and immigration, religion and sexuality, and religion and medicine, among other topics. She has published articles in *Gender and Society, Journal for the Scientific Study of Religion*, and *Contexts: Understanding People in Their Social Worlds*. Her first book, *Heartwood: the First Generation of Theravada Buddhism in America*, was published in 2005 by the University of Chicago Press.

James T. Fisher is professor of theology and co-director of the Francis and Ann Curran Center for American Catholic Studies at Fordham University. He is the author of *The Catholic Counterculture in America, 1933-1962*; *Dr. America: the Lives of Thomas A. Dooley, 1927-1961*; and *Communion of Immigrants: A History of Catholics in America*. He is completing a cultural and religious history of the Port of New York and New Jersey in the mid-twentieth century.

Lawrence Grossman, an ordained rabbi with a Ph.D. in American history from the Graduate Center of the City University of New York, is associate director of research for the American Jewish Committee and coeditor of the *American Jewish Year Book*, the standard reference work on Jewish life. Since 1988 he has written annual essays in the *Year Book* tracking trends in American Judaism. Among his other recent publications are "Denominationalism in American Judaism" in *The*

Cambridge Companion to American Judaism (2005), "Mainstream Orthodoxy and the American Public Square" in *Jewish Polity and American Civil Society* (2002), and "Jewish Religion in America" in *A Portrait of the American Jewish Community* (1998).

James Hudnut-Beumler is the Anne Potter Wilson Distinguished Professor of American Religious History and dean of the Divinity School at Vanderbilt University. He earned the Ph.D. at Princeton University. He is the author of several books including *Looking for God in the Suburbs: The Religion of the American Dream and its Critics (*Rutgers); *Generous Saints* (Alban*); and the recently co-authored *The History of the Riverside Church in the City of New York* (NYU).

Vivian Z. Klaff is associate professor in the department of sociology and criminal justice and director of the Center for Jewish Studies at the University of Delaware. His recent publications include "The Religious Demography of New York City" in *New York Glory: Religion in the City* (edited by Tony Carnes and Anna Karpathakis, New York University Press, 2001) and "NJPS2000: A Vehicle For Exploring Social Change In The Jewish Population" in *Contemporary Jewry* (forthcoming, with Frank Mott). He is currently working on a book on Jewish demography based on the 1990 and 2000 national Jewish population studies.

Mark Silk is associate professor of religion in public life and founding director of the Leonard E. Greenberg Center for the Study of Religion in Public Life at Trinity College in Hartford, Connecticut. A former newspaper reporter and member of the editorial board at the Atlanta Journal-Constitution, he is author of *Spiritual Politics: Religion and Politics in America Since World War II* (Simon and Schuster, 1988) and *Unsecular Media: Making News of Religion in America* (University of Illinois Press, 1995). He is editor of *Religion in the News*, a magazine published by the Greenberg Center that examines how journalists handle religious subject matter.